# VISITING THE NEIGHBOURS

AGNIESZKA SOBOCINSKA first set foot in Asia while still in her teens. The travel bug bit hard and she has since spent several years travelling, living and working throughout the region. She is also an historian and Deputy Director of the National Centre for Australian Studies at Monash University. With David Walker, she is the co-editor of *Australia's Asia: From Yellow Peril to Asian Century*, which is being translated into Mandarin. She's about to take on her biggest challenge yet: leading a class of university students on a study tour of Indonesia.

# VISITING THE NEIGHBOURS

## AUSTRALIANS IN ASIA

AGNIESZKA
SOBOCINSKA

NEWSOUTH

A NewSouth book

*Published by*
NewSouth Publishing
University of New South Wales Press Ltd
University of New South Wales
Sydney NSW 2052
AUSTRALIA
newsouthpublishing.com

National Library of Australia Cataloguing-in-Publication entry
Author: Sobocinska, Agnieszka.
Title: Visiting the neighbours: Australians in Asia/Agnieszka Sobocinska.
ISBN: 9781742233895 (paperback)
     9781742241807 (ePub/Kindle)
     9781742246994 (ePDF)
Subjects: Australians – Asia.
    Australians – Attitudes.
    Australia – Relations – Asia.
    Asia – Relations – Australia.
Dewey Number: 305.895094

*Design* Josephine Pajor-Markus
*Cover images* Dreamstime.com

UNSW
AUSTRALIA

All reasonable efforts were taken to obtain permission to use copyright material reproduced in this book, but in some cases copyright could not be traced. The author welcomes information in this regard.

# CONTENTS

# VISITING THE
# NEIGHBOURS

S ix months on the Hippie Trail had left their mark on 24-year-old Richard Neville. He had traded his smart luggage for a disintegrating rucksack and now wore an embroidered Afghan coat and an odd assortment of ethnic jewellery. Neville had changed in other ways, too. In the mid-1960s, the road to Kathmandu was 'paved with cannabis', and it had led him to reflect on life back in the West. The suburban monotony of Australia paled in comparison to the colour and 'fresh simplicity' he'd found in Asia, and the nine-to-five rat race seemed pointless now that he'd seen people who were happy despite owning next to nothing. Five years later, Neville published *Play Power*, a countercultural manifesto in favour of widespread 'drop out-ism'. The Hippie Trail was becoming ever more popular and he thought this might lead to revolutionary change. 'How you gonna keep 'em down', he asked, 'after they've seen Kathmandu?'

Not long afterwards, the first-ever Lonely Planet guidebook, *Across Asia on the Cheap*, was published for those hoping to follow in Neville's footsteps. It opened by asking the most important question: 'Why?' Its author, Tony Wheeler, had plenty of answers: it was cheap, it held the mystique of adventure and everyone else was doing it. By 1973, Asia was so fashionable that 'there's almost a groove worn in the face of the map'. The National Union of Students also published a guidebook, but it offered a different reason: travelling would help Australians form a bond of friendship with their regional neighbours, which was crucial as the nation groped its way towards a future that seemed to hinge on Asia.[1]

Nowadays, half of all residents leaving the country are heading to Asia. One-sixth of the entire population will travel there in a single year.[2] This adds up: almost one-third of Australians have been to Bali alone.[3] Despite the assumption that Australians are only now discovering Asia, they have been visiting their Asian 'neighbours' for well over a hundred years. They have gone there in peace and war, for business and pleasure, to visit family or to discover themselves. Some had dreamt of Asia their entire lives, while others just wanted to get away from home.

This book explores the experience of being an Australian in Asia over the 20th and 21st centuries, paying particular attention to the ways in which personal experience intersected with broader political patterns. Travel and tourism might seem frivolous at first glance, but because first-hand impressions can be more influential than academic or media accounts, even fleeting glimpses can shape an individual's views about a foreign place. Since the Enlightenment, the notion that 'seeing is believing' has become ingrained in Western thought. In an age of hypermobility, millions of Australians returned home thinking that they knew something of Asia because they had been there and seen it for themselves. Over time, this vast bank of personal experience had a substantial impact on popular perceptions of Asia and contributed to momentous shifts in the way Australians thought about their nation's place in the region and the world.

NEAR NEIGHBOURS | Since at least the 1940s, it has been commonplace to describe Asia as Australia's neighbourhood. But what does this actually mean? Some neighbours are friends who'll pop around for a chat, but neighbourly relations can be strained and more than a few heated words have been exchanged over backyard fences and communal bins. Mostly, I'm on nodding terms with my neighbours. We exchange polite greetings when we pass on the street, but otherwise stay out of each other's business. Our addresses are the only things that connect us.

The status of 'neighbour' is just as ambiguous in international relations. In the language of diplomacy, placing an emphasis on geographical proximity can subtly imply the lack of a more meaningful relationship. Referring to Indonesia or Thailand – not to mention fairly distant nations such as India and China – as 'neighbours' suggests that there is little that brings Australia and Asia together, apart from the accident of geography. But there is no escaping geography, so a 'neighbour' is also among the most important of all international relationships. Closeness can bring benefits (not least by facilitating trade), but proximity can also seem menacing. References to Asian 'neighbours' have sometimes carried a dark undertone that stirred up deep-seeded anxieties about the massive populations and increasing power of the nations to Australia's north.

Using terms like 'neighbour' serves to personalise international relations, by inviting ordinary people to draw parallels between their private lives and the sphere of international relations. In mature democracies such as Australia, what ordinary citizens think about foreign places and people can have a direct influence on foreign policy. Popular opinion obviously matters at the voting booth, but beyond this politicians and the media interpret international affairs through the lens of common stereotypes and dominant discourses. As Edward Said showed in his landmark book *Orientalism*, popular assumptions about Others come to appear as commonsense truths, which profoundly affect those individuals and organisations charged with conducting international relations, along with the rest of society.[4]

So how are dominant ideas about racial and cultural Others

created? Said traced the dissemination of discourses through the arts and in academia. The mass media, international migration and trade also played an important part during a time of accelerating globalisation.[5] Historians in the United States and Europe have recently begun to recognise the political impact of travel and tourism as part of a broader 'cultural turn' in diplomatic history.[6] This book builds on their work. It shows that, in an era of unprecedented mobility, travel and tourism are increasingly important means through which popular impressions of Others are created, perpetuated and occasionally altered, and that they are both directly and indirectly implicated in diplomacy and international relations.

In their busy everyday lives, few people have the time or inclination to carefully consider their views on international relations. An overseas journey has long acted as a catalyst that spurred Australians to think about their nation's place in the world. Travelling to the region raised pressing questions. What was Asia *really* like? Were Asians like Australians? Could Australia and Asia coexist peacefully? Or were their cultures, standards of living and values entirely incompatible? Impressions about Asian places and people – their habits, lifestyles, attitudes or even appearance or approachability – were not typically framed as questions of international relations. Nonetheless, fragmentary impressions contributed to broader ideas about what Asia was like and helped shape individuals' attitudes towards the region. Not every journey had a life-changing impact. But many did, and as the stream of travellers became a flood, their impressions fed into ongoing debates about Australia's place in the world. And politicians had to take note.

Politicians and academics alike acknowledge that popular perceptions (and misperceptions) have affected diplomatic relations between Australia and Asia. Some of the most important works on Australian-Asian relations are cultural histories examining popular perceptions. David Walker's *Anxious Nation: Australia and the Rise of Asia, 1850–1939* showed how mainstream perceptions shaped the space in which both foreign and domestic policy was devised, as have a number of historians working on specific nations and contexts.[7] This is now widely acknowledged. The Lowy Institute for International Policy, Australia's leading foreign policy think tank, measures popular attitudes towards other countries on an annual basis. Politicians and bureaucrats are also well aware of the importance of public perceptions. Diplomats on both sides of the Australia-Indonesia relationship regularly emphasise the ongoing hurdle presented by popular misperceptions.

While the importance of mainstream attitudes to foreign relations has been acknowledged, and historians have recognised shifts in popular perceptions of Asia over time, we are still working towards explaining how and why these shifts occurred. How and why did 'ordinary' Australians' ideas about Asia shift in the century or so since Federation? International politics, trade relations, globalisation, migration and many other factors are all important. But as the following chapters show, in an era defined by mobility, travel and tourism increasingly shaped the cultural context in which official relations between Australia and Asia took place.

THE PERSONAL IS POLITICAL | My first experience of Asia came during a family holiday to Bali in the late 1990s. We lived it up in a swank resort, our every whim tended to by obliging and ever-smiling Indonesian staff. My brother and I debated whether it was OK to leave our dirty clothes on the floor. I was uncomfortable with maids picking up after us; he told me that it was their job and that I had an inferiority complex – or was I being patronising? Over the next few days, we were continually confronted by situations that challenged our assumptions and tested our ethics. We felt a gnawing guilt every time we refused a hawker who obviously needed the money more than we did. I refused to watch a cockfight, but must've spent hundreds of dollars on shoes

I would never wear – surely just as offensive in a country where nearly one-fifth of the population lived in absolute poverty. Learning something about Balinese culture and Indonesian politics was also fascinating, and highlighted how little I had known before. My family's varied responses to the culture, the people and the climate made for lively discussions. Our holiday was not extraordinary, but it made a big impression. I was hooked. Since that time, I've spent several years travelling, living and working in Asia and now teach university courses on the history of Australia's relations with the region. Fifteen years on, I'm still moving along a path that can be traced back to that trip to Bali.

Other travellers had even more profound experiences that led them to reassess their opinions about Australia's place in the world. In the chapters that follow, we will meet travellers like William Wade, a middle-aged Sydneysider who set off to Hong Kong and Tokyo in 1962. A lot of his preconceptions were shattered. He found the cities to be clean and efficient; far from being backward, in some ways they were more advanced than Australia. Moreover, the Chinese and Japanese were clever, hardworking and honest. It wasn't long before he began to wonder if Australian politicians weren't being foolish in their determination to keep them out. Wade had always been politically conservative, but after only a few weeks in Asia he became convinced that the White Australia Policy should be relaxed, and relations with Asia strengthened. He returned with an entirely new view of Asia, which he increasingly summed up in one word, conveying both the spectacle and the promise of Asia: marvellous.[8] Wade's political reassessment is notable because it was so rapid and so complete and because it was thoroughly documented (he had purchased a new tape recorder in Hong Kong, and recorded a number of audio cassettes during his travels). But Wade was not categorically different from many other travellers who reconsidered their views about Australia and Asia as they visited the region.

Travel experiences take place at the personal level, but when they occur across millions of journeys over more than a hundred years they become political. Anthropologist Mary Louise Pratt coined the term 'contact zone' to refer to the spaces in which people from different backgrounds, languages and traditions encounter each other and try to make sense of the experience.[9] Pratt thought that travel writing was important because it conveyed knowledge created in the contact zone to a wider audience. Travel writing is still important, but the rise of mass tourism has made direct experience of foreign places and people accessible to a broad swath of the public. As cultural theorist John Hutnyk has shown, nowadays a good deal of knowledge (or as he refers to it, 'rumour') about a foreign place is carried in popular culture and mediated through personal experience.[10] To understand what Australians thought about Others, we need to take some account of the experiences and impressions of travellers and tourists – of individuals like William Wade – as well as prominent writers, filmmakers, politicians and diplomats.

The term 'contact zone' emphasises the fact that physical, embodied encounters are important, not least because they are revealing of broader cultural and political processes. When we approach an individual or situation in a foreign country, it's as if we are armed with a cultural roadmap that tells us what 'they' are like, which we use to interpret the situation in front of us. These preconceptions inform how we approach individual representatives of foreign societies and how we position ourselves in relation to them. Historians of colonialism have demonstrated that broader political and racial systems can be contained in the body politics of personal encounters.[11] Ethnographic historians can unpick a single contact, examining how people made sense of each other and how they attempted to communicate, in order to explain something of the societies and cultures from which they came. Identifying patterns in the multitude of encounters between Australians and Asians can be even more revealing about mainstream attitudes towards Asia and Asians, and ideas about Australia's rightful place in the world.

While the number of Australians with a direct experience of Asia is staggering in itself, indvidual journeys often had a wider impact. Eyewitness accounts gained a reputation for being 'true' following the Enlightenment. As the first-hand accounts of trusted friends or relatives, travel stories are often taken as trustworthy sources of information about foreign places and people. They can also circulate quite broadly. Travellers love to share their stories and countless tales of Asian adventure have been spun at pubs and dinner parties across the nation. Travellers have also inflicted innumerable letters, slides, photographs, home videos and, more recently, emails and Facebook status updates, upon family, friends and casual acquaintances. Even for those who wanted to do so, travellers' tales could be hard to escape.

Diplomatic historians tend to work from official records and the papers of an elite group of politicians, diplomats and bureaucrats. Tracing the experiences of 'ordinary' Australians opens up a broader archive of letters, travel diaries, memoirs and photographs recorded by visitors from all walks of life, in addition to the published impressions of professional writers, politicians and journalists. By examining these sources, we can gauge which images, stereotypes and discourses about Asia circulated in the public sphere at any one time. Moreover, we can come to understand how the experience of travel helped shift those images. The more diaries and letters I read, the more I realised that travel did not only reflect mainstream attitudes towards Asia, but was also a key way in which those attitudes shifted. Preconceptions were often confirmed but sometimes, as in William Wade's experience, they were challenged or altered by direct contact with the Asian Other.

Over time, travellers' impressions fed into key public debates surrounding diplomatic issues. Should Australia accept Asian migrants? Should it seek closer engagement with the region? Did the benefits of proximity outweigh the risks? These questions (and many more) hinged on popular attitudes to Asia and so were particularly affected by travellers' perspectives. Some travellers directly entered the political process by establishing or supporting lobby groups to demand changes in government policy. Others published letters, essays and books in which they proposed political actions based on insights into Asian society and politics they had acquired during their travels. But the vast majority limited their opinions to the intimate sphere of friends, relatives and colleagues. Although their effect on the political process is much more difficult to track, because there were so many of them, their impact on popular attitudes towards Asia assumed an increasing importance as overseas travel became mainstream.

# BEING AN AUSTRALIAN IN ASIA | In his classic *Inventing Australia*, historian Richard White branded the search for a national identity an Australian obsession.[12] Uncertainty about its place in the world lay at the heart of this obsession. Should Australia be defined by its historical ties to the West? Was it a European outpost in the Pacific, bound by blood, language and culture to Britain and the United States? Or was it time for Australia to let go of sentimental ties, acknowledge the fact of its geography and make its own way in the Asia-Pacific region? Such questions became urgent as more and more Australians recognised that their future would be increasingly shaped by Asia. Some worried about military aggression or floods of migrants; others were more optimistic, seeing untold riches in the vast untapped markets of the Near North. Either way, it was said, Australia would have to play its cards right and to project a fitting image in order to flourish in an Asian future (or more recently, Asian Century). Only one problem remained. What was this identity to be?

The national identity crisis was enacted in miniature as millions of travellers made personal decisions about how to behave with their 'neighbours'. Entering the contact zone forced them to consider what it meant to be an Australian in Asia, and assume a body politics that corresponded to their ideas. Australians travelling to Asia have repeatedly borrowed from an established repertoire of roles. In this book, I have identified and explored the roles of Imperialists, Fortune hunters, Warriors, Good neighbours, Humanitarians, Seekers, Adventurers, Tourists and Sons and daughters. I chose these labels because they are dominant and recurring, however this is not a definitive list and some individuals undoubtedly followed different scripts. Examining these roles allows us to see how travellers approached the tensions between race, culture and geography that confronted individual Australians in Asia – the same tensions that confronted politicians and diplomats on a national level.

That travellers have been striking these poses over many decades speaks to the length of time that Australians have been grappling with their regional relations. Listening to current political rhetoric regarding the 'Asian Century', one would be forgiven for thinking that Australians had only just discovered Asia. Announcing a government White Paper on *Australia in the Asian Century* in 2011, then Prime Minister Julia Gillard emphasised one point above all others: 'Australia hasn't been here before'.[13] The Liberal government under Tony Abbott has also made much of the fact that it will be 'restoring our focus and reinforcing our mindset to reflect our geographic reality' by gearing its foreign policy towards Jakarta rather than Geneva.[14]

This book proves that Australians *have* been to Asia before – and in great numbers. More Australians travelled to Asia than Europe for the first time in 1968, and this has been the case every year since 1981. Since 1998, more Australians have been heading to Indonesia than the United Kingdom. Tracing these patterns reveals that ordinary Australians have been redefining Australia's place in the world for over a century. Recognising that Australians have been here before – that there is a long and rich history of Australian-Asian contact – is an important step. Investigating how ordinary

Australians have grappled with their national identity crisis in relation to Asia, and examining how they set about resolving it as individuals and en masse, can facilitate a more coherent approach to questions regarding Australia's place in the region as we head into the Asian Century.

AUSTRALIA' AND 'ASIA' | But just who are Australians, and where is Asia? The subtitle of this book ('Australians in Asia') suggests that these categories have stable meanings. But do they? Australians held British citizenship and passports until 1948; moreover, as a nation of migrants it can be difficult to determine the point at which an individual became 'Australian'. Neither were ideas about Asia quarantined in a national bubble, but were always influenced by broader, transnational trends.[15] Nonetheless, Australia's position – geographically in Asia but culturally and historically linked to Europe – was thought to be unique and this evoked distinct responses that differed in texture and tone from those of Britons, Americans or any other national group. Moreover, travellers often reflected on national politics while travelling, so although it is admittedly problematic, a national framing is appropriate for this analysis.

Common assumptions were most directly challenged by the travels of Australians of Asian ancestry. Even though the rhetoric of White Australia occluded their presence, people of Asian descent have been part of Australian society since the mid-19th century. Chinese-, Vietnamese- or Indian-Australians make up increasingly significant communities, and many have been particularly mobile. Their travels constitute an important component of the history of Australian travel to Asia, not least by forcing a re-evaluation of widespread assumptions about 'us' and 'them'. The travels of Asian-Australians are explored in some depth in the final chapter of this book.

The term 'Asia' is even more slippery. In geographical terms, the Asian continent stretches from Istanbul to Vladivostok and the staggering variation between people and cultures makes the notion of a single 'Asia' absurd. Nonetheless, it has been customary for Australians to talk about a generic Asia for many decades. Of course, what they meant when they referred to 'Asia' changed over time. In the 19th century, 'Asia', the 'East' or the 'Orient' were used interchangeably to refer to China, Japan or India. From the middle of the 20th century, Southeast Asia came to occupy an increasingly dominant place in Australian conceptions and 'Asia' became largely reconceived as the 'Near North'. A fad for 'Eastern' religions and fashions in the 1970s was inspired largely by India; but by the end of the century, when One Nation's Pauline Hanson spoke of being swamped by 'Asians' it was popularly understood that she referred to people from East or Southeast Asia. Audiences in the United Kingdom would have interpreted it differently (there the term 'Asian' typically refers to people of South Asian descent) and 'Asia' takes on different shapes entirely if viewed from Washington, Beijing or Jakarta. Yet, even though it is largely an invented category with only a passing connection to geographical, cultural or ethnic reality, many Australians continue to speak of engaging with 'Asia' even today. It is a category that holds meaning for ordinary Australians and the chapters that follow engage with this mainstream conception.

Of course, the recognition that there is no single Asia does make it impossible to attempt to reverse the gaze and probe 'Asian' responses to Australian travellers (or indeed their attitudes towards Australia in general). The wide range and varied context of these responses renders them far too complex to fit into a single analysis and so they must fall outside the parameters of this book, which focusses on travellers' experiences in order to make sense of Australian attitudes.

As with all history, making sense of millions of journeys requires some generalisation. Personal responses could vary between destinations and over time, and depended to some extent on individual personalities and outlooks as well as social and cultural patterns. But, as noted before, they fell into distinguishable patterns, so that certain kinds of responses were particularly common at certain times and in certain places. Each chapter examines a different role from the repertoire adopted by Australian travellers in Asia. While it is divided thematically, it follows a loosely chronological structure, with those roles that were dominant at earlier periods ('Imperialists', for instance) examined before those that became commonplace later (such as 'Tourists'). This allows us to track some of the changes in popular attitudes towards the region over time.

The first chapter reminds us that early Australian contacts with Asia took place within the context of European colonial domination over almost the entire Asian continent. The fact that the culture of Asian travel emerged in a colonial context is extremely important; the body politics and attitudes that developed at this embryonic stage of tourist contact were to recur over subsequent decades. But while the logic of colonialism encouraged Australians to imagine they were racially and culturally dominant, the relative advantages of size, wealth and power were almost always on Asia's side. Several chapters chart the ways in which Australians made sense of this apparent paradox. In Chapter 2, we see how the desire to penetrate Asia's vast markets led some fortune hunters to try to ingratiate themselves with business leaders and consumers, even as many continued to think of the region with some condescension. The paradox is at the very heart of Chapter 3, which explores the complex experiences of Australian servicemen and women facing a formidable Asian foe in the Pacific War and the Occupation of Japan. It is also there in Chapter 4, which takes up the politics of 'engagement' with Asia as it was configured during the Cold War, and in Chapter 5, which examines Australian compassion and humanitarianism towards a region that was imagined to be 'backward' and 'developing' for much of the 20th century.

Even travel experiences that appear frivolous had political meanings and Chapters 6 through 8 unpick the politics of mass tourism. Australians heading to India in search of a guru or to Thailand looking for sex negotiated ideas about the relative value of Eastern and Western models and mores, and they played a role in shaping popular ideas about what Asia was 'really' like as mass tourism boomed from the 1970s. Some Australians looking for adventure found trouble instead, and popular interest in their fates reflected broader concerns about Australia's security in Asia. Chapter 8 focusses on Bali, the single most popular Asian destination for Australian tourists, to examine some of the political and diplomatic impacts of the millions of tourists who flock to the region every year. The book's final chapter, 'Sons and daughters', follows the journeys taken by Australians of Chinese descent, which signal an entirely different configuration of culture and sentiment that complicates the very notion of what it means to be an Australian in Asia. Taken together, these chapters point to the ways in which travel and tourism function as a form of people's diplomacy. Seeing Kathmandu – and Tokyo, Bali, Beijing and every point in between – may not have had the effect that Richard Neville predicted, but it did contribute to a revolutionary shift in the way Australians thought about their place in the world.

# 1: IMPERIALISTS

Born around the time of the Gallipoli campaign, Laure Falkiner spent much of her youth galloping through the golden pastures of her father's merino stud in the Riverina district of New South Wales. The landscape was so characteristically Australian it was used as a backdrop for the film *The Life of a Jackaroo*. Laure's parents were also involved in cinema and they produced iconically Australian films including *The Overlanders*. Yet the fabric of Laure's life was intricately stitched to Asia. She was still in her teens when her ship docked in Ceylon (now Sri Lanka) en route to England in 1929. On the way home, her steamer called at Batavia, Penang and Singapore, where she enjoyed the rarefied atmosphere of the famous colonial hotels. A decade later, Laure married a colonel in the British Army, and the pair settled in India after the end of World War II. Now a wife and mother, Laure's life had changed a great deal since her first visit. The world, too, had changed and the British Empire was beginning to buckle under the weight of anti-colonial sentiments. Yet Laure's views remained steady: she held that Asian 'natives' needed the guiding hand of European colonialism. Moreover, she had no doubts about her place in the colonial hierarchy; along with the other 'Europeans', she belonged in the plush surrounds of colonial clubs and hotels, waited on by 'native' staff. The fact that she had been born tens of thousands of kilometres from Europe hardly signified; nor did the fact that her own nation had only recently been a colony itself. According to Laure Falkiner, the rightful role for an Australian in Asia was that of imperial master.

While racial pseudo-science provided the justification and popular culture the support for imperialism, the experience of travelling to Asia – of *being there* – confirmed turn-of-the-century Australians' ideas regarding their place in the imperial hierarchy. Australians had come to define their nation as a 'white man's country' in the late 19th and early 20th centuries.[1] This was also a period when consistent improvements in shipping technology made foreign travel faster and cheaper. Setting foot in Asia, visitors found themselves in colonial societies predicated upon racial divides. Australians mixed with other 'Europeans' and picked up some of the habits and attitudes of colonial life in Asian ports from Singapore to Bombay. Many enjoyed the experience and found that it suited them. Like Laure Falkiner, they took away the lesson that Australians were well suited to the role of imperial masters.

G LIMPSING ASIA | Australians were never resigned to being tyrannised by distance. From the 19th century, they put up a determined struggle to overcome the vast expanse between themselves and the rest of the world. Then, as now, a communications revolution was underway. The introduction of the steamship and opening of the Suez Canal cut the travelling time from Sydney or Melbourne to London from three months to just 48 days by the end of the 1870s. By 1901 this had fallen to 31½ days, with the fact that travelling times were now counted by the half-day hinting at the perceived importance of these developments.[2]

A steady stream of Australians headed for the other side of the world seeking to re-establish family ties, to soak up old-world culture and refinement, or to try to make their fortune in the places that, to their way of thinking, really mattered.[3] Ten thousand departed for England every year at the turn of the century and this number doubled after the end of World War I.[4] But although London was considered the ultimate destination, Australian travel experiences weren't restricted to England. Most of those who travelled to Europe or America before the advent of air travel also visited Asia. The most popular shipping routes called at Singapore and Colombo before going on to Europe via the Suez Canal, and those headed for the United States usually stopped over in Hong Kong or Tokyo. For some travellers, the Orient was just as interesting as London or New York. What they saw there, how they interpreted their experiences and the stories they told after their return were important in shaping Australian ideas about Asia at a time when reliable information about the region was in short supply.[5]

Back home, attitudes towards Asia vacillated between fear and desire, as encapsulated by contrasting images of an exotic, antique Orient on the one hand and an overpopulated and menacing East on the other. Negative stereotypes dominated after the passing of the *Immigration Restriction Act 1901*. As David Walker has shown, books and newspapers began to portray Asia as the 'perfidious East' peopled by ragged coolies, opium addicts and evil masterminds plotting to invade the wide-open spaces of Australia.[6]

Australian attitudes were also refracted through an imperial lens. Nearly all of Asia had been swallowed up by European colonialism by the turn of the 20th century, and Australians' attitudes were coloured by the casual assumption that, being white and 'European', they were racially and culturally dominant in Asia. This attitude was entrenched in popular culture as well as politics. Historian John M Mackenzie has shown that British imperial attitudes were sustained by colonial imagery in mainstream literature, plays, films, songs, advertisements and colonial exhibitions, which helped establish a casual, ingrained assurance that Britons had a right to rule over 'natives'.[7] Generations of Australians were raised on the same popular tradition. Stories of colonial adventure by Rudyard Kipling, alongside scores of lesser-known boys' own tales, taught Australian children to regard Asians as 'natives' requiring the steady hand of Empire.[8] According to historian Adrian Vickers, this popular culture encouraged young Australians to imagine Asia as little more than a picturesque 'backdrop for white adventures'.[9]

COLONIAL TRAVELLERS | Laure Falkiner was certainly excited about the adventures that lay ahead as her steamer stopped in Ceylon on the way to England. Her mother, Una, was equally elated to be docking after days of monotony and seasickness. The page in her diary that describes their arrival in Colombo is dotted with exclamation marks. Even the 'scent of the misty air was delicious!' on that day.[10] Although Asian stopovers were short – usually only a few days and occasionally even a few hours – they tended to evoke strong responses. Singapore and Colombo were often the first places outside of Australia that travellers had seen and many travel diaries brim with the same breathless excitement as Una Falkiner's. After ten days at sea, Sydneysider Mabel Dowding thought it 'a joyful sight this sighting of land'.[11] Writer Ena Lilley felt 'all excited, this being my first glimpse of the tropics': so much so that she insisted she would 'never forget the sensation of wild delight and excitement upon landing …'.[12] The quixotic Sydney accountant, travel writer, journalist and popular historian Frank Clune (whom we will meet again later) was a seasoned traveller, but he was no less enthusiastic. Living by the catchphrase 'Try Anything Once', Clune was seemingly always on the move and he went on to write dozens of travel books, including a number of Asian titles. But his enthusiasm never faded. 'What a thrill to be in the East Indies at last!' he exclaimed as his plane touched down in the Portuguese colony of Timor in 1939, and he was to experience the thrill again and again as he made his way through the Dutch East Indies, British Malaya and French Indochina.[13]

Once the sheer excitement of arrival had passed, travellers began to take stock of their surroundings. First impressions were generally positive, with the lush, tropical atmosphere appealing to travellers' fantasies of equatorial exoticism. Travelling in 1874, Janey Rowe thought that Ceylon was 'just like fairyland'.[14] Thirty years later, Winifred James thought the island was so charming that it couldn't possibly be real, but was rather 'like eyesful of lovely pictures, each one more beautiful than the other'.[15] Another 40 years on, Frank Clune was so struck by Java he declared it 'the nearest thing on our globe to an Earthly Paradise'.[16]

Australians' initial impressions of local people were often positive, tending to align with images of the exotic Orient rather than the perfidious East. In Colombo, passengers craned to catch a glimpse of the athletic men who paddled up in barges and canoes to convey passengers to shore. A carnival atmosphere reigned, with hawkers paddling up to display souvenirs for sale while others performed acrobatic feats such as diving for coins tossed by passengers up on deck. Una Falkiner was delighted by the spectacle. Roused by the lush tropical atmosphere, she also noticed that the local men's 'chocolate skin shone' in the sun.[17] The fascination was sharpened by the fact that most travellers had never seen Asian people in any number before. The Immigration Restriction Act had barred most non-Europeans from entering Australia and many Australians had few opportunities to interact with Asians, apart from the Chinese market gardeners they encountered in the major cities. As May Tilton wrote in 1933, 'coming from White Australia, we were very excited to see so many coloured folk all at once' and her party was 'so vastly entertained watching them cleverly diving for pennies that we forgot to have any breakfast'.[18] Mabel Dowding was also interested in the 'natives', who were 'everywhere, of course', and she was particularly attentive to the 'very queer garbs amongst them'. She continued to observe the locals on a day trip to the hill station of Kandy. 'It was all intensely interesting', she wrote, and 'some of them looked very picturesque in their various coloured costumes, their hair in loose knots'. Watching from afar, she was impressed. The 'natives' had 'such nice faces', with 'the women and children … happy and bright'.[19]

Observing Asia from the comfort of a steamship or train was one thing, but tangible contact was another. Many travellers quickly became overwhelmed by the heat, noise and confusion of Colombo or Java. Even an experienced traveller like Clune found himself disconcerted by 'the kaleidoscope of the Orient: the crowded bazaars, the multi-colour garbed vendors and hagglers, the broad-leafed trees with vivid green foliage and scarlet flowers, the ox-carts in the streets'.[20] The sensory overload peaked during visits to markets and bazaars. Mabel Dowding thought the 'bazaars were indeed things of wonder, every imaginable thing one could or could not think of seemed to be there'.[21] Positive first impressions could quickly sour as frazzled visitors struggled to keep their bearings in an entirely foreign environment. Una Falkiner's delight at Colombo's exoticism faded after her ship docked and the 'natives simply poured on – like ants!'. Far from gazing at their lustrous skin, after a day on shore Falkiner declared that 'I never want to see or smell the blacks again'.[22] Months later, as she passed through Colombo on the return journey, Falkiner's attitudes had hardened even further; rather than delighted exclamations her diary featured only a cursory reference to the 'squalling niggers'.[23] Mabel Dowding was similarly disenchanted. Arriving in Kandy, she thought the lake beautiful, but 'as we entered the gates we were besieged by beggars of all descriptions, some only very small children' who 'were maimed in various ways'. Rather than feeling pity, Dowding found the way they 'waved their stump of arm or leg almost in our face' to be 'really revolting', and along with the insistent touts and the children who crowded around selling flowers, she found the entire scene overwhelming. 'Oh! The tawdriness of it all', she exclaimed, and after a few short hours, 'we were rather glad to get back to the boat'. On the whole, Dowding was ambivalent. While Ceylon 'was most fantastic and a picture to remember', local life had 'left an impression one could hardly define'. One thing was clear, however: 'the native mind was beyond us'.[24]

Many Australians began to think about the country they had left behind in light of what they saw in the Orient. The crowds, dirt and chaos of Asia's port cities led many Australians to reflect on the cleanliness and order of home. Being in such a different environment left visitors pining for the orderly streets of Melbourne or the fresh air of Sydney. In her 1902 novel, *An Australian Girl in London*, Louise Mack wrote of the homesickness that struck when, confronted by Oriental side streets, 'you try to remember Sydney', only to realise 'how far, far away it seems!'[25] In *The Australian Abroad*, first published in 1885, journalist James Hingston had speculated that Australians travelling in Ceylon and India would learn 'the value of the free colonies of Australia'.[26] This was borne out by Mabel Dowding's experience almost fifty years later. Having seen Colombo, she now 'realised more than we could have thought possible what it was like to live in a clean wholesome country'.[27]

POWER AND PLEASURE | Confronted by the din and exhausted by the heat, visitors were only too happy to retreat to the surrounds of plush hotels to sip tea and share their impressions of 'native' life with other travellers. The Galle Face Hotel in Colombo, the Hotel des Indes in Batavia and Raffles Hotel in Singapore were renowned for their comfortable sitting rooms and attentive servants, and many visitors whiled away their afternoons on the expansive verandas. The racial divisions and social dynamics of colonialism were both simplified and intensified by the tourism industry that was emerging to cater to both colonists and visitors.[28] Local populations were by no means passive in the face of European domination and were increasingly making their demands felt across the colonised world. Yet visitors could be forgiven for not recognising this. In the colonial hotels, 'Europeans' were masters and 'natives' were servants; white people made demands, those with darker skins responded to their every whim. This power dynamic, built on an assumption of racial inequality, framed Australian travel to Asia in the colonial period. Waited on hand and foot, some visitors learnt to take both the racial division and power dynamic for granted, and came to think that, in Asia, Australians deserved special treatment by virtue of their race.

Although we might assume that the tourism industry is a recent development, it played a major role in framing Australian experiences of colonial Asia. As Frank Clune enthused, 'You don't know what a de luxe hotel can be unless you try one in the Orient'. This 'de luxe' experience relied on servants 'numbered in hundreds', including 'six waiters to each table' and 'squads of housemen and laundresses' who ensured that everything was 'done on the Grand Scale'. For Clune, this was 'the "servant problem" solved'.[29] His comment reminds us of the dramatic contrast to the situation back in Australia. In 1900, only 9 per cent of Australians employed domestic service of any kind. Full-time domestic service was virtually unknown after World War II.[30] Most of those visiting Asia had never dealt with maids or butlers; but now, they were waited on hand and foot.

Neither was there any subtlety in the divide between those who enjoyed leisure and those who worked. Whether in Singapore, Batavia, Bombay or Colombo the division was clear to see: 'natives' served 'Europeans'. The bluntness of the division meant travellers had to situate themselves within this racial divide. Ironically, the harshness of the White Australia Policy meant that, at home, most Australians rarely confronted the race question. The Mission system removed indigenous Australians from most urban dwellers' day-to-day experiences and strict immigration restrictions meant that Asians were rarely encountered. Social divisions were experienced along lines of gender, class and religion – but race was sometimes taken for granted in White Australia. This only sharpened the intensity of the experience in colonial Asia, where the major social cleavage was premised on race. All of a sudden, everyday Australians were treated like royalty and the racial division between themselves and their servants made it patently clear that this was by virtue of their white skins alone. Exposed to an overtly racialised colonial system, many visitors came to understand that, in Asia, 'the White Man is a big fellow master – not just one of the mob as he is in Sydney'.[31]

This was particularly pronounced for those who spent extended periods in Asia, and so learnt to live according to the racial divisions of Empire. Ruby Madden, the daughter of Victorian Chief Justice Sir John Madden, spent nearly a year visiting India from 1903. She was there to see the great Coronation Durbar and divided her time between Lord Kitchener's camp in Delhi, comfortable colonial homes in Bombay and the hill station at Simla. Madden's Indian sojourn was a breathless flurry of parties, balls, luncheons and other entertainments. During the Durbar, she lived in a specially erected tent (complete with drawing rooms and warmed baths), attended by a small army of servants. At Lord Kitchener's tent, servants literally bore the mark of their master: 'all dressed in white and gold with a huge 'K' and coronet on their chests'.[32] It wasn't long before Madden had become accustomed to being waited on hand and foot by 'her' servants.

While Madden came from the established elite, many early 20th-century travellers were from the middle classes and many – women as well as men – had worked to pay for their journey. Others were on their way to find work in London or other places.[33] This only emphasised the leisure they enjoyed during their Asian sojourn. Afternoons whiled away on the Galle Face Hotel's spacious verandas took on particular resonance for travellers who knew they would soon have to go back to work, and a sumptuous rijstaffel buffet at the Hotel des Indes seemed even more extravagant to those who usually had to prepare their own meals. For people from the middle classes it was particularly evident that this level of privilege was accorded them because of the colour of their skins rather than the size of their wallets.

RICKSHAWS AND SEDAN CHAIRS | Many Australians heartily enjoyed their newfound status, and nowhere was this power more intoxicating than during a rickshaw ride or a passage in a sedan chair. A rickshaw ride was thought to be an essential component of an Oriental visit in the early 20th century, featuring repeatedly in travel diaries, letters and published travel writing. The experience could be particularly potent for women, who were often less accustomed to wielding authority. As Louise Mack described it, 'the first ride in a rickshaw is a tremendous sensation. You feel like a queen. You own the whole world. You have a *man* – a flesh-and-blood man – running in harness between the shafts of your tall, black perambulator with two big wheels'. The feeling of dominance was only magnified by the extreme strain placed on the driver. Mack noted that 'he is so thin that you fear he will break in pieces, that you will be arrested for cruelty to dumb animals'. The inequality was so great it almost stripped her driver of his humanity: rather than a human being, she came to think of him as 'a very highly-polished trotter'.[34] Ruby Madden was similarly struck by her power over the 'natives' as she was carried in a sedan chair during an excursion to Elephanta Isle off Bombay. As she explained, 'steps don't appeal to one here and I wanted to experience what it was like to be carried in a chair'. Like Mack, she dispassionately noted that '4 of the feeblest looking people carried me' up 300 stairs, a task so challenging that 'I felt I was breaking them down utterly'. The steps were steep, and 'in consequence the coolies keep changing the pole from one shoulder to another, as if they couldn't stand it another minute'. But she felt pity only for herself: the swaying created a 'most alarming sensation' and she was afraid she would be dropped. It wasn't that Madden was particularly cruel, or even particularly selfish. Her companion, Mr Hennessy, was also amused rather than alarmed by the strain on the carriers, and he 'walked up laughing at us the whole way'.[35] That the incident provoked mirth rather than concern indicates the extent to which these visitors had been initiated into the power dynamics of colonialism; it seemed only natural for 'coolies' to strain while 'Europeans' reclined. The fact that this situation occurred only days after Madden's arrival in India indicates the speed with which this initiation could occur.

While most visitors revelled in the power, a number felt less comfortable having a man for a horse. James Hingston reflected that he had never seen man 'more like an animal than when engaged in this novel conveyancing business', and admitted that 'at first it looks objectionable to be dragged about by one's fellow-beings in place of horses'. But he quickly overcame his qualms. Unable to change the societies through which he travelled, he explained that the visitor 'gets used to everything in time, and comes to look upon whatever is as being right'.[36] There were many more rickshaw rides to come.

# COLONIAL ENCOUNTERS AND THE RACE QUESTION | First-hand experience of colonial life in Asia could leave a lasting impression that affected visitors' ideas about race and power in Australia and the world. The 'race problem' was at the forefront of political discussion in Australia in the years following Federation. In the absence of a Declaration of Independence or a Bill of Rights, the Immigration Restriction Act – the first piece of legislation passed as an independent nation – served as a proclamation of Australia's core values. Australia was to be a democratic and egalitarian nation, a workingman's paradise where everyone was equal. A classless society required a level playing field and, in the thinking of the time, this meant excluding those who

were 'naturally' inferior, or were predisposed to lower standards of living by dint of their race.

Direct contact with Asians encouraged some Australian travellers to reflect on the race question. Frank Clune tried to gauge the intellectual capacities of the Javanese 'natives' while visiting the Netherlands East Indies in the late 1930s. The verdict wasn't good. 'I've only met houseboys and waiters', he admitted, 'but they are always forgetting something'. Despite the admission that he had only met a few servants, Clune had no hesitation in making statements about 'natives' in general: 'I'm disappointed in their intelligence'.[37] Some tourists went even further, and constructed entire racial hierarchies on the basis of their fleeting experiences. Vera Scantlebury Brown, a highly respected doctor from Melbourne, posited that 'as we have come up' northwards from the equator, 'the black people have ascended in the scale of humanity'.[38] Travellers extrapolated from brief exchanges with servants and hawkers in Batavia, Singapore or Colombo to make pronouncements about the 'Orient' or 'natives' in general. It is common for travellers to extrapolate outwards from fleeting personal experiences; this is the basis of the authority held by explorers, travellers and travel writers. But making confident assertions about what other people are 'like' based on very limited contact lay at the very core of Orientalism.[39]

Of course, not all Australians were unequivocally supportive of imperialism. In their studies of women travellers, historians Angela Woollacott and Ros Pesman found that some Australians, especially those involved in feminist or progressive politics, held ambivalent views about the colonial system.[40] But, like James Hingston, most travellers accepted the situation as they found it, and did not mount a sustained critique of imperialism or imperial hierarchies. At most, some diaries and letters betrayed a vague melancholy about the traditions that were being lost as colonialism introduced Oriental civilisation to modernity. Faced with the ruins of a great civilisation at Borobudur in Java, Frank Clune wondered whether it was arrogant to 'call them heathens, and consider ourselves civilised'. But such musings did not shift his support for contemporary imperialism: when it came to present-day 'natives', Clune was unequivocal that 'the influence of European overlordship has been beneficial'.[41] Una Falkiner's despondent reflections were even further removed from the political situation at hand; her concern was that the Dutch would introduce intensive tropical farming to Java, and so 'will ruin God's fairyland'.[42] Gazing upon Asia from the distance of their portholes or the comfortable veranda of Raffles Hotel, few visitors were stirred to critique the colonial system in the years before decolonisation in the wake of World War II.

KEEPING UP THE ACT | Being in Asia taught some Australians how to act the part of imperial masters. After only a few days in India, Ruby Madden had learnt to order her numerous servants around; by the time she departed Bombay she was demanding to be fanned whilst packing her trunk. Proudly egalitarian back in Australia, Frank Clune was also soon making numerous demands on the Javanese servants who served him at the Hotel des Indes. But how did they know how to behave? In the early decades of the 20th century, Australian nationhood was commonly defined in relation to England, and the prevalent 'colonial cringe' attests to the fact that Australians were not accustomed to thinking of themselves as top dogs in the imperial binary. Once they disembarked in Asia, however, they were forced to re-evaluate their place in the colonial hierarchy. Their white skins now placed them in the category of 'European', and so Australians had to learn not to act as colonials or base 'currency', but as imperial masters.

Acting in a manner befitting a colonial ruler was not straightforward. Travellers had to mediate a minefield of intricate social codes that existed to regulate interracial contact across colonial Asia. Racial superiority was something of a catch-22. Science may have 'proven' that Europeans were the most advanced race and thus fit to rule over inferior peoples, but this placed the burden of upholding the phantasm of 'White Man's Prestige' onto the shoulders of every colonist. It was feared that even a single European's bad behaviour could reflect badly on the whole race and so upset the legitimacy of the colonial system as a whole. Every individual had to act in a way that would uphold the status of the entire white race, resulting in complex codes of conduct that, as historian Ann Laura Stoler has shown, were taken very seriously in Asian colonies.[43]

Australians were aware that they were implicated in this system by virtue of their white skins. When two members of his party quarrelled during a field trip in Sumatra in 1929, for example, scientist Phillip M Chancellor checked them with the reprimand that 'there can be no displays of temper among Arians [sic] in this country'.[44] Clune was also conscious that, 'in the 'East' … we have to keep up the White Man's prestige, and try to look the part of bosses of the world, God's Chosen People, enlightening the poor benighted heathen with our culture and our commerce'.[45] But how to go about it? Unaccustomed to acting in this way back home, Clune was uncertain and self-conscious about the propriety of his behaviour. Was he inadvertently letting the side down? Some colonial governments were equally anxious that visitors did not undermine the White Man's Prestige and they issued visitors with instructions on how to act around 'natives', particularly servants. The state railways service of the Dutch East Indies issued Clune with a book of *Hints for Travellers*, in which English-speaking visitors were told to address their servants as 'Jongos' or 'boy', and to be direct and curt in their instructions.[46] Clune was pleased to have the situation on the trains clarified, but most other situations did not come with a guidebook. In their absence, travellers most often observed the behaviour of other Europeans and adjusted their own accordingly.

The lessons travellers learnt about race, and about their relative status within colonial hierarchies, were sometimes carried over even after their holidays had come to an end. Back home, radical nationalists bitterly resented Britain's colonisation of Australia, but few thought to question whether colonialism was appropriate in Asia.[47] In fact, many Australians helped advance colonialism in the region. Personal and professional networks within the British Empire facilitated a good deal of mobility between colonies, and some Australians who passed through Singapore or Colombo as tourists later returned as colonisers.

In the colonial homesteads of her mother's friends, and amidst the comforts of the Galle Face and Raffles hotels, Laure Falkiner had learnt how to dress, talk and behave so as to fit in to the exclusive world of the colonial elite during her first visit in 1929. Ten years later, Falkiner married Jack Bruce Steer, a colonel in the British Army garrisoned in India and, after World War II had ended, she joined her husband in Bangalore. Now mistress of her own colonial home, she took to the role with confidence and, by all accounts, skill. Letters to her mother reveal few difficulties in adjusting to her new role. Falkiner held no doubts about her position in relation to the 'natives', or any hesitation about how to treat her servants. Her familiarity with the niceties of colonial life helped her fit in at the Club, and she was quickly integrated into British colonial life. Falkiner employed an ayah for her young son and commanded servants at home, at the Club and in hotels. After only a year she had become so accustomed to domestic service that she was quite unable to function after her ayah quit suddenly; before she could find a replacement, Falkiner found life 'wearying to the bone'. A simultaneous intensification of the anti-colonial campaign and a food shortage contributed to the hardships and eventually led to the decision that she and her son would return to Australia in 1946, while her husband remained at his post. As he explained in a letter to her mother, Laure's life would be 'very much better in a white man's country'.[48]

India was not the only place where Australians acted in the role of imperial masters. The jewel in Australia's own imperial crown was Papua New Guinea. Queensland had attempted to annex Papua from the 1880s – when it was still a British colony itself. Australia finally acquired Papua in 1906 and was granted administrative rights over New Guinea under a League of Nations Mandate during World War I. Australians were firm and tenacious colonisers, holding on to Papua New Guinea until 1975, by which time decolonisation had swept through most of the world. As in other colonies across Asia and the Pacific, contact between white Australians and Papuans was strictly regulated.[49] One colonist recalled living 'in a bubble of our culture, isolated from the foreign world around me'.[50] Contact with 'natives' was strictly limited and Papuan domestic servants, like their Asian counterparts, were commonly referred to as houseboys and housegirls, or simply 'boys' and 'Meris'.[51] Australians also applied the principles of White Man's Prestige; indeed, anthropologist Ian Hogbin reported that Australians in Papua New Guinea were obsessed with 'what they called white prestige'.[52] This resulted in a range of laws and codes precluding Papuans from behaving in ways that threatened not only the bodies but also the dignity of Australian colonists. 'Natives' were banned from entering certain parts of Port Moresby unless they were employed in colonists' homes. They were also banned from drinking alcohol, dancing or playing drums or card games at night, and Papuan men were banned from wearing clothes on their upper bodies (this was construed as undercutting the dignity of the white men whose appearance they were thought to be appropriating). Along with the severe regulations of the White Women's Protection Ordinance, writer Regis Tove Stella argues that these regulations aimed 'to control the natives' by perpetuating the myth of White Man's Prestige.[53]

While the transmission of colonial culture from one context to another was a complex process with numerous vectors, travel and tourism certainly contributed. Travellers who had seen other colonies often felt they were in a position to make comparisons and offer suggestions in Papua New Guinea. Having experienced the British Empire in India, Malaya and Singapore, French colonialism in Indochina and the Dutch system in the Netherlands East Indies, Clune offered advice for the governance of Papua New Guinea in two books, *Prowling through Papua* and *Somewhere in New Guinea*. Clune thought 'Papua should now be intensively developed by White Australians, in the same way that the Netherlands Indies have been developed by White Dutchmen'. He suggested British Malaya's rubber plantations could be taken as another model, as well as the tea-plantation system in Ceylon. With his Asian experiences firmly in mind, Clune set out to make 'Australians wake up, take a tumble, and change the dog-in-the-manger, do-nothing policy' that kept Papua relatively undeveloped. He soon devised a scheme for 'settling from 10 000 to 20 000 White Australians on the fertile Papuan uplands', and roused his readers that 'it needs statesmanship, not Red Tape, to build an Empire'.[54]

Colonial-era travel to Asia had a further legacy. As we will see in subsequent chapters, many middle-class travellers retained the assumption that they deserved a higher level of service and comfort in Asia than back at home, and that Asians were there to ensure that this occurred. The colonial context also set the standard for much of the subsequent tourism industry in Asia. Grand colonial-era hotels such as Raffles and the Galle Face continued to operate well into the post-colonial period; indeed, they remain as edifices to colonial nostalgia even today. The travel culture that emerged during this time shaped travellers' experiences in Asia for decades to come. Although the sun was setting on Empire by the mid-20th century, the role of imperial master continued to appeal to Australians visiting Asia.

# 2: FORTUNE HUNTERS

At the start of the Asian Century, it is generally accepted that Australia's fortunes will largely depend on Asia. Announcing a whole-of-government White Paper on *Australia in the Asian Century* in 2011, then Prime Minister Julia Gillard reiterated that it is an 'Asian future we seek'.[1] All the enthusiasm about Asia's boundless markets also evoked anxiety about Australia's capacity to captitalise on its opportunities. The White Paper exhorted 'all of us to play our part' by 'becoming more Asia-literate and Asia-capable'.[2] This was the latest iteration of a recurring insecurity regarding Australians' capacity to successfully operate in Asia. Imperial culture may have insisted that Europeans were politically and culturally dominant, but the crucial advantages of size and economic power nearly always lay on the Asian side. Their economies may have been developing, and standards of living remained low throughout much of the 20th century, but capturing even a tiny proportion of China's, Japan's or Indonesia's vast markets meant making a fortune. The inducement was so great that Australians flocked to Asia hoping to make their fortune even as the ink on the White Australia Policy dried. The enthusiasm and eagerness with which Australian farmers, graziers and manufacturers looked to Asia, the effort they put in to please Asian partners and clients and the insecurities that continued to plague them, all challenge the imperial hierarchies encountered in the previous chapter.

Although it seems a recent development, the Asian business trip became increasingly common from the 1930s. A steady stream of businessmen – and occasionally professional women – set off for the commercial centres of Hong Kong, Tokyo and Shanghai. A smaller number headed to the regional hubs of Singapore, Batavia (now Jakarta) or Bombay (Mumbai). Many became enthusiastic boosters of regional trade, imploring fellow Australians to 'Wake up!' to the region's opportunities. Some became almost evangelical in their appeals to increase contact between Australians and their regional neighbours, not only in a commercial capacity but also through formal representation by trade commissioners and diplomats. They insisted that any Australian would recognise the boundless opportunities presented by Asia, if only they took the trouble to see it for themselves.

WAKE UP, AUSTRALIA! | Trade has been carried on between the peoples of Asia and those living on the Australian continent for centuries. Aboriginal Australians from the continent's northwest had built up a steady trade in trepang (sea cucumber) with Macassan islanders (from what is now Indonesia) centuries before European settlement. The Macassans then traded the trepang to Chinese merchants, thus connecting indigenous people from Arnhem Land and the Kimberley region to the imperial Chinese economy.[3] After settlement, British colonial networks linked Australia to ports at Singapore, Hong Kong, Ceylon and India. Their relative proximity meant that commerce with Asian traders was often more lucrative, and therefore more attractive, than trade with the distant motherland. By the 1830s, the Australian colonies imported tea from China and sugar from Java. In return, they sent whale oil, sealskins, horses, wool and minerals across the Asian trading world and onwards to Europe and the United States.[4]

The dramatic improvements in shipping technology outlined

in the previous chapter brought Asian markets closer and fostered great expectations. A new-found sense of proximity led far-sighted businessmen to reimagine Japan and China as potential markets, rather than distant and mysterious lands. Already in 1895 the Adelaide *Advertiser* reported that 'great things seem to be expected in some quarters from Australia's future trade relations with China and Japan'. Victorian graziers were certainly enthusiastic: as 'we can get our cattle over there in about 16 days we ought to be able to do a good business with them'.[5]

For those who could look past the British status quo, the promise of Asian markets appeared unbounded. England remained Australia's predominant trade partner: until World War I, roughly 45 per cent of Australian export trade, and some 50–60 per cent of the import trade, was with Britain.[6] While some Australians retained a sentimental attachment to Britishness, others thought that Australia needed to turn to Asia in search of new markets.[7] 'We have tried our best to make a real thing of Empire trade, and where has it led us?' asked one concerned Queenslander in a letter to the *Courier Mail* in 1934, concluding that, as 'England can't, and in some cases won't, help us … the only hope of Australia's future prosperity lies in trade with the East'.[8] In the previous chapter, we met popular writer Frank Clune as he headed to the Dutch East Indies in 1939. Although he was not himself in the export business, over and over again, Clune found his mind turning to potential trade opportunities. In Java, he began to see that 'our Nearest Neighbours of the North are … valuable suppliers and purchasers', and so 'there should be an ever-increasing volume of trade between our seven million people and their fifty-two million, if we pull up our socks, and go and get to it'. The more he saw, the more frequently he returned to a favourite catch cry: 'Wake up, Australia!'[9] A few years later, he visited India, and picked up the refrain. 'What a lot of mugs we have been!' he exclaimed. 'It is quite clear that Australia's future is in the Pacific and Indian Oceans, rather than in the Atlantic – and the sooner we recognize this fact, the better.'[10]

The business trip to Asia entered Australian commercial culture in the 1920s. It was facilitated by the intensification of shipping services between Australia and East Asia, with British lines including P&O, Blue Funnel and China Navigation as well as the Japanese line NYK running fast and efficient services between Australia and Japan via Hong Kong and the Philippines. The rise of commercial aviation in the late 1930s saw the options multiply. Qantas flew between Sydney and Singapore three times a week, the Dutch company KNILM flew the Sydney to Batavia route twice a week and Airlines of Australia flew from Cairns to Batavia on a fortnightly basis. Passengers could catch connecting flights onwards to Shanghai, Tokyo and Hong Kong, among other places. In 1938, as he planned his next trip, the ever-intrepid Frank Clune decided he would travel to Shanghai entirely by air.[11] At this time, even conservative politicians including Robert Menzies began to refer to Asia not as the 'Far East' but the 'Near North'.[12]

Many travellers were optimistic about the commercial promise of Asia, particularly as the Great Depression dampened prospects in other parts of the world. Newspaper reports increasingly referred to Asia as 'Australia's Future', and the region's markets as its 'Great Opportunity'.[13] Media interest was so great that reporters sometimes met returning businessmen as they disembarked from their ships or planes, and their impressions commanded inches of column space in metropolitan and regional newspapers. In 1931, the local representative for American motor manufacturer Studebaker-Pierce Arrow, C Scott-Fletcher, declared 'that there are vast markets in the Far East for Australian products'.[14] The following year, another 'motor man', AC Aubry of Willys Overland, reported that he 'really thought Australia had good prospects in the East'.[15] The enthusiasm was not limited to manufacturers. During the course of his 1932 visit, HV Foy of the noted Sydney department store Mark Foy's had become persuaded that, although 'the

Chinese market has not been fully explored', Japan would prove to be the real prize as it was 'very prosperous at the present time, and the more they improved themselves the better it would be for us'.[16] Perth businessman L Masel was also 'most eulogistic' in his praise of Japan after a 1934 visit.[17] Politicians were just as impressed. Tasmanian Senator RJ Payne travelled to Japan in 1935, reporting that the nation 'had made wonderful strides in industrial matters', with factories 'beautifully equipped' and filled with 'the most up-to-date machines'. Like Foy, however, he was less impressed with China, which presented a 'direct contrast to the conditions in Japan'.[18] His reports reached a wide audience. More than a year after his return, Payne was still giving public lectures on 'Japan as I Saw It', and his praise of its industries, as well as 'wonderful' scenery and 'magnificent' buildings had lost none of its fervour.[19]

Farmers and graziers were among those most excited by Japan's market potential. In 1932, the periodical *Farmer and Settler* reported that Japan was already the second largest consumer of Australian wool after Britain and 'if our merchants have sufficient enterprise [it] should become one of the largest purchasers of much of our primary produce'.[20] The following year, the secretary of the Wheat Pool of Western Australia, Mr HE Braine, toured Japan and China. He gained a sense that 'any happenings there … would exert a profound effect on Australia's future'.[21] Not long afterwards, grazier WT Atherton returned with reports that both China and Japan had 'enormous possibilities as a market for Australian wool'. Atherton sat on the executive of the United Graziers' Association of Queensland, so his impressions had some influence on trade deliberations.[22] The South Australian Minister for Agriculture, SR Whitford, also returned from an extended 'business and pleasure trip' 'impressed with the possibility of Australia expanding her trade in the East, and particularly with Japan'.[23]

Not every returned visitor was optimistic. Tasmanian accountant TA Stump was one of the few visitors who did not foresee the potential for Australian trade after visiting Japan in 1933. 'The Japanese masses do not earn enough money to buy goods at Australian prices', he noted; moreover they seemed 'perfectly happy and content to lead a simple life, free from the extravagances and luxuries which have become second nature to most of the Western nations'. Yet even he thought Australia should increase trade with Asia, noting that Java held 'great opportunities for developing markets, provided that the Australian goods ... are up to standard'.[24]

Returned visitors often became travel evangelists, encouraging other Australians to visit China, Japan, Hong Kong and, occasionally, the Dutch East Indies or India to explore their potential for themselves. As one report in *Farmer and Settler* had it in 1932, 'from a business point of view a trip to [Japan] should provide the traveller with a great fund of information that should be of value for the expansion of trade'.[25] Perth businessman L Masel agreed that travel was important for those seeking to capitalise on foreign markets; but just as importantly, Japan was 'wonderfully interesting and comparatively cheap, so cheap, in fact, that ... you live like a lord from the time you leave here until the time you get back'. All in all, he thought that a visit to Japan was 'undoubtedly the most suitable foreign trip for Australians at the moment'.[26] As the *Farmer and Settler* noted, charming scenery, magnificent temples, and 'quiet gentle, soft-mannered people' combined to make 'a holiday in Japan ... an experience that no one should miss'; one which would provide 'unlimited enjoyment'.[27]

Australia did not have direct diplomatic representation in Asia at this time, and the impressions of returned business travellers assumed great importance as a source of direct information on social and commercial conditions in the East. While they enjoyed the authority this bestowed on them, many travellers called on the government to establish formal ties. For AC Aubry, it was clear 'that better commercial representation was necessary'. He thought Australians needed commercial offices in Hong Kong, Manila and

Shanghai, where 'things were very good'.[28] A 'well-known Brisbane business man' made a similar demand in Brisbane's *Courier Mail* in 1934, noting that 'there were markets for Australian goods in China and Japan', but 'a comprehensive selling and advertising campaign should be developed'.[29]

The government was prepared to listen to the first-hand reports of prominent businessmen. In 1932, industrialist and government adviser Herbert V Gepp returned from a five-month tour of Japan, China and Hong Kong brimming with enthusiasm for the potential presented by Asian markets. He presented the Prime Minister with a report recommending the despatch of an official trade delegation, building towards permanent trade representatives across the region. Professor Melbourne of the University of Queensland also tabled a report calling for similar action after his return from China and Japan. The two accounts helped influence the 1933 decision to appoint Trade Commissioners to Japan, China and the Netherlands East Indies, and to despatch the first Goodwill Mission to Asia, headed by the Minister for External Affairs, John Latham. These represented the earliest moves towards independent diplomatic relations with Asia.

# THE 'EAST-MEETS-WEST COMPLEX' | If Asian markets were to be taken seriously, Australians had to overcome the casual assumption that Asia was backward, underdeveloped and industrially primitive. Where in the last chapter we saw the ways in which colonial-era travel could strengthen these stereotypes, visiting the region could also shatter them. Commercial imperatives encouraged business travellers to regard Asians not as backward 'natives' but as increasingly sophisticated consumers. Upon return, they roused other Australians to 'Wake Up!' and recognise that Asia was a vital and modern marketplace. Returning from China and Japan in 1933, for example, FA Wicks reported

that 'the departmental or chain stores are a revelation' which 'make our largest Australian stores look very small in comparison'.[30] Frank Clune wrote of Asia as awakening 'from dreams and lethargy to the boom, bang and burst of Big Business'.[31] A repeat visitor, Clune was stunned by the pace of development. In the Dutch East Indies, he wrote, 'where I expected to see nothing but primitive coconuts and kampongs, I was amazed by displays of modern micrometers and microscopes'. Even on the streets, 'among the sarong-clad throng of Sundanese natives ... may be seen studious professors, engineers, technicians and physicists'.[32] Touring a research facility in Bangalore some three years later, he again thought it an 'eye-opener' to discover that 'in the very heart of "darkest India" a team of "heathen native" scientists were carrying out researches ... which are followed with bated breath by scientists throughout all the civilised world!'. Having visited modern engineering plants, irrigation projects and factories, Clune found himself imploring, 'Wake up, Australia! Learn a lesson from that "backward" country, India!'[33]

Clune used irony to convey his sense of shock. Deep-seeded assumptions that the West was modern and the East was backward had been shattered. Having seen signs of modernity even in 'darkest India', Frank Clune began to wonder whether 'it's all rot to say that "East is East and West is West, and never the twain shall meet"'. Instead, he began to think of an 'East-meets-West complex', in which the latest in modern consumer goods were peddled alongside 'all the strange and wonderful merchandise of Hindostan'.[34] The sense that East and West were in the process of meeting became a recurrent theme in Cold War travel accounts, which are explored further in Chapter 4. Clune's account, which formed an early example of this trope, reveals that commerce as well as politics provided an inducement for Australians to abandon the assumption that 'never the twain shall meet'. Another traveller, businesswoman Ethel Ranken, returned from a 1937 buying trip with the striking sense that Japan 'looked and smelt exactly like England'.[35] At a time of enduring sentimental connections with Britain, there could be no stronger statement of the 'East-meets-West complex'.

Such epiphanies could lead Australians to recognise that, far from being 'backward', some parts of Asia were actually striding ahead of Australia. Returning from a four-month trip of Japan, China and Java in 1933, TA Stump reported that in Tokyo, roads 'were among the finest on which he had ever travelled', vehicles were directed automatically by traffic lights and trains were electrically powered. Australians had 'much to learn from the Japanese in the organisation of tourist traffic', he concluded – before adding that they had plenty to learn 'in the matter of courtesy and attention', too.[36] The comfortable and efficient trains in Japanese-occupied Korea were also a revelation for Frank Clune. He concluded that 'Australia could learn a bit in Manchukuo ... we should put our own house in order'.[37] Admonitions for Australians to learn from Asia could be confronting. Such statements challenged entrenched assumptions that European civilisation stood at the apex of a cultural evolutionary hierarchy. Far from upholding the White Man's Prestige, these travellers questioned the extent of the difference between East and West, and even began to contest the division in the first place. Travelling to Asia for business had led some travellers to see things differently. They looked for – and found – market opportunities and economic potential where other visitors saw only backwardness; and found progress where others saw stagnation. In doing so, they undermined some of the claims by which Europeans justified colonial domination over Asia, as explored in the previous chapter.

THE AUSTRALIAN DIASPORA | All this enthusiasm lured a number of enterprising and ambitious Australians to search for their fortunes in Asia. Most fortune hunters eventually came home (some with heavier pockets; others not) but some remained. Although this book focusses on travellers rather than migrants, the fluid nature of Australian expatriation to Asia requires some recognition of this important subgroup.

The extent of Australian expatriation to Britain, Europe and the United States has been well documented, but historians are only now beginning to chart the experiences of Australians residing in Asia. Yet, so many Australians had settled in interwar Shanghai that an Anzac Society was established in 1931; by 1939 it distributed 900 copies of its quarterly magazine, *Down Under*.[38] That same year, a review of Clune's *Sky High to Shanghai* noted that 'in nearly every place he visited he found an Australian filling some important post'.[39] In Japan, Clune was welcomed by Peter Russo, then a lecturer at the Tokyo College of Commerce and later a journalist and respected commentator on Asian issues in Australia. In Tokyo, he also caught up with Mark Gallard, editor of the Sydney *Truth*, and noted anaesthetist and Boer War hero Rupert Hornabrook; in China he met Les Lawrance, responsible for the Transport Section of the Shanghai Telephone System, and Bill O'Hara, who had settled in Shanghai after serving with the Australian Light Horse during World War I. Seemingly bumping into a 'fellow-marsupial' at every turn, Clune declared that 'the place is alive with Australians'.[40] Significantly, this assertion didn't take into account the thousands of Australians of Chinese heritage who regularly shuttled between China and Australia throughout this period, as explored in Chapter 9.

A number of Anglo-Australians reached positions of some standing in Republican China. Lithgow-born William Henry Donald was at the peak of his influence at the time of Clune's visit. Known to posterity as 'Donald of China', he had begun working as a journalist for Hong Kong's *China Mail* and Shanghai's *Far Eastern Review* before rising to a position of influence as adviser to the Kuomintang government of Sun Yat-Sen, and later Chiang Kai-shek. The extent of his influence is the subject of some debate, but he has been credited with inspiring some reforms and he certainly played a key role in a number of critical political incidents during the 1930s. His biographer, Earl Albert Selle, was confident that readers had 'heard about William Henry Donald, the "Donald of China"' who was 'an almost legendary character' and 'the only foreigner since Marco Polo to live and break bread with China's rulers'.[41]

'Donald of China' was in some respects following in the peripatetic footsteps of GE 'Chinese' Morrison, who we'll meet again in Chapter 7. Morrison's legend was established with a 4800-kilometre journey from Shanghai to Burma, as recounted in the 1895 book *An Australian in China*, and he went on to become China correspondent for the London *Times* before taking up a position as government adviser to the Nationalist government from 1911. His son, Ian Morrison, was also influential, firstly as an English lecturer at Hokkaido Imperial University in Japan and later as the China correspondent for the London *Times*. After World War II he moved to Singapore, where his affair with a doctor, Han Suyin, was recounted in her semi-autobiographical novel (later made into a successful film), *Love is a Many-Splendored Thing*. Morrison continued as correspondent for *The Times* after the outbreak of the Korean War, where he was killed in action in 1950. Others found commercial success. Sydney-born VG Bowden was an influential businessman and a member of both the European-only Shanghai Club and the mixed-race Hsui Club. His standing in the trading community was such that he was chosen to serve as Australian Trade Commissioner to Shanghai in the years before World War II disrupted trade.

Not all expatriates struck gold. Historians Kate Bagnall and Sophie Loy-Wilson have discovered that a good number of Australians lived in decidedly straitened circumstances in China during the 1920s and 1930s. Unable to find work in Depression-era Australia, they made their way to Hong Kong and Shanghai hoping to find their fortune – or merely find a job. Their presence reminds us that movement between Australia and Asia was not as rare as we might assume; nor was it the preserve of the wealthy. Australians from all classes made their way to the East in search of opportunity. Like all fortune hunters, only a few succeeded. The rest lived in rundown boarding houses, struggling to make ends meet. Some found the situation so difficult that they turned to charity. The Hong Kong Benevolent Society assisted Australians in desperate circumstances from the early decades of the century and the Anzac Society in Shanghai established a special Benevolent Fund in the 1930s 'with the object of assisting Australians, particularly those who were destitute'.[42] The situation was so dire that in January 1934 the Lyons government issued a warning discouraging Australians from heading to Shanghai in the hope of finding work.[43]

Those who did not turn to charity sometimes turned to crime. As Loy-Wilson recounts, Australians were implicated in Shanghai's notorious underworld, including its gambling, prostitution and narcotics rackets. One Australian, Mrs VV Johnson, was arrested and deported for manufacturing and selling commercial quantities of opium, cocaine and heroin in 1935 in a case that was reported as 'one of the most sensational cases in Shanghai's criminal history'.[44] Indeed, Australians were so prominent in Shanghai's underworld that segments of the Chinese-language media thought that they were particularly prone to criminality and speculated whether this was due to their convict heritage. After all, they wrote, what could you expect from 'that place where the British sent their prisoners'?[45]

According to Loy-Wilson, the presence of so many Australians sharpened anti-colonial sentiments amongst the local Chinese population. Reports in radical newspapers such as the *China Critic* fumed: 'To them we say "Go home and scatter your white man's pride to the wind and remove your immigration discrimination against Asiatics and cultivate your goodwill for the Chinese people before you come to do business here"'.[46] While tracing the Asian view of Australians is beyond the scope of this book, it is important to remember that Australians in Asia elicited a range of responses from local populations. The Australians' bad reputation also sharpened colonists' anxieties. Colonial life in Hong Kong was strictly bound by concern for White Man's Prestige, as explored in the previous chapter. Those fortune hunters who lived hand-to-mouth found it difficult, if not impossible, to maintain a way of life in keeping with imperial standards, a fact that was noted with some concern by the British residents of Hong Kong and Shanghai.[47] By living at a standard decidedly below the imperial standard, these Australian fortune seekers were seen to be disruptive to the colonial order.

OPPONENTS | The repeated calls to 'Wake Up!' point to a deeper story. Markets with this much potential shouldn't need boosterism. If Asia presented such a golden opportunity, why were Australians so slow to get on the bandwagon? The White Australia Policy, and the racial prejudice that sustained it, presented one major obstacle. The union movement feared competition from Asian labour and so was particularly virulent in its opposition to Asian trade. Unionists were concerned that closer trade ties would lead to demands that Australia open its borders to Asian migrants and they feared that a flood of Asian labourers would undermine Australian working conditions, which, they proudly asserted, were the best in the world. For supporters of the White Australia Policy, businessmen who encouraged trade with Asia were selling their country, and their race, down the river for a few (or even a few thousand) pounds.

Opposition to commercial ties was also motivated by anxieties for Australia's security. Some Australians became wary of Japan after its stunning 1905 victory over Russia – the first time an Asian power had defeated a European one. Even enthusiastic remarks about Japan's surging economy could betray the shadow of unease. Interviewed in 1933, business traveller FA Wicks was effusive about the Japanese market but he also noted that, if it weren't for Singapore's British defences, 'Japan would have been a real menace to Australia long ago'.[48] Five years later, Australian waterside workers refused to load metal bound for Japan, arguing that it would be used to manufacture weapons that could be turned against Australia. They argued that Australians risked the ultimate irony by enabling their own invasion.

The Pacific War seemed to bear out the waterside workers' fears and it affected popular perceptions of trade with Japan for years to come. Official trade relations with Japan resumed in 1947, but the prospect of trading with the enemy remained an unsurpassable hurdle in many minds. An editorial in the *Australian Women's Weekly* pulled no punches: Japanese wartime atrocities had 'left an undying hatred of the Japanese people and deep repugnance of all their work'. While it admitted that trade must resume 'for our own benefit', the editorial seethed at the prospect.[49] Nonetheless, Japan quickly rose to become Australia's premier trading partner in the years following the Pacific War. In 1957, Australia and Japan signed a formal Commerce Agreement. By the late 1960s, one quarter of all Australian exports was bound for Japan, and these figures rose over the following decades as the Japanese economy experienced near-miraculous rates of growth.[50]

FUMBLING WITH CHOPSTICKS | Economic historians have argued that trade underpinned warmer diplomatic relations with Japan.[51] Booming trade certainly encouraged more travel. Following a post-war lull, the Asian business trip re-emerged to become firmly established as part of Australian business culture from the late 1950s. Japan and Hong Kong again became prominent destinations for entrepreneurial businessmen. Business travel was encouraged by new direct flights between Australia and Asia. By 1961 almost 90 per cent of all Asian business trips were taken by air, compared to only 42 per cent of leisure trips.[52] The business market was so strong that Qantas hoped it could be used to expand leisure travel to Japan, so it encouraged commercial travellers to 'explore profitable opportunities for expanding overseas trade, and enjoy a colourful holiday' at the same time.[53]

Australians hoping to establish trade relations had to build cordial relations with Asian counterparts and they had to conduct themselves in a way that would be gratifying to their hosts. The body politics of business contact were very different from that of colonial tourists who, as we saw in the previous chapter, learnt to be haughty and imperious in their contacts with 'natives'. Businessmen were placed at a disadvantage in that they had to conduct themselves according to Asian business culture, which many found baffling. Merchant WJ Ledger was exasperated after a buying trip to Japan in 1933. As he told the *West Australian*, Asian business culture was strange and 'rather tiring'. Great reserves of patience were required for 'the Japanese merchants' manner of doing business'. Firstly, one had to endure 'a great deal of bowing' and, although 'you cannot fail to be bewildered at the lavishness of the surroundings' the long, drawn out discussions, conducted through translators, soon made visitors uncomfortable and impatient.[54] Ledger's account shows that the Japanese way of doing business was entirely foreign to Australians; moreover the fact that the *West Australian* published his comments in full reveals that it considered the problem of conducting business with Asians to be of broad interest at a time of expanding economic ties.

Australians continued to struggle with Japanese corporate culture as trade relations intensified from the 1950s. In the official diary documenting a 1963 business trip to Tokyo, the chairman of the mining conglomerate BHP Sir Colin Syme noted that his 'main problems were chopsticks, geishas, slippers and language'. The language barrier was perhaps the most serious problem; Syme admitted that 'a number of questions and answers [were] probably misunderstood' during the course of his visit.[55] Sydney-based engineering executive William Wade found his inability to speak the language bred a broader confusion, as it was 'very strange coming out of a hotel you don't know, among people ... not one in the vicinity who spoke English, and getting into a cab with someone who didn't speak English'. Unable to control the situation to the extent he was accustomed, he found 'the lack of language ... quite an experience'.[56]

Business contacts needed to be wined and dined, but dining etiquette – particularly the use of chopsticks – presented a litany of problems for Australian visitors. Many businessmen worried that their inability to eat with chopsticks made them look foolish and placed them at a disadvantage. Syme was a frequent business traveller, and a booster of Asian trade relations who went on to chair the Private Investment Company for Asia. Yet he never overcame his awkwardness and preferred to use Western cutlery to avoid the risk of fumbling with chopsticks.[57] Others were more adventurous. Wade did his best to pick up local customs: 'I keep my eyes open and try to do the right thing'. Although he suffered some embarrassing setbacks, by the time of his second visit to Japan in 1963 he boasted that 'the Japanese waitress remarked how well I use my chopsticks'.[58]

Asian corporate culture was strictly men's business in the mid-20th century. In Japan, entertainments involving geisha or hostesses were common to many corporate negotiations. The presence of geisha was another stumbling block for Australians who were unsure about the boundaries of acceptable conduct. Judging from travel journals and corporate reports, the quandary of which women to approach, and how to behave, consumed a good deal of business travellers' energy. Syme noted the fine distinctions between hostesses ('paid by the Club and not usual to tip them') and geisha (whose 'services were expensive' and so 'used largely to entertain visitors out of expense accounts') for the benefit of the other BHP executives who might read his report. As well as cost and tipping etiquette, he made note of their sexual availability. Even with hostesses it was 'not to be assumed that they are of easy virtue'. Geisha were 'said to sleep with men only from inclination' and advised that the money side should be 'handled with tact'. Professional travel writers also explained the process of procuring and paying for sex. Best-selling travel writer Colin Simpson explained it in some detail in his best-selling Japanese travelogue, *The Country Upstairs*. 'The function of a hostess … is to talk to and drink with the customer, dance with him and generally keep him happy so that he stays and spends money', but 'if the happy customer should have ideas of a more intimate relationship … he may or may not be able to make arrangements'.[59]

REORIENTATIONS | The business trip introduced thousands of Australians to China and Japan, as well as to other trading hubs such as Hong Kong and Singapore. Although they had gone there in search of profit, most came back with a bounty of impressions and experiences about Asia and its people. Senator Payne was evangelical about the impact of travel. He thought Australians were 'apt to have wrong ideas altogether about other countries', and so 'every public man, if possible, should see the conditions prevailing in other countries', particularly those Asian countries with which Australia traded.[60]

Many business travellers had privileged access to local elites and some found that, far from feeling disgust at their 'native' customs, they enjoyed the company of their Asian counterparts. Their generally positive impressions formed significant threads of counter-opinion at a time when popular prejudices prevailed. In the 1930s, when prominent businessmen such as HV Foy 'said that the Japs were the dominant people of the East, and he had a great liking for them', the newspapers listened.[61] Twenty years later, with popular perceptions of the Japanese at a new low following the Pacific War, Colin Syme found the people to be 'hard working, pleasant and happy', and he also admitted he enjoyed their company.[62] As he was leaving, William Wade noted that his visit 'has given me a better understanding of Japan and Tokyo than I ever had before'. As we will see in Chapter 4, Wade became enchanted by Asia and this was largely because of the friendliness and good humour of the people he met. While his warmest regard was for the people of Hong Kong, he found that people in Japan were also 'very pleasant', as they 'tend to smile all the time'.[63]

Such positive impressions were particularly significant in the context of the continuing suspicion with which many Australians viewed their former enemy. A visit to Japan could help convince travellers that the Japanese were not the barbarous fiends of wartime propaganda. Colin Simpson wrote that, arriving in Tokyo for the first time, his mind had been crowded with 'thoughts about the past', which were 'grim with the memory of … Australian prisoners of war, sick and starving [being] machine gunned'. But he soon came to see a different picture, in which the Japanese were decent, ordinary people. This was the 'picture … we see when we go there, by plane or ship or armchair'.[64]

A number of travellers retained ties to Asia in subsequent years, returning both for business and leisure; others became boosters of Asian trade at home, encouraging the next generation of ambitious Australians to turn their gaze north. The increase in contact led to formal attempts to direct regional business relations, with groups such as the Australia-Japan Business Co-operation Committee launched in 1962 to co-ordinate the steady flow of capital and people between the two nations.

ENGAGING THE DRAGON | The Chinese Revolution of 1949 precipitated a break in official relations between Australia and the People's Republic of China that lasted for over two decades. The resumption of diplomatic relations in December 1972 aroused an explosion in Australian interest. Journalist and sex therapist Bettina Arndt quipped that, by the 1980s, China had become as exciting as sex.[65] A good deal of optimism regarding China focussed on its market potential. Historian David Goldsworthy called the 1980s a 'China Bubble', as politicians, business people and media figures came to espouse buoyant – even 'romantic' – views of China's potential.[66] Chief among the enthusiasts were prime ministers Bob Hawke and Paul Keating. Hawke removed a range of tariff barriers to encourage regional trade and oversaw the launch of Asia-Pacific Economic Cooperation (APEC) in 1989. He was also a singularly enthusiastic traveller, making dozens of trips to China.

Australia's exports to China soared. Valued at $63 million in 1972–73, they rose to $555 million in 1981 and $1.59 billion in 1986.[67] This helped encourage a 'benign view' of China and according to Sinologist Edmund Fung, elevated the relationship with China 'to a status second only to the American alliance in Australian foreign policy'.[68] The first 'China Bubble' burst in June 1989, as the Chinese government turned against pro-democracy demonstrators in Tiananmen Square. In the wake of the attack, even Australia's first Ambassador to China, Stephen FitzGerald, began to fear that Australian enthusiasm had been built on 'a large measure of illusion' and regretted that the 'national embrace' of China had been so 'craven' and 'obsequious'.[69]

By the first decade of the new millennium, Australian business had regained its enthusiasm for China. The value of Australia's exports to China soared: $5.4 billion in 2001, $60.9 billion by 2010.[70] China was now Australia's largest trading partner and although the riches were dug out of Australian soil, China assumed the mantle of El Dorado. In 2011, the Director of the Lowy Institute for International Policy, Michael Wesley, wrote *There goes the neighbourhood: Australia and the rise of Asia*. Focussing on China, and particularly its likely impacts on the Australian economy, this was a book of its time. But the language was strangely familiar. Addressing his Australian readers directly, Wesley had one piece of advice: 'wake up!'[71]

And again, fortune seekers set out in search of riches. Over one million Australians now live and work overseas, and a growing number are settling in Asia. In 2003, Hong Kong hosted the fifth-largest Australian expatriate community, and the Australian diaspora in Shanghai has substantially increased over the past decade.[72] Yet, this does not mean that the edges of cross-cultural interaction had been smoothed. Judging by the shelves of business etiquette guides to China available for purchase in Australian bookstores, doing business with the Chinese in the 2000s was thought to be even more difficult than dealing with Japan in previous decades. In 1990, Kevin Sinclair's *Culture Shock! China* portrayed Chinese culture as an 'enigma', and his guide as an attempt to answer 'baffling queries' about the 'mysterious Chinese'.[73] The number of guidebooks mushroomed, advising Australians on *Communicating with Asia*, *Doing Business in China*, *Doing Business in North Asia* and *How to do Business in China: 24 lessons in Engaging the Dragon*, among many other titles.[74] The anxiety was palpable: one guidebook warned aspiring tycoons that the corporate climate was so complex that '80 per cent of deals that fall over in China are the direct result of the mistakes made by western companies', so Australians had to work hard to learn 'the way of the dragon'.[75] Of course, Australians weren't the only ones struggling with Chinese business culture. The *China Business Guide*, for example, was published simultaneously in Hong Kong, London, Chicago, Singapore, Melbourne and Kuala Lumpur and it portrayed 'venturing through the open door in search of opportunities' as 'a torturous and difficult process'.[76] But the sheer number of guides published for the Australian market suggests a distinctively anxious cohort, concerned about their capacity to function in Asia.

While they may provide some comfort to anxious first-timers, as a genre these etiquette guides perpetuate, rather than minimise, the sense of difference between Australia and China. Many recent publications echo Orientalist tropes by over-generalising 'Chinese behaviour' and claiming it was 'governed' by mysterious systems such as 'Li' or 'the way of the dragon'.[77] Others even draw tenuous links to classical texts such as Sun Tzu's *Art of War* to suggest that to succeed in contemporary business, Australians needed 'to know your Chinese 'enemy' as well as you know yourself' – which required 'both close study and close scrutiny'.[78] In only a couple of pages, the foreword of Sinclair's *Culture Shock! China* claimed that 'the Chinese are different': 'baffling people' with 'significant differences in outlook, manner, work ethics, eating, entertainment, dress, ways of relaxing and even in such simple areas as saying hello' – altogether 'different from much of the rest of the world'.[79]

Portraying China's culture as baffling and complex serves the interests of etiquette guide authors. As Sinclair concluded, 'understanding China and the Chinese is never easy' but 'this book will help unlock some of the loops in this complex Chinese puzzle'.[80] But their popularity speaks to the continuing fears of Australian business people forced to communicate across cultural divides. Ironically, Australians became more anxious about their performance in Asia, even as the El Dorado began to pay. This was the result of greater appreciation for cultural sensitivity as well as a fuller recognition of the importance of the Chinese market – and so the consequences of getting it wrong. But the rising anxiety perpetuated the idea that a great gulf separated Chinese and Australians, and that bridging the divide required a lot of work. Business travellers may have been among the first to overcome the geographical distance between Australia and Asia, but they continued to cling to a sense of cultural distance well into the 21st century.

The anxiety felt by Australian businessmen was mirrored in broader concerns about whether Australians were 'Asia literate', and whether they would succeed in a future shaped by Asia. Exhortations for the nation to 'Wake Up!' were often accompanied by demands that Australians learn more about their region. The *Australia in the Asian Century* White Paper of 2012 roused 'all of us' to facilitate Australia's economic integration with the region by becoming more Asia-literate and Asia-capable.[81] Fears about the nation's lack of Asia literacy, or more recently, 'Asia capacity', continue to accompany the economic narrative. In a recent book examining the Sino-Australian relationship, for example, academics James Reilly and Jingdong Yuan argued that 'Australia's deepening economic interdependence with a rising China poses a national test'.[82] Successive governments have publicised their attempts to prepare for that test. In July 2013, the Rudd government pledged an investment of $36 million over 10 years to develop a National Centre for Asia Capability, based at the universities of Melbourne and New South Wales. Prime Minister Tony Abbott signalled his resolve to invest in Asia literacy while still in Opposition. 'It should go without saying that geography won't keep Australia prosperous even in the coming Asian century', he noted, and expressed concern that 'Australia's moment could easily be missed through complacency'.[83] Since assuming the prime ministership, he has made the Reverse Colombo Plan, which sends Australian students to universities throughout the region, a flagship policy.

The optimism with which Australian business travellers regarded Asia in the early 20th century can appear surprising. But alongside racial prejudice, invasion anxiety and imperialist disdain lay a solid streak of Australian enthusiasm for Asia. The previous chapter showed that many Australians came to think of Asia as backward and requiring European colonial control. But few visitors could refer to Asian backwardness in Shanghai or Tokyo, which were buzzing, modern metropolises from the early 20th century.

More often, they were astounded by their progress and prosperity, not least because the citizens of these bustling cities represented millions of potential consumers. Some of this was configured around geography. By referring to a single 'Asia' (or 'region' or 'neighbourhood') Australians have tended to think of a hugely diverse region as a single entity. Yet, perceptions of individual nations and regions within this category always varied and East Asian cities evoked a unique set of responses. The imperatives of business also saw commercial travellers interact with Asian elites on terms that suggested a greater level of social equality than most tourists did in their interactions with servants. Even so, some visitors continued to regard the local people as 'coolies' and 'natives', and many held that colonial intervention in Hong Kong, or the concession system in Shanghai, was right and proper. The imperative for trade complicated the bank of assumptions about Asia, but the range of individual experiences of the region always reflected an ambivalence.

The rhetoric that the nation's future would be determined by Asia led Australians to look north with anticipation. While in the economic context this often provoked enthusiasm, the recognition of Asia's proximity, size and power could also rouse profound anxiety. Australians looked north anticipating danger as well as benefit, and their concerns are explored further in the next chapter.

# 3: WARRIORS

Melbourne-born twins Phil and Jack Lavery were 21 when they enlisted with the RAAF in 1942. The Japanese were advancing south through Papua; it was widely believed that they were headed for Australia. On 28 July, the *Argus* published a rousing editorial urging a deeper thrust into Asia. The Pacific conflict was more than a war, it claimed, it was a crusade, and 'the surest way of preventing the enemy from carrying the fight to us is to carry the fight to them'.[1] The Lavery twins enlisted later that day and over the next four years they served in Papua, New Guinea and the Dutch East Indies, where their paths crossed with their older brothers Reg and Harry, also serving with the RAAF. Along with hundreds of thousands of others, the war introduced all four Lavery boys to Asia for the first time.

They say that history doesn't repeat itself, but you'd be forgiven for thinking otherwise with the Lavery family. The next generation brought another set of twins, and again they fought a war of forward defence in Asia. When Joe and Gerard Lavery went to Vietnam in January 1970, however, it was not of their own choosing: their numbers had come up in the macabre lottery that regulated National Service – conscription – from 1965. All the Lavery boys, from both generations, survived their deployments; in this they were lucky. They were also united by the ambivalence with which they regarded Asia. In letters home, they sometimes complained about the 'god forsaken hole' to which they'd been posted, but there were moments of real appreciation, too. By the end of his service Reg had begun to learn some Malay; almost 30 years later Joe contemplated taking a formal course in Vietnamese. War had introduced two generations of an otherwise unexceptional Australian family to Asia and they all came back with a new interest in their nation's role in the region.

While rarely so colourful, family histories such as this are not unusual. Before the tourist booms of the 1970s, the greatest number of Australians who travelled to Asia did so as warriors and peacekeepers. Australian military personnel have been deployed in the region almost continuously since the 1940s. They were there from the very start of the Pacific War in 1941, the Korean War in 1951 and the Vietnam War in 1962. They served in lesser-known Asian conflicts, including the Malayan Emergency and Konfrontasi and they were also extremely active in regional 'peacekeeping' roles. They enforced Japan's surrender for seven years after 1945; they were in Indonesia to arbitrate its path to decolonisation in 1947; in India and Pakistan to enforce Partition from 1950 (staying until 1985); in Cambodia to oversee its transition to democracy during the 1990s; and in East Timor as it declared independence in 1999.

Why was Australia's military so consistently engaged in Asia? In the early days of the Pacific War, Prime Minister Robert Menzies declared that Australia's role in the region was a 'tranquilising' one. The claim was echoed in subsequent years. The editors of a recent volume of military history even called Australia a 'peacekeeping nation'.[2] Yet, far from tranquilising or peacekeeping forces, some local populations regarded a number of Australia's military interventions as an intrusion, assault or even invasion. Framing military involvement as peacekeeping (or even as forward defence) was also problematic on the home front, provoking questions about whether other people's problems were worth the toll in Australian dollars and lives. These questions are reflected in the titles of histories of Australia's Asian engagements, such as *Other*

*People's Wars, Imposing Peace and Prosperity,* or *Reluctant Saviour.*[3]

In fact, Australia was not only in Asia because of altruism, but also because of widespread fear. Anxiety underpinned official relations with Asia throughout the 20th century. Again, the titles given to history books encapsulate broader patterns: *Anxious Nation, In Fear of China, Fear of the Dark, Fear of Security: Australia's invasion anxiety.*[4] Long-standing fears of Asian invasion lent weight to arguments supporting military deployment throughout the following decades.[5] Under the oxymoronic doctrine of 'forward defence', Cold War operations were also driven by fear that Asian nations would 'fall' to communism, as anticipated by the Domino Theory that underpinned strategic thinking at the time.

This chapter looks at the earliest major deployments in Asia: World War II and the Occupation of Japan that followed it. It examines the motivations behind these deployments, weighing up rhetoric about altruism and the desire to maintain peace against the impetus provided by deep-seeded fears of Asia. It also looks at the experiences of the hundreds of thousands of 'ordinary' Australians who came to know something of Asia through their military service. What were their experiences of Asia? What roles did they assume when confronted with the region? And how did their service affect their views and attitudes towards the region, both in the short term and over time?

T HE ASIATIC MENACE | At the end of the 19th century the population of Australia was only four million – less than one per cent of the population of China alone. And they were well aware of the fact: Australian culture at all levels was marked by apprehension about 'Rising Asia', which threatened invasion, either of armies or migrants. Some of this fear had arisen in response to Chinese migration. The middle decades of the 19th century saw one of the greatest waves of emigration in human history, as a chain of tragedies including civil war, drought and famine impelled millions to leave China's southern provinces in search of a better life in Southeast Asia, the Pacific Islands, the Americas and further afield. Viewed from a global perspective, the number of Chinese settlers who reached the Australian colonies was relatively small. But they provoked a strong reaction because their numbers grew suddenly (45 000 arrived in Victoria during the years 1854–58 alone); furthermore, the Chinese were visible amongst a small and overwhelmingly Anglo-Celtic Australian population.[6] To some, it appeared as if the Australian colonies faced an Asiatic invasion. Images of Mongol hordes and Asiatic tides began to haunt labourers and prime ministers alike.[7] They came to think of the Chinese with a blend of arrogance and apprehension, an almost schizophrenic mix captured by the noted historian and politician Charles Pearson in his *National Life and Character: A Forecast*. 'We are well aware that China can swamp us with a single year's surplus of population', he wrote, and so 'we are guarding the last part of the world in which the higher races can live … for the higher civilisation'.[8]

Having only just secured their tenure on the great southern continent, some Australians worried that their foothold may prove as tenuous in the face of the coming invaders as that of the Aboriginal inhabitants had been before them. Others worried that the Chinese would undercut wages. The dream of a workingman's paradise was based on ideals of social justice in which every worker had dignity, political representation and a good standard of living. But that depended on excluding outsiders. Because they felt they were fighting for a just cause, radicals and unionists were particularly prone to aggressively anti-Chinese diatribes. Their lexicon of filthy, vice-ridden and iniquitous Chinamen, as well as dehumanised images of flooding populations, teeming insects and insatiable octopuses or dragons, established the vocabulary of Australian racism.[9]

Where popular fears initially focussed on the Chinese, official anxieties soon turned to the region's emerging industrial and military superpower: Japan. Widespread enthusiasm for all things Japanese had swept the Western world in the mid-19th century. Japanese silks, slippers, fans and kimonos adorned drawing rooms from Paris and Berlin to New York and Sydney. While the fashionable rejoiced, more 'serious-minded' citizens began to sound a warning about the strategic threat Japan might pose to Australia. As David Walker has shown, the rising anxiety was expressed in a stream of invasion novels such as William Lane's *Yellow or White?: The Race War of AD1908* and *The Coloured Conquest* by 'Rata', a pseudonym for labour historian Thomas Roydhouse.[10] The fear of Asia also lay at the heart of Australian military and naval planning from the beginning of the century.[11]

KEEPING PEACE IN THE PACIFIC | On 3 September 1939, two days after Hitler unleashed the invasion of Poland, Prime Minister Robert Menzies took to the radio to announce that Britain had entered the conflict and, 'as a result', Australia was also at war.[12] The decision to become involved was based on strategy as much as sentiment; Japan was not far from Menzies' mind. He feared that the war in Europe was the 'slow beginning of a greater and vital struggle' in which Australia 'will be the first prize'. In his words, 'If Britain wins then we win. If she loses we are gone'.[13]

It seemed as if Australians' darkest fears were coming true after the Japanese began their assault on Southeast Asia from December 1941. Colonial defences in French Indochina, British Malaya and the Dutch East Indies buckled and the Japanese advanced southwards with frightening efficiency. The 'impregnable' fortress of Singapore fell on 12 February 1942 and Japanese forces soon entered Australian territory in Papua and New Guinea. Darwin came under direct air attack from 19 February. The Curtin government announced that Australians faced 'the gravest hour of our history'.[14]

The Department of Information instigated a propaganda campaign that was so fierce it came to be known as the 'hate' campaign. It claimed that 'the Jap as he really is' came from 'a bespectacled ape-like race', which was 'physically short-sighted' and 'mentally myopic'. Radio segments finished with the rousing cry, 'We've always despised them, now we must smash them!'[15]

The Japanese advance saw a rush to enlist; the Lavery twins were among the surge. All in all, more than half a million Australians served overseas during World War II (out of a total population of 7 million).[16] Soldiers heading for service in the Middle East passed through Singapore, Bombay or Colombo; others were stationed across Southeast Asia, the Indian subcontinent and the Pacific. More than 22 000 fought a different kind of battle in prisoner-of-war camps across Thailand, Malaya, Indonesia and Japan itself. The Pacific War facilitated a great deal of personal experience of Asia, which contributed to longer-term shifts in popular attitudes.

WARTIME ADVENTURES | The majority of soldiers had never left their state, let alone their country, upon enlistment.[17] Most could only dream of the kind of holidays enjoyed by Laure Falkiner, or the business trips of HV Foy. In a letter home, Reg Lavery admitted he 'probably would never have seen coral islands, reefs, equators, jungles and natives & things if weren't for the war'.[18] Soldiers' preconceptions about Asia were largely based on images circulating in popular culture. Most of those who saw service in World War II had grown up in the 1920s and 1930s and, as noted in Chapter 1, the popular novels, histories and films of the time painted Asia and the Pacific as an exotic backdrop for white men's adventures.

The outbreak of war could prove alluring for those who longed for adventure. Author John Barrett estimates that roughly half of all recruits signed up at least partly because of a longing for adventure.[19] Edward 'Weary' Dunlop enlisted because he yearned 'for the high romantic ground for adventure in strange lands'.[20] Others, including commando Brian Walpole and FF Fenn, also enlisted out of 'the sense of adventure'.[21] Others still set off hoping for the exotic sunsets and romantic encounters of Hollywood blockbusters. Historians Sean Brawley and Chris Dixon have shown that many soldiers framed their experiences of Asia and the South Pacific through preconceptions based on movies.[22] Like most young people at the time, the Lavery brothers were keen moviegoers, and their letters home contained references to films such as 'Honeymoon in Bali'.[23]

Soldiers bound for the Middle East began to call at Colombo and Bombay from 1940, and the 8th Division assembled in Singapore from February 1941. In the months before fighting began in earnest in early 1942, many felt as if they were enjoying a holiday rather than fighting a war. Wartime requisitioning saw servicemen and women sail on the same comfortable cruise liners that had previously conveyed wealthy tourists. Not only were they heading overseas for the first time, but also the fact they were doing so on ships such as the famed *Queen Mary* 'made the voyage all the more appealing'.[24] In port, servicemen (and women) were often served by the same staff, enjoyed the same meals and maintained the same refined idleness as colonial-era tourists.[25] This encouraged soldiers to behave like tourists, engendering a level of continuity between peace and war. At Singapore, soldiers tossed coins in the water and watched the 'natives' jump after them, much as Una Falkiner had done in Colombo.[26] Some of those deployed to Batavia in early 1942 stayed at the lavish Hotel des Indes, where they ate decadent meals washed down with 'as much good French champagne as we could consume'.[27] Those in India were treated to grand repasts at which servants washed the guests' hands at the table, before serving dishes on plates 'two feet wide and three feet long'.[28]

Sensual pleasures were not limited to the table. Private Roy

Maxwell Poy devoted himself to 'having a good time' during the five months he spent stationed in Singapore, and his definition of a good time meant taxi girls (who charged a small fee for a dance) as well as encounters with women who offered more than just a waltz. All in all, Poy admitted to doing 'a lot of things I can't tell you about!!!!'[29] Private Don McLaren was not so reticent. He admitted that 'life in Singapore was excellent', mostly because of the 'thousands of gorgeous Chinese girls', one of whom 'even deflowered me!'[30] Private Ivor White also 'broke my maid' in Asia, thanks to an encounter with a 'little dark sheila' as his ship stopped over in Bombay on the way to the front in the Middle East.[31]

Preconceptions of Asia as a colonial space, where white men enjoyed comforts beyond their usual standards, appeared to be confirmed for many servicemen. It is striking that soldiers in Asia had servants for the menial jobs they would normally be expected to do themselves. Letters home brimmed with details about servants, as did memoirs published after the war. Training at the Command and Staff College in Quetta (now in Pakistan), Tom Wyett was assigned a 'native' bearer who even took his shoes off for him at the end of each day. Wyett was not an exception: the college retained 'dozens of white-clad servants … moving silently and efficiently' to take care of the trainee Officers.[32] Even lower ranks had servants. Privates stationed in India were assigned 'room boys' to do the cleaning and washing and bring cups of tea to barracks.[33] Soldiers in Malaya were served by Chinese launderers referred to as 'coolies' or, in a telling transfer of the language of the Raj to Southeast Asia, as 'dhobi'.[34] Moreover, 'coolies' were on hand for the kind of manual labour that rank-and-file soldiers would usually do for themselves. The Australian War Memorial holds numerous photographs of RAAF personnel resting while Indian labourers loaded their bags onto troopships, brought tea or built aerodromes.[35] In Asian theatres, the colonial hierarchy superseded some of the structures of the military.

As a result, thousands of Australian soldiers were introduced to colonial modes of travel, akin to those described in Chapter 1, during their deployment. Media reports emphasised the colonial flavour of these deployments. Reporting on the arrival of Australians in Malaya in 1941, the *Australian Women's Weekly* depicted a scene where 'the Malays are the willing slaves of the diggers', so that 'when one trainload of soldiers was getting under way a tall, good-looking boy strolled on to the station ... with no fewer than four Malayans carrying his kit and fussing round their tanned Tuan (master) as though they had been his servant for years'.[36] Such reports situated Australian soldiers within colonial frames, confirming assumptions about Asia as a space of colonial comforts to broader audiences back home.

There were other similarities with pre-war tourists. Like their leisured predecessors, Australian servicemen and women were preoccupied with rickshaws and their drivers. Their letters brimmed with tales of rickshaw rides, races and spills, sometimes accompanied by photographs of themselves being drawn across Singapore, Colombo or Calcutta. While some felt 'more than a little guilty' at being 'pulled by the poorest specimen on two legs I have ever seen', others thought it 'the funniest sight imaginable to see a couple of 15-stone soldiers in a rickshaw with the poor coolies dragging them along'.[37] Historian Lachlan Grant concludes that 'for many, the rickshaw evidently reflected the right relationships between whites and others in colonial society'. In his view, this contributed to a wider process by which soldiers 'discovered their own whiteness' whilst serving in Asia.[38] This echoed the discoveries of prewar tourists and hints at striking continuities between Australian experiences of Asia during peace and war. It also points to the strength of colonial images, which framed Australian ideas about Asia and Asians, even at this time of upheaval.

The good times continued during intermittent lulls in the fighting. Letters home brimmed with Hollywood clichés and tourist images. Reg Lavery wrote that the twinkling fireflies and glow worms of his camp in Dutch New Guinea were 'rather Disneyish', evoking the whimsy of recent films such as *Fantasia*.[39] Special correspondent for the *Australian Women's Weekly* Adele Shelton Smith concluded that, surrounded by such picturesque scenery, 'everybody was happy' in the 8th Division in Malaya.[40] Shelton's preoccupation with the comfortable quarters and 'Tip-Top Tucker' of Asian theatres provided a sharp contrast to contemporary reports of the hard fighting and dire conditions in the Middle East.[41] Before long, the 8th Division had acquired a reputation as 'glamour boys' and 'Menzies' Tourists', which they bitterly resented.[42] Although it was primarily aimed at maintaining morale, such reporting served to confirm the prewar image of Asia as a place where white men lived lives of luxury, and reinforced the casual presumption of racial and cultural superiority.

While Australians liked to portray their experiences through colonial frames, personal experience didn't always align with expectations. Some soldiers came to feel demoralised when they were ignored – or even shunned – by the British and Dutch civilians living in colonial Malaya and the Dutch East Indies. Many soldiers agreed with author Russell Braddon's depiction of the typical European resident in Asia as 'the most calculated snob'.[43] They were particularly dismayed by their exclusion from colonial hotels such as Raffles and the Galle Face. Imagining themselves in the role of tourists, many servicemen had beaten a path to these fine establishments, but lower ranks found themselves turned away by a management determined to preserve colonial prestige even under wartime conditions. Some soldiers felt so slighted that they began to question why they were risking their lives to defend people who were too haughty to even admit them into their presence. As we will see later in this chapter, such experiences led a proportion of soldiers to develop a growing distaste for colonialism.

ASIAN CHALLENGES | On 7 December 1941, the Japanese Army attacked Pearl Harbor in Hawai'i, and simultaneously landed forces in Malaya and Thailand. Two days later, the destroyers HMS *Prince of Wales* and HMS *Repulse* were sunk, crippling the British Navy in Southeast Asia. Over the next two months, the Japanese advanced southwards. By the end of January 1942, they had reached Singapore as well as Australian-mandated New Guinea, quickly capturing its capital, Rabaul. Singapore was surrendered on 15 February, the Dutch East Indies fell within a month and the Japanese advanced further into Australian territory in Papua.

The contrast with previous months was striking. As Les Atkinson, later a POW, remembered, 'the good life was over – we were back in the army with a vengeance'.[44] Days at leisure were replaced with fighting and tourist excursions became a thing of the past. The colonial languor of battalion life in Asia disappeared seemingly overnight and Atkinson had trouble reconciling the bombed out, bloodied clutter of Orchard Road with the Singapore he had previously enjoyed.[45] As nurse Mona Wilton wrote in December 1941, 'we miss the outings we were getting used to … but guess that war is war'. The siege on Singapore had finally forced her to recognise that 'we haven't come here on a Cook's Tour'.[46]

The Japanese advance challenged some of the basic assumptions that underpinned the colonial system. An Asian power not only threatened European colonies but also was vanquishing them with alarming ease. This upheaval was underscored by the capture of over 22 000 Australians as prisoners of war. The Japanese military system did not hold those who surrendered in high regard and felt no obligation to ensure their wellbeing. Prisoners starved on minimal rations and many fell gravely ill from dysentery, malaria, dengue, beri-beri, cholera and other diseases. Australians were also subjected to beatings and other corporal punishment, which the Japanese inflicted seemingly 'just to let us know who was boss'.[47]

The body politics of captivity confirmed the total power of the Japanese and served as tangible evidence that the prewar colonial order had been overturned.[48] As one captive remembered, now that the Japanese were in charge, 'we had to take it'.[49]

Many POWs feared that their captivity would strike a permanent blow to White Man's Prestige. They kept a keen eye on the 'native' populations, trying to gauge whether they recognised the wider political meanings of white men being held at the power of Asian captors. Sergeant Stan Arneil kept a diary as he was transported north to the infamous Burma–Thailand railway. The sweltering journey in an overcrowded cattle truck was an ordeal, but for Arneil, the worst part was that Thai civilians observed the Australians under degrading conditions. The 'most humiliating experience' came when white men were forced to eat inside their sweltering train carriages, while 'almost black Thai guards … lounged on the cool platform'.[50] Christopher Dawson remembered being marched into a POW camp by the Japanese as a 'humiliating procession with the native people and Chinese watching us'.[51] Richard Cahill similarly thought the Japanese did 'everything to humiliate' their white captives 'in front of all the people'.[52] During her years in captivity, nurse Betty Jeffrey resented being forced to work 'while natives sit around smoking straws and watch and laugh at us'.[53] Another Australian nurse, Wilma Oram, was similarly affronted when forced to travel in the back of a truck, which she believed was done 'for the benefit of natives who jeered and cheered at the sight of so many captive white women'.[54] Flying to Hong Kong near the end of the war, John Balfe, an RAAF transport pilot, concluded that 'the cloak of British superiority had fallen' now that locals had seen white men dominated by Asians.[55] Russell Braddon prophesied that this would unleash a brutal war of 'Asia against the white man' that would continue for a hundred years or more.[56]

The political implications were widely recognised upon the POWs' release following Japan's surrender in August 1945.

Australians were shocked by the physical condition of returning POWs. Approximately one-third of Australian prisoners of the Japanese had perished and the bodies of many survivors revealed that theirs had been a narrow escape. As journalist Creighton Burns wrote in the *Argus*, the captives' suffering was 'written in their bodies and broken bones in the language of scars, weals, duodenal ulcers, jaded nerves' as well as amputated limbs and emaciated, skeletal frames.[57] The Sons of Anzac were returning home looking less like bronzed heroes than like the Holocaust victims so recently liberated from Europe's death camps. As historian Christina Twomey has shown, these were profoundly troubling images that carried a number of challenging questions. Did their broken bodies, evidence of their powerlessness and passivity as captives, undermine the POWs' masculinity and their claims to the Anzac legacy?[58] And, just as troubling, did they not undermine the presumption of European racial superiority on which the entire colonial system depended? Would it be possible to reassert European colonialism after the Japanese had so thoroughly undermined the premise of White Man's Prestige? Country Party MP Joe Abbott was troubled by these insinuations and he introduced a motion in Parliament urging journalists to stop publishing images of frail POWs. He believed that 'no earthly good' could come from reproducing images of Australian men brought low by Asians; the House agreed, resolving the question in the affirmative. Nonetheless, public fascination prevailed, and reports testifying to the mistreatment of POWs continued to find their way into print.[59]

Abbott needn't have worried as far as domestic popular opinion went. From the vantage point of victory, the Japanese offensive was construed as evidence not of strength, but of ferocity, which was the very opposite of true civilisation. Returned POWs portrayed the Japanese as cruel fiends in best-selling memoirs including Rohan Rivett's *Behind Bamboo*, WS Kent Hughes' *Slaves of the Samurai*, Roy Whitecross' *Slaves of the Son of Heaven* and Russel Braddon's

*The Naked Island*. The narratives of female POWs, including Jessie Simons' *While History Passed* and Betty Jeffrey's *White Coolies*, were equally pejorative. POW memoirs captivated the public and their portrayals of the Japanese spread widely. *White Coolies* was reprinted six times in 1954, then again in 1955 and 1956.[60] *The Naked Island* was reprinted 13 times within 20 years by Pan Books and had sold over a million copies by 1958.[61] The total Australian population at this time was less than ten million.

These memoirs were concerned with the power dynamics of POW camps, in which Australians were forced to obey Asian masters. Their success suggests a widespread fascination with the nightmare scenario of Australians falling under Asian domination. But the Allied victory, and the ultimate survival of POWs in spite of their mistreatment, was thought to reinforce rather than undermine previously held assumptions about 'European' superiority. The Japanese may have been ferocious and brutal, but the Australians' courage and valour – the true markers of civilisation – held firm even in the face of death. This reframing excised many of the troubling political messages of the POW captivity and bestowed returned soldiers with the dignity they had been denied in detention. Furthermore, far from forcing a reappraisal of imperial and racist assumptions, POW narratives reserved a place for anti-Japanese vitriol during the 1950s. Japan's postwar co-operation with the United States, as well as its booming economy, saw it rehabilitated from the status of enemy to firm ally in only a few years. Yet, popular anxiety remained and POW memoirs provided a space for the expression of ongoing resentment and suspicion. POWs often claimed that their captivity had given them an insight into the 'true character' of the Japanese, which was 'ruthless, brutal, inhuman'.[62] Such descriptions carried an undertone of warning, suggesting that Oriental cruelty would ultimately reassert itself – and that Australia would come under threat once more.

THE POLITICS OF PERSONAL CONTACT | As the next chapter explores in more detail, the postwar period saw a widespread surge of popular interest in Asia. Some of this interest was motivated by wartime experience. Lachlan Grant argues that personal contact facilitated a new awareness and empathy for the political and economic situation of civilians in Southeast Asia and precipitated a 'reorientation towards Asia' for many soldiers.[63] Many servicemen became enthusiastic supporters of decolonisation in the Dutch East Indies, which became Indonesia after independence was declared on 17 August 1945. Approximately 50 000 Australian servicemen and women remained in Southeast Asia at the end of the war and they witnessed the Republican struggle at first hand. While the majority of soldiers, including most POWs, had only transitory contact with the local people, some were very much alive to their Asian surroundings. Reg Lavery, for example, had begun to learn some rudimentary Malay so that he could communicate with the locals more directly.[64]

Many returned servicemen and women took a special interest in postwar debates about Australia's place in the region and the world. Having seen something of Asia for themselves, soldiers began to reflect on the region and Australia's place within it. Where many had begun their deployments by cultivating colonial pretensions themselves, by the time they returned home a number had become sympathetic to Asian demands for independence from European colonialism. Seeing the determination of those fighting for freedom from the colonial yoke encouraged a good deal of support.[65] Some soldiers had also been dismayed by the arrogant and overbearing attitudes of the Dutch colonists who refused to let them take part in 'European' society.[66] The Army magazine, *Salt*, reflected the interests of returned soldiers and it regularly featured articles and letters on developments in Southeast Asia, with the situation in Indonesia a particular concern. A rancorous debate arose after Driver Ronald Lewis wrote in to state that 'it is none of Australia's business what treatment the natives get after the war – it is Holland's concern'.[67] Lewis' letter reflected the views of the recently formed Liberal Party and would have likely gone unnoticed if it had been published in the mainstream media, which took a conservative stance towards Indonesia in the immediate postwar years. But *Salt* was inundated with responses, suggesting that the servicemen who formed its readership were more taken with questions of Australia's place in the region than the general public. *Salt*'s international affairs editor was roused to enter the fray, arguing that 'far from being no concern of Australia's, the future of Indonesia, Malaya, Indo-China and the other SE Asian lands urgently concerns this Commonwealth and its 7 000 000 people'.[68] A stream of letters agreed. A number testified to Indonesians' political sophistication, a view that was rarely expressed in mainstream political or media discussion and so was most likely informed by personal experience.[69] Others argued that Australia owed a debt to those who had shown generosity to POWs, often at great risk to themselves. Others still supported decolonisation because of ideological reasons, arguing that 'the bill for the Atlantic Charter is being presented. It must be paid in full', or that '[t]he present intervention against the Indonesian people violates the principles for which so many Australians have given their lives'.[70] The activism of returned soldiers was not restricted to the pages of *Salt*. Sympathetic letters from those who had served in Indonesia occasionally appeared in mainstream media including the *Australian Women's Weekly*.[71] Others supported the Black Armada campaign that blockaded Dutch shipping in Australian ports. Eventually extending to hundreds of ships and preventing the transport of weapons and other crucial provisions to the Dutch East Indies, the Black Armada has been credited with providing vital support to the Indonesian Republican cause.[72]

While some former servicemen chose to retreat to the safety of home and hearth, many others continued to be interested – sometimes even involved – in Asian issues. They formed an important contingent in a nation that was sharply divided on the question of Indonesia. A Gallup poll in December 1945 showed that some 70 per cent of men, and half of all women, were interested in the question of Indonesia's future.[73] The Labor government was sympathetic to the Republican position, but the Liberal opposition (and much of the metropolitan media) vehemently opposed Independence. Their arguments relied on colonial-era stereotypes of Indonesians as 'natives' requiring the steady hand of Dutch colonisation, and belittled Indonesia's uprising as a mere 'hubbub'.[74] As Leader of the Opposition, Robert Menzies argued that Indonesians were not ready for self-government as 'the truth is that in the Netherlands East Indies, those who, by reason of intellectual development, are fit to cope with the democratic instrument could probably be numbered by hundreds, certainly not by millions'.[75] Others worried about the possible threat to Australia. Using apocalyptic imagery, Liberal MP (later Minister for External Affairs) Percy Spender thought of Australia as 'a handful of white people in a coloured sea', and he feared that it would be impossible to hold back the tide once it had been whipped up by decolonisation and communism.[76] Personal experience of Asian lands and people led some soldiers to see the situation in a different way. Their views, carrying the force of eyewitness accounts, were conveyed to friends, family, and broader audiences through letters to *Salt*, the *Australian Women's Weekly* and through direct activism.

## KEEPING THE PEACE? POSTWAR DEPLOYMENTS

As the debate over Indonesia shows, the postwar years were marked by indecision about the shape of Australia's future relations with Asia. Diplomatic and trade relations were established with Asian nations through both bilateral and multilateral frameworks. But, with the Japanese advance still fresh in many minds, the fear that diplomacy would not be enough saw the Australian military deployed in a number of regional engagements. The earliest, and perhaps most curious, of Australia's Asian 'peacekeeping' missions to Asia was the commitment of some 16 000 soldiers to the British Commonwealth Occupation Forces (BCOF), which assisted the United States in the Occupation of Japan from 1946 to 1952. This deployment reflected broader ambiguities in Australian ideas about Asia. It wove together a popular desire for vengeance against the Japanese with Cold War imperatives brought about by Australia's alliance with the United States. It also reflected the desire to restore and even extend Western imperialism in Asia.[77]

The extent of American interference – which restructured Japan's government and economy, redistributed land and assets and even encouraged the uptake of Western popular culture – has led its pre-eminent historian, John Dower, to brand the Occupation as 'the last immodest exercise in the colonial conceit known as the "white man's burden"'.[78] After the war, the Americans preferred to carve out neo-colonial 'spheres of influence' rather than imposing direct colonial control. But the Occupation's Supreme Commander, General Douglas Macarthur, was an admirer of the old colonial style once practised by his father, who had been Governor-General of the American-occupied Philippines. According to Dower, Macarthur invoked his father's example and 'reigned as a minor potentate in his Far Eastern domain'.[79] In annexing parts of Tokyo (known as 'Little America') for the exclusive use of the Occupation Forces, in his refusal to meet Japanese on a basis of equality and in the strict controls he imposed over every element of Japanese political, economic and civilian life, Macarthur consciously applied colonial models onto occupied Japan.

The Australian military leadership also saw the Occupation as an opportunity to reassert the prestige of the British Empire following the humiliations of the Pacific War. Initially composed of British, Indian, Australian and New Zealand troops, BCOF was explicitly identified with the British Empire. Press reports casually referred to them as 'Empire troops'.[80] Arriving in Japan, soldiers were advised that their role was to 'maintain and enhance British Commonwealth prestige'.[81] They were also advised that they were there because the Japanese had 'caused deep suffering and loss in many thousands of homes throughout the British Empire'.[82] Australian policies were formulated with an eye to building and maintaining national, as well as imperial, prestige. As historian James Wood has shown, the military leadership was concerned that the Australian contingent be visible to a broad swath of the Japanese population and it organised parades and intricate 'showing the flag' ceremonies 'at every opportunity'. These ceremonies, which represented a good proportion of BCOF's activities in Japan, had no purpose other than 'as a reminder to the Japanese of the formal nature of the occupation' and the authority held by Australians.[83]

Following imperialist logic, it was thought that BCOF forces would remain in Japan indefinitely, and from 1947 Australian soldiers serving in Japan were joined by their families. The presence of nearly 500 wives and some 600 children, and the erection of suburban-style family homes to house them, lent a sense of permanence to the Australian deployment. The ever-peripatetic Frank Clune visited the BCOF deployment and he compared the settlement to a British garrison at the high point of the Raj. He thought that the orderly homes symbolised the strength of the Occupation, which 'should be a lesson to the "coloured" peoples of East Asia, and elsewhere, that the Anglo-Saxon, or the White Man generally, is terribly tough and ultimately invincible'.[84] In doing so, he repositioned the heart of the British Empire from India to Japan; he also shifted Australians into the role of colonisers. This is all the more interesting for coming at the very point when the British Empire disintegrated, both globally and within the BCOF deployment. The Indian deployment pulled out following Independence in 1947 and its departure was quickly followed by the New Zealand and British contingents. For more than four years from 1948, Australia *was*

BCOF, and it worked alone to secure a place for the British Empire in East Asia.

Like the colonial tourists described in Chapter 1, Australians serving in BCOF took it for granted that they deserved a higher standard of living than Asians. Soldiers lived a more luxurious life-style in the Army than many civilians back in Australia. All officers, and even many lower ranks, had Japanese 'housegirls' and 'house-boys' who looked after the cooking, cleaning and other domestic chores. Those with children usually had more than one servant. Domestic service was almost unknown in Australia by the 1940s and so BCOF troops, their wives and even children had to learn how to manage servants whilst in Japan. In her study of BCOF women, historian Christine de Matos found that many modelled their behaviour and language on colonial models – or rather, on their impressions of colonial life, as patched together from popu-lar culture as well as limited personal experience. Historian Robin Gerster notes that even 'BCOF kids' invoked colonial models when lording their power over Japanese nannies.[85] The attempt to intro-duce a model of behaviour developed in colonial South and South-east Asia into postwar Japan aroused some resistance among the local population, many of whom were immensely proud of their heritage as one of the few Asian nations to have escaped Euro-pean colonialism. The Australian Commander-in-Chief was soon receiving complaints about a 'deliberately arrogant and bullying attitude towards the Japanese civil population'. As the number of complaints grew, he began to fear that, by acting in such an impe-rious way, Australians were actually endangering, rather than pro-moting, Empire prestige.[86]

As with the entire US Occupation, the BCOF deployment was an attempt to reinforce European domination over Asia and this extended to individual contacts. The military leadership was unu-sually sensitive to the body politics of Australian-Asian encounters. Official policies urged soldiers to maintain a 'correct' order by insisting that Japanese civilians bow to them and address them as 'sir'. The social division was enforced by a strict non-fraternisation policy that sought to prevent personal contact between Australians and Japanese. Troops were directed to be 'strictly correct and coldly polite' with locals and regulations prohibited close physical contact – even shaking hands – in case this was interpreted as a symbol of equality. Australians were also prohibited from entering all local restaurants, bars, cabarets and cafés, as well as cinemas, theatres, geisha houses, public baths and private homes.[87] This became particularly important after rumours of a high VD rate began to spread back in Australia, arousing widespread criticism that soldiers were getting too familiar with their former foes.[88] Careful of its reputation, BCOF Command paid press reporters and popular writers – including the *Australian Women's Weekly's* Dorothy Drain and Frank Clune – to come to Japan to scuttle these rumours. Their reports emphasised the physical and social distance that separated Australians from the Japanese. One 1946 article in the *Australian Women's Weekly* took readers through the home of an Air Vice-Marshal (requisitioned from a Japanese viscount) to show that a vast gulf separated Australians from the civilian population. It paid particular attention to formal relations the Vice-Marshal maintained with his many 'housegirls'; readers were assured they 'bow low' whenever in the Vice-Marshal's presence. Accompanying the article was a series of photographs, including one depicting a Japanese 'housegirl' kneeling down in order to tie the Vice-Marshal's shoes for him.[89]

Of course, the lived experience was much more complicated than the non-fraternisation policy and its publicity would suggest. A whole range of relationships developed over the five years that Australians served in Japan. Some Australians became friendly with servants or secretaries. Sexual liaisons were common and ranged from casual, drunken encounters with prostitutes to long-lasting, monogamous unions and marriages. Historian Keiko Tamura estimates that around 650 Japanese wives eventually came to Australia after the BCOF deployment withdrew in 1952.[90] The extreme difficulty involved in bringing Asians to White Australia means that this number represents the very tip of a much larger iceberg. Only the most solid, serious unions could withstand the years-long process of migration; the number of relationships that didn't survive would have been far higher. As Walter Hamilton has shown, the children born of liaisons between Allied troops and Japanese women during the Occupation period reveal a broad tableau of intimate contact.[91]

Some soldiers even came to sympathise with the Japanese and critique the BCOF deployment. Allan S Clifton was scathing in his controversial service memoir, *Time of Fallen Blossoms*. Formerly working as a BCOF translator, Clifton had become sympathetic to the plights of the civilian population and he railed against those Australians who treated the Japanese with an arrogant callousness that, in his account, sometimes descended into barbarism. He was so critical of the Australian deployment that his memoir caused a great deal of controversy when it was published in 1951.[92] While Clifton's opposition was particularly vehement, many other Australians returned from Japan with a similarly sympathetic attitude towards Asians. As one Army padre noted, being in Japan had led him to recognise that, far from being inscrutable Orientals or cruel beasts, 'the Japanese at home are people much like ourselves'. Returning to Australia, he now thought that 'Australia and Japan should try to become friends'. His attitudes ran far ahead of both official and popular sentiment in Australia; the *Sunday Herald* report carrying his story presented such views as a 'shock'.[93] Japanese War Crimes trials and the publication of POW memoirs continued to stoke the fires of hate well into the 1950s and writer Colin Simpson found that many returned BCOF soldiers had learnt to keep their views to themselves, as 'you just can't talk to the people at home'.[94] Only the experience of being there could convince Australians that the Japanese were people 'much like ourselves'.

By settling in Japan, and consciously cultivating a form of

colonial culture, the BCOF deployment embodied the view that Australia should work to restore – and even extend – European imperialism in postwar Asia. This view became increasingly untenable as decolonisation swept through Asia. Not only were Asians becoming more forthright in demanding sovereignty but also colonising powers – including Britain – were actively retreating from their former imperial strongholds. International affairs were increasingly mediated by the United Nations, which was premised on principles of racial equality and self-determination. Any hope of expanding Western dominance over Asia began to look absurd in this context, and from the 1950s Australian deployments to the region were portrayed in the new lexicon of peacekeeping and the Cold War rather than in imperialist language. The United States devoted substantial economic and military resources to limiting the spread of communist influence across the continent, and the Occupation of Japan shifted its focus to strengthening the nation as a bulwark against communism. The BCOF deployment became geared towards supporting the troops fighting the Korean War.

Although BCOF was finally dismantled in 1952, Australia's military forces remained in constant deployment in Asia throughout the entire Cold War period, and beyond. During the 1950s, the twin issues of decolonisation and communism drove Australia's deployment to the Malayan Emergency and Konfrontasi. They also underpinned involvement in the Vietnam War, to which we will return in Chapter 6. The Cold War came to dominate official and expert deliberations about Australia's relations with Asia. As the next chapter shows, it was also a pressing concern for the growing number of Australians who set off to visit the region during this period.

# 4: GOOD NEIGHBOURS

In 1962, middle-aged Sydney businessman William Wade visited Asia for the first time. In Hong Kong, he bought a state-of-the-art cassette recorder and began to record a travel diary for his wife and daughters. At first, Wade assured them that all was well. His hotel was plush, with every need met by attentive servants. After a few days, however, the recordings began to betray a less confident tone. Wade had been disoriented by the crowds and unfamiliar language and had got lost several times. Rickshaw drivers had demanded two dollars even though he had heard, somewhere, that you weren't supposed to give them more than one; public arguments had ensued. The brashness and confidence of the people forced him to recognise that, even though Hong Kong was still a colony, there was no longer any trace of servility – 'not even among the coolies'.

Wade had never given a great deal of thought to Asian politics. In Hong Kong, however, he began to pay attention and soon became 'fascinated by it'. The experience was so powerful it led him to review his political beliefs: 'the whole thing makes one think', he mused. Wade was troubled by the sight of appalling poverty existing alongside great wealth and the stark inequality forced him to recognise that, rather than simply being a projection of Chinese power, communism may have held legitimate appeal in Asia. Perhaps even more profoundly, this brief visit led the conservative voter to question core elements of Australian foreign and domestic policy, including the White Australia Policy. Having seen the industriousness and intelligence of Hong Kong's residents, Wade began to wonder if Australia wasn't 'acting very foolishly' in refusing Asian migration. After only a few weeks, Wade returned to Australia with an entirely different view of what Asia was like, which he now summed up in one word conveying both the strangeness and promise of Asia: marvellous.[1]

A NEW NEIGHBOURHOOD | The world seemed to shrink in the middle decades of the 20th century. As popular writer Frank Clune wrote, by the mid-1940s there was no doubt that the aeroplane was 'making short work of long distances'. This new proximity demanded a shift in the way Australians thought of their place in the world and the language they used to express it, as 'thanks to air travel, the Far East has now become the Near North'.[2] Popular interest in Australia's relations with Asia intensified in this context. As we saw in the previous chapter, some soldiers became interested in Asia after serving in the region. Decolonisation and the Cold War kept Australians' attention focussed on Asia. The communist victory in China in 1949, and the United States' determination that communism would not spread further, saw the Cold War expand to Asia. Newspapers devoted more space to regional issues and most mainstream media – even the *Australian Women's Weekly* – regularly featured stories with an Asian angle. For journalist George Johnston, it seemed evident that Asia 'more certainly than any other continent, is the continent of tomorrow'.[3]

International politics demanded a conceptual shift. The racial hierarchies that had once been taken as simple commonsense became increasingly disreputable after the Holocaust. The Atlantic Charter and the United Nations made racial equality a core principle of the international order. In this new world, casual assumptions about racial hierarchies or relative levels of civilisation became inreasingly unacceptable. This put many Australians in a bind. As journalist Clive Turnbull noted in 1948, 'a majority of Australians still subscribe to the exclusionist policy of the Immigration Restriction Act. But it is obvious that a large number of Australians does not subscribe to its implications of racialism'. Looking at the situation, he concluded that 'the time has come for a restatement'.[4] The search for a way to restate the continuing desire for social and cultural unity without invoking race was among the most urgent, and most difficult, problems facing mid-20th century Australia.

Attitudes to Asia were further complicated by the spread of the Cold War. The Cold War was framed as a battle for 'hearts and minds', and politicians across the Western world began to exhort the public to take greater notice of world affairs.[5] In Australia, metaphors of Asia as the 'neighbourhood' became part of the national mainstream and they encouraged ordinary Australians to feel personally involved in their nation's foreign affairs. Books with titles referring to *Our Pacific neighbours*, *Our Asian neighbours*, *Our neighbours in Netherlands New Guinea*, *Our neighbours in Indonesia*, *Northern neighbours* and *A thousand million neighbours*, competed for space on Australian bookshelves.[6]

Conceptualising Asia as the 'neighbourhood' demystified and, in a sense, domesticated Asia. Homely imagery was appealing in the context of the postwar baby boom and suburbanisation.[7] It also placed ordinary Australians at the heart of diplomacy. If Australia's foreign relations were predicated on neighbourliness, then individuals could imagine themselves as active participants in the relationship. Otherwise ordinary citizens were encouraged to think of themselves as 'people's diplomats'. Many did begin to consider their nation's reputation abroad, and set out to win hearts and minds as they travelled through their newly-discovered neighbourhood.

THE TWO ASIAS | The idea that everyday citizens could help shape Australia's regional relations was prominent in professional travel writing. Travelogues consistently topped best-seller lists during the 1950s and 1960s, providing some armchair escapism at a time when many Australians were conserving their money for the suburban dream. Writing about Asia was particularly popular. Two of the three best-selling authors of the post-war period, Frank Clune and Colin Simpson, wrote a number of Asian travelogues (the third, Ion Idriess, wrote fiction set in the South Pacific). Frank Clune has already featured a number of times in this book. He was not only prolific but also staggeringly popular; he was also increasingly interested in Asia and his 1938 bestseller, *Sky High to Shanghai*, was followed by 12 more Asian travelogues over the next 20 years. Clune's writing had extensive reach. Most titles debuted with print runs of 10 000 copies, and several of his Asian travelogues were reprinted or released in second editions.[8] His influence also stretched beyond his sales, with one librarian estimating that he accounted for half the loans from Australian collections.[9] Furthermore, Clune did not limit himself to books. He wrote for several newspapers and magazines and told his travel stories to a weekly radio audience estimated at over one million.[10] As journalist EW Tipping noted at the time, this immense reach meant that Clune 'taught tens of thousands of Australians most of what they know about the Near North'.[11]

In terms of popularity, Clune's major rival was Colin Simpson. *The Country Upstairs*, Simpson's bestseller about Japan, sold approximately 50 000 copies in the ten years after its publication in 1956, which, as Simpson liked to claim, made it the most successful travel book ever published in Australia.[12] While they never reached quite the same heights, Simpson's other Asian titles, including *Asia's Bright Balconies* (1962), *Bali and Beyond* (1972) and *Off to Asia* (1973), achieved respectable sales.[13] Peggy Warner, wife of prominent foreign correspondent Denis Warner, was also a popular travel writer focussing on Asia. In addition to feature articles in newspapers including the *Courier Mail* and the *Mail*, Warner published the book-length travelogue, *Asia is People*, in 1961; it ran to three editions by the end of the decade.[14] Although few other writers enjoyed the same success, Clune's, Simpson's and Warner's books were joined on Australian shelves by Asian travelogues from authors including FJ Thwaites, Peter Pinney, Marie Byles, Norman Bartlett and Ronald McKie.

While they were meant to entertain, these books were also profoundly political. In the United States, the government encouraged conservative academics, journalists, writers, filmmakers, playwrights, artists and photographers to produce works that supported its pursuit of the Cold War.[15] The Australian government was less dynamic in its public diplomacy. Yet, writers and journalists from both the left and the right stepped into the breach, taking it upon themselves to encourage ordinary Australians to take account of developments in Asia.

The popular appeal of travel writing, and its potential as a weapon in the battle for hearts and minds, was recognised by writers on both sides of the Cold War's ideological divide. They had different – and often conflicting – goals. Conservative writers such as Clune, Simpson and Warner hoped to secure popular support for US-led campaigns aimed at preventing the region from 'falling' to communism. On the other side of the political divide were those who wrote about their travels through communist Asia, particularly China (and to a lesser extent North Vietnam), in the hope of arousing ordinary Australians' sympathy for socialist ideals. Many Australians were curious about life behind the bamboo curtain, but the absence of diplomatic ties until 1972 made gaining accurate information about China difficult. Travelogues and first-person reports purported to fill this gap. Accounts by well-known authors and respected figures such as Myra Roper, Dymphna Cusack and Ross Terrill were the most popular. But the public interest was such that books by otherwise 'ordinary' people – doctors, farmers, teachers – who wouldn't normally be expected to release written accounts of their travels, were also published throughout the 1960s and into the 1970s.[16]

Travel writing was an important conduit of Asia-related knowledge to mainstream audiences and it was for this reason that it formed a battleground for the Cold War's competing ideologies. Travel writers on both sides of the political divide attempted to inform – and not merely entertain – Australian readers. Clune positioned himself as 'an unofficial fact-finder for the Australian public on the history and geography ... of all those countries nearer to us than Europe or America, which our official education system sometimes ignores'.[17] He thought his role was to depict how Asians 'actually live and act, so that Australians will get to know their "Neighbours of the Near North" a little better'.[18] According to his publishers at Angus & Robertson, this was an important political contribution; by encouraging Australians to engage with Asia, Clune did nothing less than help 'arrest the movement of communism throughout South-East Asia'.[19] On the other side of the political spectrum, novelist Dymphna Cusack also thought Australians needed to 'accept the fact that we belong to Asia' and wrote in an attempt to educate Australians about the need to 'enlarge our policy into a peaceful good neighbourliness'.[20] Respected Melbourne author Myra Roper explained that she had written *China: The Surprising Country* because 'we have to get to know [China] better,' as 'she is so near and so powerful'.[21]

Far from being factual reports, most Cold War-era travelogues were steeped in politics. Those on the right wrote travelogues that endorsed Australia's support of American Cold War containment strategies in the region. A core task lay in shifting Australian popular opinion with regard to Japan. By the early 1950s, the United States had shifted its policy to strengthening Japan so it could be an effective bulwark against communism. Convincing the Australian public that its recent foe was now a worthy ally proved a difficult task. As Clune's 1950 travelogue *Ashes of Hiroshima* explained, 'the idea of alliance and consequent friendship with Japan is hard to swallow; but in world politics there is no law greater than that of military necessity'. Clune was in a distinctly uncomfortable position. He had made no secret of his hatred of the Japanese in previous books; now he had to portray them in a positive light. The tensions were evident in *Ashes of Hiroshima*. The majority of the text, written in 1948 – during the Tokyo War Crimes trials and before the communist victory in China – portrayed the Japanese in blisteringly negative terms. Clune used the word 'stupid' so often that he felt it needed an explanation: 'some people still think that the Japanese are clever' and they needed to be shown their error. Yet, a postscript added just prior to publication in 1950 – after the United States' strategic shift – revealed a dramatic change. In striking contrast to the rest of the book, Clune now claimed that Japan had 'become truly democratic and fully civilised in … a short period of time', and so deserved Australia's trust.[22] This positive tone continued in subsequent travelogues.[23]

Travellers to the newly established People's Republic of China (PRC) were no less political; however they portrayed the Chinese, and not the Japanese, as being worthy of Australian sympathy. The earliest reports came from committed socialists. Approximately 70 members of the Communist Party of Australia (CPA), including prominent party figures Eric Aarons, Laurie Aarons, John Sendy and Keith McEwen, went to Peking for ideological study during the 1950s.[24] Journalist Wilfred Burchett, who had achieved fame after filing the first 'eyewitness' report of the devastation of Hiroshima, was already a strong advocate of communism in China by the time of his 1951 visit. But the most popular first-person accounts were written by people who were not members of the Communist Party. Myra Roper, who went to China 15 times between the 1950s and the 1980s, was certainly not a socialist radical. Principal of the Women's

College at the University of Melbourne and a well-known radio and television personality, Roper was the very epitome of respectability: so much so that, despite her many visits and sympathetic accounts of China, it seems that she never attracted a personal ASIO file. Neither did filmmaker and author Maslyn Williams, who produced a slew of films and books about Indonesia and Papua New Guinea as well as China. Ron Wright was the Deputy Chancellor of the University of Melbourne when he travelled to China in 1972; his wife was Executive Director of the Myer Foundation. Novelist Dymphna Cusack and her husband Norman Freehill lived in China for two years during the late 1950s and returned again during the early 1960s. They did attract an ASIO file – indeed, ASIO considered Cusack a communist sympathiser and 'fellow-traveller' – but there is no evidence that she ever joined the CPA.[25]

While presenting contrasting views of communism in Asia, both camps followed a strikingly similar strategy, in which they attempted to dispel Australians' fears and arouse their sympathies towards Asia. The first task lay in debunking the stereotypes that portrayed Asian people as mysterious and inscrutable Others. As Myra Roper wrote, 'if this awareness of our common humanity were everywhere accepted, not as a sentimental concept but as the main cold, hard fact of international relations, the chances for peace would be brighter'.[26] In a notable departure from previous depictions, Cold War travel writing focussed less on the exotic Otherness of Asia and instead highlighted the similarities between ordinary Asians and their Australian counterparts. Warner's *Asia is People* depicted Asian women going about their everyday lives: buying and cooking food, looking after children, having their hair set. Warner sought to encourage Australian women to identify and empathise with their Asian sisters by revealing that a woman's lot was the same across racial and cultural divides.[27] As a long-time Anglo-Celtic race patriot, Clune had a more difficult time equating Asians with Australians. In earlier travelogues, he had depicted

Japan and China as 'strange places ... with strange people'. In line with Orientalist convention, Clune had not typically depicted individual Asians, but rather portrayed a 'vast yellow conglomerate of the Orient', which shared a mysterious Oriental 'mind'.[28] Yet, as we have seen, the imperatives of the Cold War brought about a dramatic shift. Now, Clune profiled selected individuals – Christians, family men, democrats – whose lives largely resembled those of his readers, and he exhorted 'ordinary' Australians to identify with their counterparts in non-communist Asia.

Most Chinese travelogues also depicted everyday life in the People's Republic. Like Peggy Warner, a number of progressive writers paid special attention to women's personal lives in an attempt to build sentimental bonds between Australian and Asian women. Cusack's *Chinese Women Speak*, for instance, was peppered with depictions of instant friendship and 'instinctive sympathy' between women hailing from different worlds.[29] Countless visits to 'typical' workplaces and apartments, schools and theatres were also recounted in order to portray the Chinese as not too dissimilar from Australians.

In doing so, Cold War travel writers contested the Orientalist stereotypes that had underpinned Australian ideas about Asia for the best part of a century. In *Anxious Nation*, David Walker has shown that, although Asia evoked a complex range of images and reactions, it was always imagined as fundamentally Other.[30] The geopolitical demands of the Cold War required that this change; accordingly, East and West met on the pages of Australian travelogues. Simpson was blunt: 'Kipling was wrong'. While 'side-street Tokyo is still Oriental ... mid-town Tokyo is largely a modern city of the kind we know'. He even tried to overturn 'the commonest of Western assertions' by insisting that 'the Japanese are not slant-eyed'.[31] Peggy Warner was even more strident, arguing that very little remained of the East at all: 'old Japan' had 'practically disappeared beneath all the westernized innovations which have appeared since the Occupation'. In 'new' Tokyo, 'everyone was eating Western food', so that 'when we asked for something Japanese we were told proudly that all the food in the restaurant was American'. According to Warner, this had wrought a dramatic change on the Japanese. Eating less rice and more meat, Japanese children were growing taller and the girls had 'much larger' chests. Their legs were also longer and straighter now that they sat at desks rather than on the floor. According to Warner, the new generation was no longer Japanese but a 'new race', half-Asian and half-Western.[32] The inference was that they were no longer the same Japanese who had been responsible for the atrocities of the Pacific War. Rather, this new race was fully deserving of Australians' sympathy and co-operation.

SEEING IS BELIEVING | Travel writing relies on the notion that personal experience is a reliable source of information about foreign places and people, an idea that has been widely accepted since the Enlightenment. The widespread propaganda and misinformation of the Cold War heightened the perceived value of eyewitness accounts. Travellers to China almost inevitably prefaced their reports with claims that, in an age of misrepresentation, only eyewitness accounts could be considered credible. The official China International Travel Service certainly encouraged visitors to think that 'to see once is better than to hear a hundred times'.[33] An eyewitness report was often valued above other forms of expertise. Despite substantial academic knowledge and professional experience, Colin Mackerras and Neale Hunter foregrounded their roles as eyewitnesses in the 1967 *China Observed*, even claiming that it was impossible to really understand China without a personal encounter.[34]

Because of the political nature of their visits, travellers went out of their way to establish their credibility as reliable and unbiased eyewitnesses. John Jackson, who went to China as part of the 'ping pong diplomacy' phenomenon of 1971, insisted that his account was credible because his visit 'had no political significance to me personally'.[35] As a Labor MP, Leslie Haylen had a harder task in convincing readers of political neutrality, yet he too prefaced his account, *Chinese Journey*, with claims that 'I sought to please no man or party ... I wanted it only to tell the truth'.[36] Travellers were also determined to prove that their accounts were completely unbiased. Jackson assured readers that his every claim could be substantiated, as he had recorded 'everything I saw, heard or did in China' by taking notes for 15 hours a day – emptying nine pens in the process – as well as shooting 500 photographs and seven reels of film.[37] Similarly, Myra Roper claimed she had made sure to 'look round every corner, under every bed, sift every statement, check every claim' so that her account could be trusted as an accurate portrayal of the 'real' China.[38]

Yet, no matter how much they worked towards an unmediated experience, visitors' access to the 'real' China was strictly regulated. Historians have now established that the Chinese government, working through the China International Travel Service, carefully manipulated visitors' experiences.[39] Tourists were ferried between model factories, hospitals, schools and universities, to museums, theatres, Friendship Stores, model homes and towns with names like 'Happy Village'. Visits were closely supervised by a team of specially trained guides and, as direct communication with locals was forbidden, even fluent Mandarin speakers had to conduct all conversations through an interpreter.[40] Not that there were many opportunities to speak to locals in the first place: Chinese citizens had to be formally accredited before they were allowed to meet foreigners. After the Cultural Revolution, approaching foreigners could be taken as an indication of inappropriate enthusiasm for the capitalist world, and so was rarely attempted. Tourists were also physically separated from ordinary citizens. Foreigners ate in private dining rooms, travelled in private cars and sat in specially designated sitting rooms at the theatre and the opera. Friendship Hotels were miles from anywhere and, as taxis were non-existent, visitors were dependent on their appointed drivers. The frenetic pace of their itineraries also kept visitors from making unusual demands and ensured they were too tired to ask many questions. Myra Roper's itinerary in June 1974 was so crowded that she did not have a single unplanned hour over a 20-day visit.[41] In his 1978 expose of these various subtle forms of control, Belgian–Australian academic Pierre Ryckmans (writing under the pseudonym Simon Leys) concluded that those 'who pretend they describe Chinese realities ... only deceive their readers, or worse, delude themselves'.[42]

Visitors to communist China certainly had a first-hand, direct experience, but what constituted that experience had been manipulated to ensure they were impressed with what they saw. Accordingly, they wrote glowing accounts in which social ills including drug abuse, child abuse, domestic violence, divorce, the black market, prostitution, organised crime, teenage delinquency and even road accidents, disabilities and stomach ulcers were 'all but non-existent in China'.[43] For over 30 years, visitors wrote of their astonishment at discovering that there was no theft under communism. Crossing the border from Hong Kong they were advised that, now they were in the People's Republic, they could leave their luggage unattended and doors unlocked. Not only was nothing ever stolen, but a cast of over-zealous hotel concierges tracked visitors over thousands of kilometres to return old biros, used razors and worn slippers, just in case they had been left behind by accident. Visitors were inevitably charmed by such ostentatious examples of honesty and extrapolated from them to conclude that China had, indeed, undergone a dramatic transformation under Maoism. In Cusack's account, even revolution was 'too simple a term for what is happening here. It is resurrection'.[44]

This was not disingenuous propaganda – these eyewitness reports were based on genuine, first-person experience, as corroborated by notes, statistics and photographs. All travellers extrapolate from their singular experiences to entire cities, cultures, or continents. Travellers aren't typically experts, and they base their accounts of foreign places on their own experiences. Extrapolation is also at the very heart of all travel writing. Travel writers have to make broader claims if their travelogues are to be relevant to a wider readership. As literary critic Paul Fussell has recognised, travel writing spans 'the individual physical things it describes, on the one hand, and the larger theme that it is "about", on the other.'[45] Those who travelled to communist China were not being dishonest – they reported what they saw; furthermore, they could provide evidence to corroborate their stories. Yet, the credibility of writers such as Cusack and Roper suffered a serious blow when the system was revealed in the late 1970s. After this time, they were ridiculed as gullible 'fellow-travellers' who had seen China with 'two left eyes'.

Travel writers on the other side of the political spectrum made similar claims, but they were not brought to task in the same way. Frank Clune had said he had gone to Asia 'to find out the facts, by independent investigation on the spot', and insisted that *Flight to Formosa* was credible because he 'saw and heard what these pages describe'. Yet, Clune's personal experiences were also skewed by ideology. He referred to Taiwan as the 'land of democracy' despite the fact that it was under one-party rule. He also claimed that the number of refugees from the PRC was evidence both of Taiwan's freedom and mainland China's tyranny, despite the documented series of abuses perpetrated by Chiang Kai-shek's regime.[46] Like Roper and Cusack, Clune wrote his travelogues to support a particular political cause, and he too was guilty of extrapolating outwards from his single, highly contingent experience. Yet, largely because he did not challenge the official strategic outlook of Menzies-era Australia, his experiences were never subjected to the same level of scrutiny.

P EERING OVER THE FENCE | The 1950s and 1960s are often considered tourism's glamour age. International travel became increasingly accessible and desirable. Globally, the number of people taking an overseas trip grew from 25 million in 1950 to 166 million in 1970.[47] Australians were particularly eager travellers, with the number heading overseas nearly tripling every five years between 1960 and 1975, to reach nearly 632 000 departures.[48] Australians still preferred to spend their time and money getting to England: more than 15 000 travelled 'home' in 1955. Family connections, along with its convenience and affordability, drew a similar number to New Zealand.[49] In contrast, fewer than 3000 Australians set out for Singapore, and less than 2000 to Japan, in that year. Yet, only five years later, the number travelling to Singapore had doubled and by 1970 it had surged to almost 35 000: a rise of almost 1200 per cent in 15 years.[50] Tourism to Southeast Asia soared further after travel agents began to offer discounted, all-inclusive package tours in the early 1970s. In 1975, at the peak of the package-tour boom, almost 125 000 Australians travelled to Singapore and Malaysia alone – more than to the United Kingdom.[51] While mass tourism forms the subject of later chapters, it is important to note that by the time these packages were offered in the early 1970s, Asia held mainstream appeal as a tourist destination. The discursive groundwork for this shift took place during the 1950s and 1960s, even as the political volatility brought on by the Cold War and decolonisation peaked.

The vast majority of Australians travelling to Asia during the 1950s and 1960s went to Japan, Singapore or Hong Kong. Indonesia, the Philippines and Malaya (Malaysia after 1963) also attracted a growing proportion of Asia-bound visitors. However, something like 1000 Australians entered the People's Republic of China between 1949 and the resumption of diplomatic relations in 1972.[52] Australian passports were not valid for China and those wishing to enter the PRC had to apply for special permission, which could attract the attention of ASIO. The Minister for External Affairs had the discretion to refuse a visa and could even deny the re-issue of passports; Wilfred Burchett was denied a passport for 17 years on account of his sympathy for the North Korean and Chinese regimes. But most Australians did not face anywhere near the same difficulties, and requests for passports to be validated for China were usually granted.[53] Despite the regulatory burdens, many teachers, academics, engineers, unionists, farmers and other 'ordinary' Australians applied for permits after receiving an invitation to visit China as part of a professional delegation. Although commercial tourism was generally not permitted in China until the 1970s, some Australians, including the prominent retailer Kenneth Myer, also managed to gain entry as part of a private group.[54]

Following the cues provided by professional travel writers, visitors on both sides of the bamboo curtain came to think of their visits as fact-finding missions to uncover the 'real' Asia. Many visitors' diaries and letters betray an unusual attentiveness to local politics. Docking in Surabaya during a cruise through Indonesia and Malaya in 1955, barrister Joan Rosanove kept a keen eye for political posters and slogans, particularly those featuring the 'Hammer & Sickle'. Her travel diaries also brimmed with details about the local standard of living, leading her to reflect on the region's political situation. Rosanove was concerned that the basic wage was so low that 'about 90 per cent are poor', and she thought this would lead to communist victories in the upcoming elections in Singapore and Malaya. In Kuala Lumpur, she noted that communism was already so widespread that tourists were warned to stay within 'White Areas', which had been 'cleared from [communist] bandits'.[55] Visiting Singapore in 1958 on one of his numerous business trips, BHP Chairman Colin Syme also made careful inquiries about the city's population, ethnic distribution, age breakdown, average wage and unemployment rate. Like Rosanove, he was concerned that the poverty he saw could enable a communist success.[56]

William Wade also worried about the standard of living in Asia in his audio letters home. 'One has to be careful not to paint too glamorous a picture of Hong Kong', he warned his wife. While the major thoroughfares thronged with shoppers, 'the side streets seem to be so much poorer'. He was particularly troubled by the colony's many beggars and, as the father of three young girls, by children living on the streets. He worried that 'the little ones look so pathetic'.[57] As Peggy Warner had expressed it, while Hong Kong could be 'as the advertisements insist, a shopping paradise and a "little bit of Heaven", it is also a large slice of hell for many of its inhabitants', and this left the island open to communist subversion from the mainland.[58] The people were certainly poor enough, but Wade did not sense an impending revolution; indeed he declared that Hong Kong's citizens seemed content with their government. He supposed that, if the locals felt satisfied 'it's almost by comparison, because when they think of the people on the other side of the border [in communist China] … they realise that in many ways they are well off'. But he remained uneasy. The 'thing that one wonders about', he mused, 'is the future of the whole place. Will the mainland of China ever repossess this section which is under lease? Or will they leave it as it is?'[59]

Politics was, without a doubt, the major tourist attraction in China. As all visits were regulated by the Chinese authorities, travellers to the People's Republic were guided through the same exhaustive itinerary of model factories and co-operatives as prominent writers. Commercial tour operations began to be admitted in the late 1970s, but politics remained the major drawcard. A 1979 joint venture between Thomas Cook, Qantas and Ansett advertised 'ample time … to visit a commune, see an assembly-line factory, witness the enthusiasm of students … '. Tour companies also advertised the 'chance for you to draw aside the mythical 'bamboo curtain' and see for yourself the emerging China of today'.[60] Such advertising appealed to ordinary Australians wishing to conduct a

Cold War fact-finding visit of their own. Departing in 1977, hotel manager Gordon Aldridge explained that he was eager to see 'the proper China which has been shrouded in mystery to us for so long'. He also wanted to meet the people and find out what they really thought. Of course, the experience didn't always live up to expectations. Having set out to find the 'real' China, Aldridge was disappointed by the rigorously trained cadres and 'model citizens' he encountered. He became disenchanted with political tourism, and it wasn't long before he wrote describing 'the usual please come back and see us and bring back your family and your friends because we are friends of the Australian people' routine.[61]

Tourists to Hong Kong or Singapore may not have been so obviously regulated, but many found it just as difficult to access the 'real' Asia. Many visitors were unwilling to venture too far into the unknown, and the comfort of their hotels made the heat and confusion outside seem less appealing. The moment he stepped out of the plush, air-conditioned Peninsula Hotel, Wade found himself disoriented by the 'melee of people and buildings and signs and traffic running in all directions'. The contrast was so great that the normally effusive Wade could 'hardly find words' to describe what he saw. He turned to stock phrases and images – Hong Kong was 'a thriving mass of humanity', a 'colossal number of people', and a 'terrific population'. He was similarly overwhelmed as he stepped outside his Tokyo hotel on a second Asian trip the following year. Again, his senses were overloaded: there was a 'tremendous amount of people, a colossal amount of traffic, and the activity that is going on in the street' was overwhelming. His words became jumbled in conveying the confusion of 'the neon lights, and the amount of traffic, the tooting of horns, road construction work going on every-where, streets up all over the place, wooden planks down, and off the main streets, hundreds and hundreds of these small streets, a mass of little lights and little shops and eating places and bars and of course the signs in Japanese'.[62]

Reading their diaries, it is rare to find Australians having sustained contact with Asians outside the tourist industry. Far from gaining an insight into how their 'neighbours' really lived, and gauging what they thought, their role as tourists enforced a distance that limited visitors' capacity to build genuine connections with locals. Wade had set out with an enthusiastic desire to be a Good Neighbour, and had even hoped to find an Asian penpal for his young daughters. This proved difficult, however, as he lived and ate in tourist establishments that effectively segregated him from the people on the streets. He felt assaulted by the heat, the confusion and the congestion, and he sometimes longed to be back inside the hotel where the servants were invariably polite and friendly to paying guests. Like so many others, Wade was captive in a tourist bubble and his hopes of bridging the gulf of misunderstanding between Australia and Asia were ill-fated. The prospect of finding a penpal for the girls diminished, and the only Asian voices to feature in his audio-letters home were the voices of servants.

POLITICAL RE-EVALUATIONS | Although long-held generalisations about race and type still structured some views, tourism sometimes facilitated new insights. Colonial-era racial divisions had begun to fall away by the 1950s and 1960s and many Australians observed or met educated, middle-class Asians who did not conform to their ideas of 'natives'. In her diary, Rosanove mostly referred to local people as 'natives', but she occasionally departed from the script when describing local elites. At a cocktail reception in Surabaya, she was part of a mixed-race group that she described as 'a United Nations ... Australians, Americans, Swiss, Dutch, Indonesians, Indians and Eurasians'.[63] This metaphor located Asians on a basis of equality with Westerners and so was loaded with political meaning. William Wade did not have much social contact with locals, but he also developed a new respect for the people of Hong

Kong. Wade was particularly impressed by the tailor who stayed up all night to deliver his suit by the following morning and by the tailor's charming daughter, who chattered away brightly despite English being her second language. In Australia, discussion regarding 'Asiatics' took place within the context of the White Australia Policy and so tended towards the negative. Yet, these individuals were clearly decent, hard-working people. Even this brief encounter forced Wade to recognise that not all 'Asiatics' were the same, and encouraged him to re-evaluate his preconceptions.

Australia's immigration policy was a major site for reappraisal. Tourists were regularly confronted by questions about immigration restriction, so much so that Frank Clune warned all Australians heading to the region 'to get ready to be quizzed on the White Australia Policy'.[64] Direct questions forced visitors to consider the White Australia Policy from the Asian point of view and to weigh it against the rhetoric of Australia as a good 'neighbour'. Arriving in India, Colin Syme was advised that Indians did not like to hear reference to 'White Australia', although he was also assured that Australia was 'popular … despite our immigration policy'.[65] It wasn't long before an Indian business contact confronted Syme about 'Australia's policy of excluding Indians' especially in the light of 'its big area and lack of population'.[66]

Such encounters could provoke profound re-evaluations. At the time of Wade's 1962 visit, both major parties supported the White Australia Policy. A lifelong political conservative, Wade had never thought to oppose immigration restriction before his departure.[67] After travelling in Asia, however, he began to re-think his attitudes. He began to think it 'strange' that the White Australia Policy forced Colombo Plan students  – who could enter Australia in order to study at its universities – to leave after graduation. 'We seem to be acting very foolishly,' he mused, as 'we're not ready to take advantage of the outstanding pupils that come out of our education system'. Having witnessed the work ethic and good humour of the Chinese through brief personal encounters, Wade came to 'think the right thing to do is for Australia to retain some of them, and then to use them'. Not only would this give Australia the benefit of these 'outstanding pupils', but would also help secure its place in the region. By acting as a bridge between East and West, Asian graduates could help in 'maintaining our sphere of influence in these countries', and would encourage 'greater co-operation between Australia and the eastern neighbours'.[68] In only a few short days, a business trip to Hong Kong had led Wade to reconsider one of the keystones of Australian government policy, which had been in place since Federation.

Some business travellers had been wrenched from the misconception of Asian 'backwardness' after seeing the vitality of interwar Shanghai or Tokyo, and these epiphanies continued in the Cold War period. Colin Simpson was transfixed by the television set in his Tokyo hotel room in 1955, 'while Australia, so typically, was still making up its mind whether the country could afford it'.[69] Twelve years later, writer Gordon Bleeck marvelled at the colour television in his Toba hotel, having never seen the technology before.[70] He wrote letters gushing about the speed of Japan's fast train service, known as 'The Bullet', and at automatic car doors that opened and closed at the push of a button.[71] Wade was just as impressed. 'While some people say it's a dirty place', in some respects Hong Kong was actually better maintained than Sydney; furthermore, there was 'progress galore everywhere you look'.[72] The recognition that in some things 'backward' Asia was actually more advanced than Australia was an unexpected outcome of many visits to Hong Kong, Shanghai or Tokyo. As Donald Horne wrote in *The Lucky Country* in 1964, it came as a shock to realise that 'Australia is not the most "modern" nation in "Asia"', and only the act of seeing it for themselves could convince a number of Australians to overcome that long-held conceit.[73]

Of course, politics was not at the top of every visitor's to-do list.

Many preferred to go shopping. In 1966, the Hong Kong Tourist Association (HKTA) conducted a survey of tourists. It found that Australians were particularly enthusiastic shoppers: no less than 94 per cent did some shopping during their visits and, astoundingly, 72 per cent admitted that they had done nothing else but shop and eat – significantly higher than the average for international visitors.[74] Although her stated concern was with politics, Peggy Warner reserved her greatest enthusiasm for Asia's shops. In *Asia is People*, she described shopping 'like crazy', with Japanese department stores and Filipino craftsmen alike offering wares so far above the Australian standard that she bought up 'almost hysterically'.[75] Visitors' purchases were not limited to souvenirs. The HKTA report found that ready-to-wear clothing and electronic goods were the most common purchases, suggesting that Australians were buying serviceable, practical items to use back home.

Yet, even apparently frivolous impressions could contribute to broader patterns of political and economic 'engagement', as it was becoming configured at this time. William Wade was struck by the vitality of Asia's commercial sector. 'There's so many shops, you can't imagine', he reported to his wife: 'not just thousands of shops, there's tens of thousands of shops. And they're everywhere, all over the place, and some of them have the most delightful things, some beautiful, some things expensive, some things cheap.' Moreover, he was pleased that, 'contrary to what a lot of people tell you about Hong Kong', there was 'really no trickery' but rather 'quite a co-operative spirit' of commerce. Wade was in Hong Kong and Japan in his capacity as Director of a Sydney-based engineering firm and the buzz of commerce, combined with his new-found respect for the hardworking people, made him eager to do business with Asia. He returned on another business trip the following year.[76]

Of course, not all visitors were impressed by Asia. While many came home brimming with tales of the latest technology and bustling markets, others continued to propagate Orientalist stereotypes of backward, inefficient and lazy 'natives'. Some of this was configured around geography, with visitors to East Asia's urban centres generally more enthralled than those travelling to regional areas, or to South or Southeast Asia. Travelling to inspect BHP's Indian operations in 1946, Syme declared that 'the Indian is a poor technician and requires much supervision', and combined with the political upheaval that accompanied decolonisation, he declared that doing business in India was next to impossible.[77] As we have seen, Syme was a strong proponent of deepening economic ties between Australia and Asia. Yet he remained wary of doing business in India and more than 20 years later he was still remarking that Indian workers were generally thought to be 'very idle' and 'corruption rife'.[78] Neither were all travellers' views about race and politics necessarily affected in the same way. Frank Clune's many visits to Asia only strengthened his support for immigration restriction: he thought that 'the example of what has happened in Malaya, through unrestricted immigration of Chinese and Indians, should be a warning' for Australians.[79] Clune serves as a reminder that, although travel was a spur to reassessments of Australia's relations with Asia, not all travellers came to the same conclusions.

WIDER IMPACTS | Insights and epiphanies were typically shared beyond immediate family and friends. Wade punctuated his audio-letters with instructions about which sections his wife should replay to others. Unlike personal journals, travel diaries were often regarded as semi-public productions. Rosanove typed her diary to make it more legible, and it accompanied her legal papers to the National Library of Australia after her death. Business travellers like Colin Syme routinely submitted official travel diaries (that sometimes contained a surprising range of personal reflections) to their companies. Travellers were also eager to share their experiences with a broad group of friends and acquaintances. Slide nights, at which travellers screened photographs they had taken during their holidays, formed a staple of Australian middle-class social life in the mid-20th century. Travel stories about Asia inevitably reached an ever-wider audience as the number of Australians visiting the region grew during the 1950s, 1960s and into the 1970s.

While the impact of personal stories can be difficult to assess, the influence of visits by prominent Australians can be traced more directly. In his biography of historian Manning Clark, Mark McKenna writes of the influence of an extended visit to Indonesia, Singapore and India in 1955–56. At a university in Singapore, students demanded to know why Australia supported Dutch colonialism in West New Guinea and why Australia retained Papua New Guinea as a colony. He was also repeatedly interrogated about the White Australia Policy. McKenna writes that, 'after facing so many questions from Asian students … he saw Australia's history in a much more critical light'. Clark began to weave a narrative that seemed to satisfy his Asian interlocutors, in which Australia's history was framed by its own anti-colonial struggle against England. Presenting Australia's history in a way that would appeal to his Southeast Asian audience, Clark explained that, far from being embraced as the mother country, England was 'resented and even hated in Australia – though not by all people'. The ideas that germinated in Asia went on to shape his seminal *History of Australia*.[80] Donald Horne, the prominent editor of the *Observer* and the *Bulletin*, also attributed his most influential ideas to insights he'd had while travelling. Being in Asia 'seemed to make it possible to evaluate my own country all over again'. The result of these re-evaluations was *The Lucky Country*, a publishing 'phenomenon' that had a profound impact on how Australians thought about their own country.[81]

Personal experiences could also encourage direct political action. Traveller Daniel O'Brien was not alone in returning to Australia feeling 'a bold challenge to do something'.[82] Ken Rivett became convinced of the need for change after facing endless questions about the White Australia Policy during a trip to India in 1957. Returning home, he met Jamie Mackie, who had become strongly opposed to the White Australia Policy through professional and personal contact with Indonesia. Both men had learnt just how unpopular the White Australia Policy was in Asia, and had found the arguments they rehearsed in its defence to be unsatisfying to their listeners and, increasingly, themselves. The experience helped inspire the pair to form the Immigration Reform Group, which played a central role in rousing opposition to the White Australia Policy with its 1960 pamphlet, *Immigration: Control or Colour Bar?*[83] The Immigration Reform Group was composed of academics, writers and activists who were united by the belief that the White Australia Policy had no place in Australia's future. A number of them were also united by the experience of travelling or living in Asia; indeed several, including Mackie and Ailsa Zainu'ddin, had spent several years volunteering in Indonesia as part of the Volunteer Graduate Scheme, an early expression of Australian compassion and goodwill towards the region, which is the subject of the next chapter.

It is important to recognise that these reassessments worked in creative tension with official policies of Asian engagement. As we have seen, influential travel writers exhorted ordinary Australians to engage with their regional neighbours from the 1940s, and a growing number of travellers came to press for deeper diplomatic engagement well before the official reorientation of government policy towards Asia which occurred in the late 1960s and 1970s.[84] Travellers' experiences and insights, and their influence on broader Australian perceptions of the region, helped shape a public climate that was receptive to shifts in foreign policy towards Asia by the time they were tabled. The growing concern for the lives of 'ordinary' Asians also had another effect, arousing a sense of compassion that increasingly translated into organised humanitarian and benevolent action.

# 5: HUMANITARIANS

Australians have long peered over the fence with concern. The image of Asia as an overcrowded, destitute and backward place was well entrenched by the turn of the 20th century. Some Australians rushed to shut the gates in the face of so much misery, maintaining immigration restriction policies to ensure that Asia's poor could not flood south in search of a better life. But other Australians' concern was motivated less by anxiety than by compassion, goodwill and a strong sense of social justice. While a small number of missionaries had worked in the region since the 19th century, a growing range of well-meaning Australians headed to Asia from the 1950s in the hope of improving the lives of millions of their neighbours. They styled themselves as humanitarians, effused altruism and goodwill and behaved in ways that spoke to racial equality and international friendship. In many ways, they were pioneers who put themselves on the frontlines of the international campaign to banish racism and overcome the legacies of colonialism. But, as with religious missionaries, their crusading desire to assist Asian development can also be seen from other, more critical, perspectives. From the early 1950s, the nation's reputation in Asia became a pressing concern. Humanitarianism and foreign aid became tools of foreign policy, regarded as a means of improving Australia's image amongst the newly independent nations of Asia and therefore improving the nation's regional security. These policies were motivated by self-interest along with altruism. More critically, although volunteers

and aid workers went to Asia in the spirit of international broth-
erhood, the assumption that they knew best could, at times, imply
paternalism rather than fraternity. Many Australians liked to think
that they approached Asia with a heart of gold, but to others, it
looked like the heart of darkness.

Asia's proximity, and the widely held assumption that the region
was poor and backward, has meant that Australian humanitarians
have long targeted the region with their goodwill. In the early years,
this concern was often imbued with missionary fervour; the most
devoted headed to Asia under the aegis of missionary organisations including the London Missionary Society and the Catholic
Church. By the middle of the 20th century, well-meaning Australians increasingly expressed a secular spirit of goodwill.

NEIGHBOURLY ASSISTANCE | Decolonisation
unleashed a wave of progressive idealism. Entire nations
were being built from scratch and an optimistic language of progress and equality pervaded the international sphere. Many Australians were inspired by the enthusiasm of post-colonial leaders
such as Indonesia's President Sukarno, who spoke of the need
to raise his people up from poverty with conviction and passion.
Australia's earliest official relations with the emerging Indonesian
Republic were characterised by idealism and a genuine desire to
help. The Chifley Labor government acted on Indonesia's behalf at
the United Nations, and it was also among the first to establish full
diplomatic relations with Jakarta.

The enthusiasm extended beyond government. As we saw in
Chapter 3, returned soldiers and the unions formed significant
pockets of domestic support for Indonesian independence. While
public opinion was initially wary, polls found that a majority of
Australians had come to support Indonesia's independence by the
late 1940s.[1] Some became passionately and actively involved in the

cause. One young Sydneysider, Molly Warner, began campaigning for an independent Indonesia after meeting Indonesian soldiers stationed in Australia during the Pacific War. She married one of the activists, took on his nationality, and followed him to Jakarta under her married name of Molly Bondan in 1947. Once there, she set about building a new way of life that embodied the post-colonial ideals of racial equality and international fraternity. Unlike the Dutch colonists and European tourists who sought to maintain the illusion of White Man's Prestige, Bondan based her life on the principle of equality with Indonesians. She took up work in the Republic's civil service at the same rate of pay as her Indonesian counterparts. She lived in an Indonesian-style house, ate Indonesian food, and spoke Bahasa Indonesia at home. Her lifestyle was frugal – some have even called it austere – which made a sharp contrast not only with the colonisers of the recent past, but also the tennis-and-cocktails circuit frequented by other expatriates, including Australians attached to the new Embassy in Jakarta. Rather than maintaining a social distance between 'natives' and 'Europeans', Bondan wanted her actions to convey the fundamental equality between Indonesians and Australians.

Like so many others, Bondan was conscious of the fact that her individual behaviour carried broader messages about Australians in Asia. She knew Indonesians would interpret her personal identity as revealing something about the Australian national character, and she wanted to broadcast an image of an egalitarian Australia that did not discriminate between races. Conscious of the eyes on her, she not only shared in the lives of locals but was careful to be seen to be doing so. Bondan was a savvy communicator and a subtle master of public relations. She attained a high profile through her role at the Ministry of Information, which included working as President Sukarno's speechwriter. She used this profile to transmit the image of an Australian who was on Asia's side in the struggle for decoloni-sation; someone who wanted to help but not to dominate. Bondan continued her personal campaign for international friendship over many years, and her efforts were recognised and appreciated both in Indonesia and Australia. After her death in 1990, Minister for Foreign Affairs and Trade Gareth Evans called Molly Bondan 'a living symbol of the sympathetic links between Australia, the land of her upbringing, and Indonesia, her adopted country'.[2] Through her actions, Bondan helped pioneer a new role for Australians in Asia: the well-meaning humanitarian.

THE VOLUNTEER GRADUATE SCHEME | Molly Bondan's example inspired a small but growing cohort of enthusiastic young Australians who shared her post-colonial politics and egalitarian ideals. Melbourne University students John Bayly and Alan Hunt became friendly with a number of Indonesian students as the group sailed to an international conference in India in 1950. They learnt that years of war and civil disorder had left Indonesia with a severe skills shortage, which was exacerbated by the departure of Dutch administrators who had filled key posts in the colonial administration. Although Indonesians were being trained, in the meantime the public service relied on expatriate staff who demanded exorbitant wages that the emerging nation could hardly afford to pay. Returning to Australia, Bayly and Hunt discussed the problem within their network of student activists and Christian groups. They devised a scheme to send Australian graduates to work in the Indonesian civil service for a period of two years at the Indonesian rate of pay.

The Volunteer Graduate Scheme (VGS), as it was called during these early years, appealed to a range of idealistic young Australians who were motivated by a combination of progressive politics, humanitarian ideals and Christian notions of service. The scheme's first volunteer, political science graduate Herb Feith, arrived in Jakarta in 1951. At the airport, Feith was greeted by Molly Bondan, who was one of the scheme's earliest supporters. She took Feith in and, over the next few weeks, introduced him to her views about Australia's place in relation to post-colonial Asia, and demonstrated a way of life that was in keeping with these ideals. Feith came to consider Bondan his mentor and role model and largely adopted her lifestyle. Through Feith, Bondan's brand of post-colonial body politics came to have a profound influence on the VGS as it grew over the coming years.[3]

The VGS program was a success, attracting dozens of young Australians to Indonesia during the 1950s and 1960s. Many modelled their behaviour on Bondan and Feith. They received local wages, which didn't stretch to luxuries, and many did their best to become integrated into the Indonesian way of life. Volunteers took Bahasa Indonesia lessons, lived in Indonesian homes, ate local food and made a determined effort to become a part of the community. In 1965, author Ivan Southall wrote an account of the Volunteer Graduate Scheme as part of his travelogue, *Indonesia Face to Face*. He reported that VGS volunteers were proud to be 'the first Europeans not only to accept but to ask for beds in Indonesian dormitories and places at communal tables', and that they proudly contrasted their behaviour to that of other Westerners, who would consider this 'an affront to the dignity of the white race'.[4]

Living at an Indonesian standard was an important statement against colonialism, but such a statement was only effective if it had an audience. Like Bondan, volunteers were eager to be seen performing the role of concerned humanitarians in order to ensure that the message of Australia's goodwill was received by the broadest possible range of spectators. There is a certain dramatic quality to the way former volunteers recount their experiences. Southall enthusiastically retold some of the volunteers' favourite stories, in which their asceticism came into sharp contrast with the lavish lifestyles of other expatriates. Similar stories were recounted for years to come; researching her recent biography of Herb Feith, historian

Jemma Purdey came across a number of such tales. One recalled a picnic in 1954, in which VGS volunteers ate with some Americans as well as a group of Indonesians. The Australians watched as the Americans unpacked a meal so elaborate that it seemed they had 'brought everything ... except the refrigerator, with them'. After the Americans had unrolled the tablecloths and arranged their cutlery, the Australian volunteers unpacked their own simple lunch of rice and vegetables, wrapped *bungkus* style in a banana leaf, and proceeded to eat with their fingers. The Americans' astonishment at their piety was gleefully emphasised as the story was retold in later years.[5] The positive impression of unassuming egalitarianism lay at the heart of this VGS tale, as of many others.

VGS grew over the 1950s and 1960s, and as an institution it became increasingly concerned with the impression conveyed by volunteers. The literature issued by the Scheme reveals that living at an Indonesian standard, and being seen to do so, soon became the rationale for the scheme over and above any benefit to the Indonesian nation. As a 1962 manifesto stated, 'by sharing in manual work, washing dishes, splashing down muddy kampong tracks and so on, one is protesting against the perpetuation of hierarchies fostered by feudalism and colonialism'. As a result, 'our most important job ... is just to live normally and naturally in the Indonesian world and to make friends, not standing on the sort of superiority ideas which so many of the Western community in Indonesia still practice'.[6] By the 1960s, the initial impetus for the scheme – helping Indonesia overcome a skills shortage – had been overtaken by the task of projecting a body politics that conveyed international friendship and racial equality. As Molly Bondan reflected, the volunteers 'did a lot in the way they used their knowledge to help others, but what they did in promoting friendship between Indonesia and Australia in those difficult early days cannot be measured'.[7]

Even at this early stage, the fundamental tensions inherent to the role of regional humanitarian were becoming evident. While the initial motivation had been to help Indonesia, institutions such as VGS increasingly cultivated the role with an eye to the benefits for their own nation's reputation. Shifting the focus to volunteers' lifestyles rather than their work emphasised Australia's goodwill, rather than any concrete results. The Australian government approved of this image and it supported VGS, including with financial backing, from 1952. In return, the Department of External Affairs used VGS for public diplomacy purposes. Official photographers were despatched to capture volunteers as they set off for their postings, and their formal compositions, depicting well-groomed young Australians beaming with goodwill, spoke to the kind of image the government wished to project to its neighbours in Asia.[8]

The image projected by well-meaning student volunteers was particularly valuable as a weapon against ongoing charges that Australia was a racist society, which dogged the nation as long as the White Australia Policy remained in place. As influential journalist Peter Russo wrote in 1956, 'if there is any better way of "showing the flag" in Asia' than the VGS, 'I have not heard of it'. Moreover, a positive reputation would benefit the nation's regional security; as Russo put it, 'these young Australians … are our leading insurance salesmen in Asia'.[9]

VGS aroused the interest of ordinary Australians who wanted to contribute to the region's development. From the mid-1960s, it expanded its scope beyond Indonesia, posting volunteers throughout Asia and the Pacific. It underwent several name changes before becoming Australian Volunteers International (AVI) in 1999, and it continues its work today. Since its inception as VGS in 1951, the program has deployed over 6000 Australian volunteers to developing nations around the world, with the vast majority posted to Asia.[10] The experience of living and working in Asia was intense and often profound, and it could shift the course of volunteers' lives. Many maintained a lifelong interest in Southeast Asia, and tried to share their insights with as many of their fellow-Australians as possible.

Herb Feith, the Scheme's first volunteer, went on to become a leading expert in Indonesian politics, and remained a vocal proponent of Indonesian-Australian academic and community engagement until his death in 2001. As we saw in the previous chapter, a number of core members of the Immigration Reform Group, including Jamie Mackie and Ailsa Zainu'ddin, were former VGS volunteers. Feith, Mackie and Zainu'ddin all worked at Monash University, teaching Bahasa Indonesia and Indonesian Studies to thousands of young Australians over several decades. They are remembered as dedicated teachers who generously shared their knowledge and insights about Australia, Indonesia and how to live between the two, with colleagues and students.

Other volunteers united Australia and Indonesia in more intimate ways. Joan Minogue spent 18 months as an English teacher at a school in Central Java in the late 1950s before returning for a second VGS posting. She stayed on, married an Indonesian man, and the couple's daughter Ratih Hardjono grew up to become a prominent Indonesian journalist and Presidential Secretary to Abdurrahman Wahid. Hardjono was also vitally interested in Australian-Indonesian relations and addressed the topic in a 1993 book, *The White Tribe of Asia*. The VGS legacy continues to bear on Australian-Indonesian relations even today.

The role of humanitarian appealed to governments and volunteers alike and the VGS model was mirrored by a number of international volunteering programs established in subsequent years. The United Kingdom introduced Volunteer Service Overseas (VSO) in 1958, and similar schemes now operate in a number of countries, including Canada and Norway. The best-known program is the Peace Corps, initiated in the United States by President John F Kennedy in 1961. In setting up the Peace Corps, Kennedy looked to young volunteers to project an idealised American national identity in much the same way as the Volunteer Graduate Scheme had done a decade before. In her account of the Peace Corps, historian

Elizabeth Cobbs Hoffman writes that it 'symbolised what America wanted to be': 'superhero, protector of the disenfranchised, defender of the democratic faith'.[11] Volunteers did good work, and also projected a positive national image. Western governments were aware of the international goodwill that could be generated by these idealistic young volunteers and increasingly sponsored their activities abroad.

The Menzies government was also cognisant of the value of a reputation as a regional humanitarian, and it instigated its broader foreign aid program with a firm eye to the goodwill it could arouse in Asia. Introducing Australia's earliest major foreign aid program, the Colombo Plan, Minister for External Affairs Percy Spender insisted that it was 'not a policy of mere humanitarianism; it is also a policy of serious self-interest'. Australia would build up the region's 'latent goodwill' with foreign aid programs, which could also serve as 'an antidote to unfavourable publicity'. Furthermore, the image of Australian humanitarianism appealed across the political spectrum. As historian Daniel Oakman has noted, the Colombo Plan was one of few postwar policies that 'allowed the humanitarian internationalist and the Australian nationalist, fearful of the world, to come together'.[12]

Publicity and public relations activities were a core component of the foreign aid program as it developed from 1951. A separate publicity wing within the Colombo Plan Bureau was established in 1954. By the mid-1960s, around 6.5 per cent of Australia's commitment to the Colombo Plan was spent on radio equipment alone, so that residents in Asian nations could access Radio Australia and learn more about Australia and its way of life.[13] As with VGS, investing in foreign aid was certainly important, but being seen to be doing so was thought to be essential.[14]

T HE POLITICS OF CONCERN | Projecting Aus-
tralia's humanitarian role in Asia became more urgent as the
Cold War escalated. International development and foreign aid
became active fronts in the ideological conflict between capitalism
and communism. The battle for Asia's hearts and minds saw a dramatic expansion in the number and range of Australian aid projects, especially after the Vietnam War began to take its dreadful toll
on civilians in Southeast Asia. Minister for External Affairs Paul
Hasluck oversaw an exponential increase in Australia's foreign
aid budget during the years of the conflict, hoping that it would
'present to Asian opinion a constructive and humanitarian side to
the Australian involvement in Vietnam'.[15] For maximum publicity value, some humanitarian aid was delivered by Australian soldiers deployed in the Vietnam War. Although the military's Civil
Aid Program accounted for a fraction of the contingent in terms of
personnel and funding, it received a disproportionate amount of
publicity. Images of soldiers solicitously aiding Vietnamese civilians captured by official Army photographers appeared on the front
pages of mainstream newspapers across Australia. Historian Rachel
Stevens has argued that this coverage was so prominent that the
overall character of the Australian deployment could be taken as
one of 'noble humanitarianism' rather than a military contingent.[16]

Public concern about the standard of living in Asia, and Australia's regional responsibilities, rose as the scale of the humanitarian crisis in Vietnam was revealed. Australian non-government
organisations (NGOs) Project Concern, Australian Catholic Relief,
the Asian Aid Organisation, World Vision Australia and Austcare
were among many that were founded during the Vietnam War.
Established NGOs, including Community Aid Abroad and the Red
Cross, also underwent substantial growth during this time. Popular
interest rose further as Third World issues intersected with popular culture. Celebrities including musicians and film stars mounted
prominent publicity campaigns for the Biafra civil war and famine

of the late 1960s and the Concert for Bangladesh in 1971. By suggesting that ordinary people in the West could help alleviate poverty in the Third World, these campaigns encouraged everyday citizens to imagine themselves as agents within the international system.

Thousands of Australians have travelled to Asia as aid workers in the years since. The complex politics of humanitarianism have played out in any number of ways through their experiences. While some were keenly attentive to their image and reputation, others were resolutely devoted to their tasks, with little regard to how they were perceived either back home or amongst the local population. Their actions did not always meet with a positive reception. Some scholars and activists have long been wary of Western humanitarian impulses. They have regarded the good intentions of aid workers as paternalistic and arrogant, carrying the implication that Westerners – even those with little expertise or practical experience – know what is good for the 'Third World' better than local communities. Some critics have even likened foreign aid to the colonial rhetoric of a White Man's Burden.[17]

High-profile individuals are often implicated in these systemic critiques. One aid worker, Rosemary Taylor, operated an orphanage in Vietnam at the height of the war. With so many children orphaned or abandoned as a result of the war, Taylor set out to rescue as many as she could and place them with new families in the West. Taylor organised 1132 overseas adoptions over four years, and in 1972 she co-ordinated the famous Operation Babylift to evacuate hundreds of Vietnamese children from the war-torn country. Conducted with great urgency, many of the adoptions were lightning-fast and ad hoc, often arranged outside the usual processes and with little documentation. As Taylor saw it, she was saving the lives of children who had been abandoned by their parents and Vietnamese society. Nonetheless, children were whisked out of Vietnam, sometimes without the correct immigration clearance, to parents who had not always been fully vetted through the usual channels. Taylor was adamant that it was impossible to get the necessary permits due to the rampant corruption and the scale of the crisis in Vietnam. Forced to choose between due process and the unfolding humanitarian emergency, she chose to save lives. However, her actions elicited constant criticism, and occasional reprimand, from Vietnamese authorities who resented her apparent disregard for local laws and authorities. Criticism intensified after a plane carrying 243 children crashed, killing 78 children and severely injuring many others. The ethical and moral quandary is obvious and immense. On the one hand, Taylor had shown compassion and courage and had borne numerous personal sacrifices. Many people – both in Australia and Vietnam – supported her actions. But, as she admitted in a memoir published more than a decade later, her uncompromising attitude evoked criticism and resulted in conflict with Vietnamese counterparts and authorities.[18]

This quandary reminds us of the complexity inherent to the role of regional humanitarian. Although it has been portrayed as an expression of Australian compassion and concern, Australia's role in the foreign aid system is premised on the notion that Australia is a modern and developed part of the First World, while Asia is Third World, backward and underdeveloped. It also situates individual Australians in a position of direct authority and power over Asians. Westerners have assumed positions of authority even if they were not experts – VGS mostly recruited young people with academic qualifications but little work experience, and Rosemary Taylor had been a nurse who had never worked with adoptions before arriving in Vietnam. Furthermore, some foreign aid projects (as well as large-scale economic development schemes) have been imposed without the full consultation of local communities. Increasingly, foreign aid agencies and NGOs have changed their operations in response to criticism. Organisations such as CARE Australia are careful that their projects are now 'guided by the aspirations of local communities'.[19] However the ambiguities of the foreign aid system have not been resolved, and these tensions became increasingly pressing as a broader range of Australians took on the mantle of humanitarianism and set off to Asia.

# THE VOLUNTOURISM PHENOMENON | I was 24 when I spent a year volunteering in Cambodia. In the early years of the 21st century, humanitarianism was having its moment in the spotlight. Musicians including Bob Geldof, Bono and Chris Martin publicised campaigns such as Live 8 and Make Poverty History, and celebrities like Angelina Jolie and David Beckham lent a touch of glamour to international humanitarianism as United Nations Goodwill Ambassadors. Volunteering overseas had become increasingly popular in this context, and by the time I set off it was not unusual for Australians to devote weeks, months or even years to projects across Asia and the developing world.

I went to Cambodia as part of the Australian Youth Ambassadors for Development (AYAD) program, funded by the Australian Agency for International Development (AusAID) and largely based on the VGS model. I worked at the Royal University of Phnom Penh, the nation's largest public university, which had been razed during the terrible years of the Khmer Rouge and was still recovering almost 30 years later. Initially posted to a role in university administration, before long I had been seconded to the history department. I was enthusiastic but, halfway through a PhD and with a couple of years' tutoring experience, certainly not a seasoned expert. Teaching history in Cambodia was politically fraught and, along with the language barrier and chronic lack of resources, the job was both immensely challenging and incredibly enriching. Some mornings, I began lecturing at 7.30 am and trying to keep my students interested despite the stifling heat was exhausting. But most of my days weren't so taxing, and the three-hour lunch breaks were positively luxurious. I found the work rewarding; but there was very little of Mother Teresa in what I did.

The AYAD program is funded out of Australia's aid budget, but as with VGS, much of the focus is on improving Australia's image overseas. As the program's name suggests, volunteers are Youth Ambassadors, helping spread the word that Australians are clever, polite and eager to help. At the pre-departure training session I attended, then Minister for Foreign Affairs Alexander Downer insisted that, above all else, the AYAD program was there to serve Australia's national interest. Our chief task was to improve our nation's image abroad; anything we could do in the specialist roles to which we had been assigned was a bonus. The AYAD program's website confirmed this order of priorities: it stated its dual purpose was to 'strengthen mutual understanding between Australia and the countries of Asia, the Pacific and Africa and also make a positive contribution to development'.[20] Some of my fellow-volunteers had already worked in the foreign aid sector and they were disappointed that AYAD prioritised image projection above development goals. Nonetheless, many relished the opportunity to advance Australia's reputation in the region.

Inevitably, there were moments when the responsibilities of improving Australia's image slipped from our minds. Cambodia levies no taxes on alcohol, and the sombrero-wearing barman who poured tequila at the Riverhouse Lounge was as much a feature of my volunteering experience as the long, hot teaching days and earnest discussions about development indicators. On the whole, most volunteers did their best, and many did leave a good impression. Many are still working in development roles across the region and the world. But the truth is, we did not face much privation, and our lifestyle as volunteers was still well above that of most Cambodians. Over the 12 months of our posting, we all learned a lot about Cambodia, and about ourselves. We also learnt that Australian humanitarianism in Asia was built on the best of intentions, but the lived reality could be a lot more complicated.

Humanitarianism has become a commodity and Australians are eager consumers. Like me, tens of thousands have gone overseas on volunteering assignments for periods ranging from a few days to several years. The Australian government's 2009 review of volunteering programs noted that it had supported over 12 000 volunteers, mostly to Asia, since the 1960s.[21] On top of this are the thousands of volunteers who went through non-government organisations. The tourism industry began to offer 'voluntourism' (volunteer tourism) products in the 1990s and 2000s. Although they borrowed the mantle of humanitarianism, these operations exploited a niche in the market for profit. Major industry players such as STA Travel and Student Flights began to offer holiday packages that included a short volunteering stint, and operations such as Projects Abroad and Volunteer HQ were established specifically for voluntourism. By 2005, the travel supplement in Sydney's *Sun-Herald* reported that voluntourism was 'one of the hottest trends in travel'.[22]

The market growth testified to ordinary Australians' desire to take on the role of humanitarian whilst in Asia. As travel journalist Louise Southerden reported in 2007, 'you don't have to be Bill Gates to be a philanthropist; all you need is a couple of weeks and a willingness to give some time and energy to the place you're visiting'. Even a short project was enough to get 'that warm inner glow' that came with being a humanitarian.[23] Yet, the warm glow did not necessarily translate into benefits for those at the receiving end. Unlike the tourism industry, which stands to gain from its expansion, a number of tourism academics have mounted vehement critiques of voluntourism. Scholars including Eliza Raymond and C Michael Hall argue that the model perpetuates colonial mindsets by encouraging untrained volunteers to assume authority over locals simply because they came from the 'developed' West. At its worst, they argue, voluntourism 'can be seen to represent the neo-colonial construction of the westerner as racially and culturally superior'.[24] The tensions inherent to the role of regional humanitarian are amplified as an ever-growing number of Australians set off on voluntourism assignments.

The mantle of humanitarianism has become so attractive that segments of the tourism industry, and some travellers, have come to portray tourism as a form of altruism in itself. Asia's tourism industry suffered a series of severe shocks during the early years of the 21st century. As Chapter 8 discusses in more detail, the Bali bombings, SARS epidemic and the 2004 Asian tsunami contributed to a dramatic (albeit short-lived) downturn in tourist numbers. In the wake of the Bali bombings, travel journalists suggested that the best way to help the Balinese was to 'spend, spend, spend ... you'll be doing everyone a favour'.[25] A similar refrain came in the wake of the tsunami, with articles suggesting that 'it's hugely comforting to think that another glass of Singha beer, another foot massage or another night in a hotel is going to percolate through the economy to help the people of Phuket get back on their feet'.[26] *The Age* reported on the recovery effort by claiming that Thailand's most 'desperate need is a share of the world's tourism dollars'.[27] While the travel industry clearly stood to gain from such rhetoric, it's important to note that these articles appeared in the mainstream press, not in tourism brochures.

Some individual travellers came to think of their journeys in this way. Tony Abbott was a minister in the Howard government when he travelled to Bali in 2006. In a piece for the *Sydney Morning Herald*, he portrayed his holiday as a form of aid. 'It was gratifying to think that indulging in a five star lifestyle at a fraction of what it would cost in Australia and enjoying some remarkably good value shopping might be helping to reduce world poverty and equalise the gap between rich and poor', he wrote. 'Tourists have never been accorded much moral standing', he summed up, 'but it seems they are just as necessary as aid workers and might be of more long-term benefit for the world's poorest countries'.[28] There is some evidence that ordinary Australians were also receptive to rhetoric that reframed their holidays as altruistic pursuits. Interviewed by the *Sydney Morning Herald* as he boarded a flight to Bali in 2004, Townsville local Rohan Geyser explained that he was going because 'the Balinese need us'.[29] Interviewed the following year, tourist Andy Boucher, who had lost a number of friends in the 2002 bombing, stated that 'I don't think in this particular instance with a community that's been very good to us, we can say "Sorry, we're not coming anymore"'.[30] The economic and social impacts of mass tourism in developing nations are hotly contested. Rather than pointing to the reality of the situation, this rhetoric testifies to the continuing appeal of the role of regional humanitarian for Australians in Asia.

HELPING THE REGION | The image of Australians enthusiastically and selflessly helping their Asian neighbours is an attractive one. There is no stronger refutation to charges that Australians are imperialist or arrogant than Molly Bondan's lifelong dedication to the Indonesian people, and no greater counterpoint to accusations of racism than Herb Feith's enthusiasm for cross-cultural identification. Australians are clearly eager to project an image of beneficence to the region, and the role of humanitarian fits nicely. But alongside altruism and a desire to improve the nation's image sits a more troubling idea, that Australians have been attracted to the role of humanitarian because it fits with deep-seeded prejudices about Asia as backward and developing and Australia as modern and developed. This mirrors broader critiques of the foreign aid system, which hold that it perpetuates notions of Western superiority. Some nations – notably the rising superpowers of China and India – bristle at the suggestion that they need Western assistance. India has long refused some forms of Australian aid (including volunteers sent through government programs such as AYAD), and AusAID programs in China were officially terminated in 2013. The suggestion that China (with an economy that dwarfs Australia's, nuclear weapons and an active space program) is backward and in need of Australian aid can appear improbable. Indeed, by the time the aid program was concluded, Australia was economically dependent on China. While foreign aid and international development are important components of Australia's regional relations, the power dynamic has never been as clear-cut as that between donor and recipient.

The Australian government's review of its overseas volunteering programs found that returned volunteers had an impact 'at the local, family and community level'. Many returned volunteers and aid workers retained a lifelong interest in Australian-Asian issues, and they went on to share their experiences in their capacity as teachers, activists and writers. The government's report claimed that the overall impact of its volunteering programs was 'positive', but it does not define what this means.[31] In his work on images of Calcutta, post-colonial theorist John Hutnyk has shown that volunteers and aid workers help perpetuate the 'rumour' that Asia is backward and in need of Western assistance.[32] Stereotypes of Asian backwardness become increasingly problematic as the Asian region becomes more prosperous. The continued appeal of the humanitarian role in Australia, and its increasing accessibility through the booming voluntourism industry, points to an ongoing disparity between popular perceptions and geopolitical realities. This disparity is at the heart of the following chapter, which turns to Australians heading to Asia because they imagined it as a place where they could find enlightenment, or more earthly pleasures.

# 6: SEEKERS

Marie Obst was eager to discover a world beyond safe, dependable Australia when she set off on the Hippie Trail. It was 1972; she was 22 years old and working as a nurse in Brisbane; her boyfriend, Nick Ribush, was a doctor at the same hospital. Through the travellers' grapevine they heard of a Buddhist monastery in Nepal that ran meditation classes for Westerners and it wasn't long before they had signed up for a month-long course of study and reflection. Deep in the Himalayas, they discovered a rich spiritual tradition that contrasted with life back home. They were still there two years later, by which time they had been entirely transformed. Marie was now Yeshe Khadro, a fully initiated nun in the Tibetan tradition. Nick was a Buddhist monk. Their relationship gave way in the face of strict discipline, but over the coming years they remained firm in their faith, helping spread Buddhist teachings and encouraging thousands of Australians to discover the wisdom of the East. More than 40 years later, they both remain pillars of the Tibetan Buddhist community in Australia. That youthful trip to India left a deep imprint.

In the previous chapter, we met Australians who believed they had something to offer Asia. Others thought that it had more to offer them. While it may have been economically poor, it was rich in the things that mattered. Inspired by Orientalist images of Asia as the 'Mystic East', spiritual seekers made their way to Asia as pilgrims seeking enlightenment and spiritual fulfilment. Others carried a different, though equally alluring, image of Asia as the erotic Orient: a place of untold sensual and sexual pleasures. Oriental women were imagined to be beautiful butterflies, delicate and truly feminine; the men regarded as passionate and sensual lovers. These fantasies drew Australians looking for love, or just sex, far from the watchful eyes of home. Regardless of whether they had come in search of heavenly wisdom or more earthly pleasures, many Australians found themselves succumbing to the sensory overload of vibrant colours, sounds and flavours that they discovered in Asia, which presented an alluring escape from the familiarity of life back home.

SPIRITUAL AND SENSUAL | Travelling to India in search of spiritual enlightenment became popular during the 1970s, but Australians have been doing it for a surprisingly long time. Among the earliest pilgrims was Alfred Deakin. The two-time Prime Minister and leader of the Federation movement nurtured a life-long interest in the spiritual and the mystical. He met his wife Pattie during a seance, and published articles on spirituality and Eastern religion throughout his journalistic career. In 1893, he set off to India. His stated intention was to study the irrigation systems the British had installed across the Raj, but he also yearned for a mystical experience. This dual purpose is reflected in the two books published on his return. *Irrigated India* described the modern engineering bestowed by the British Empire, while *Temple and Tomb in India* explored elements of 'native' life. Deakin had a profound respect for Buddhist philosophy from afar, but he wasn't always impressed by the reality of Indian religious practices when seen with his own eyes. He was especially scornful of Hinduism, which he thought bred a 'mental and moral miasma', but was also disappointed that the purity of Buddhist teachings had been polluted by the confusion and disorder of day-to-day life in India. But he was not deterred. Returning to Australia, Deakin helped establish the Toorak branch of the Theosophical Society, a semi-occult organisation that attempted to bridge Eastern and Western traditions, and retained an abiding interest in Eastern spirituality throughout his life.[1]

Marie Byles was another prominent pilgrim. She was a remarkable woman: the first female solicitor in New South Wales and a keen mountain climber, Byles embarked on a spiritual quest after a foot injury left her battling chronic pain. In 1953, she set off to discover deeper wisdom in the ashrams in India; after much searching she eventually found a fulfilling practice at the Maha Bodhi Meditation Centre in Burma. On her return, she built a small ashram back in Australia and spent much of her life trying to share her discoveries with other seekers. Byles also went on to travel through Asia in search of other Buddhist practices and published a number of books detailing her quest, including *Journey into Burmese Silence* (1962) and *Paths to Inner Calm* (1965).

Why were Deakin and Byles driven to seek spiritual fulfilment in Asia, rather than looking to Christianity or other Western traditions? While they were earnest in their search for spiritual and religious wisdom they were no less drawn to the sensual palette of Asia's bright colours, striking people and exotic cultures. Images of the 'Orient' had stirred Deakin's imagination since childhood. He thought that the very word 'India' was a 'magic name … before which the throng of unimpressive words falls back as if outshone by a regal presence'. Its colour and exoticism made India 'the most picturesque theatre in the world'. Yet, the very abundance of colour and noise seemed to threaten chaos at the same time as delighting the senses and Deakin found the extravagant sensuality of 'native' life disquieting. According to Indian scholar Ipsita Sengupta, the tension between attraction to India's exoticism and revulsion at its disorder helped shape Deakin's political stance towards Asian immigration. Seeing something of day-to-day life in India reinforced his support for the Immigration Restriction Act. He appreciated the spiritual and sensual aspects of India during his visit, but thought that admitting 'the yellow, the brown and the copper-coloured' to Australia would stain its whiteness and tarnish the pure with 'the unclean'.[2]

Where Deakin was overcome by the sensual abundance of Asian life, Byles was drawn to a different sensory landscape. Hers was a 'search for a quiet retreat' as reflected in the title of her first spiritual travelogue, *Journey into Burmese Silence*. Although she sought a different kind of experience, Byles' quest was nonetheless sensual as much as it was spiritual. She delighted in the 'light, joyousness and colour' of Buddhist rituals: the 'shrines open to the fresh air and sunlight, and gaily adorned with gold and silver and coloured things, and little umbrellas brought by the worshippers, as well as flowers, candles and incense'. The discovery of inner calm also brought its own kind of sensual ecstasy. For Byles, perfect stillness brought 'a violent heart-palpitation and breathlessness as if climbing a terribly steep mountain at a high altitude and at too fast a pace', before settling to a 'delicious relaxation ... complete stillness, perfect rest without sleep, as if being lulled on gentle waves of the ocean of all being'. This sensation was so powerful she 'almost wept with the beauty and bliss of it'.[3] Peace and stillness may have represented a different kind of sensual palette to the colour and chaos that overwhelmed Deakin, but both seekers had been drawn by the sensory experience of Asia as well as its promise of spiritual fulfilment.

# ENLIGHTENMENT ON THE HIPPIE TRAIL |
Mainstream interest in Eastern religion came with its integration into the youth counterculture of the 1960s and 1970s. The 'spirit of the Sixties' has been so heavily mythologised that it can be difficult to define. Entailing a generational rebellion against political

traditions and social conventions, the counterculture is nearly impossible to contain in a single definition. Adding to the difficulty is the fact that the counterculture was extremely dynamic, varying over space and time and comprising both political and cultural facets as well as a number of radical offshoots. In general, it privileged youth over age, innovation over tradition and personal freedom over social responsibility.[4] At its core lay a widespread rejection of 'ordinary' life in the West. As Australian artist Ken Whisson recalled, this was based on the sense that 'any sort of spiritual relation with the world is very difficult … because of the sort of environment we've created for ourselves and the world view that science has created'.[5]

With a binary logic reminiscent of 19th-century Orientalism, many young people came to conceive of the East as the opposite of the West. The counterculture imagined the West as materialistic and the East as spiritual. Older Orientalist and Romantic notions about the wisdom of the East enriched their tableau of preconceptions. Jack Kerouac's *Dharma Bums* and Allen Ginsberg's *Indian Journals* revived long-standing Romantic ideas about Eastern spirituality, and the Beat poets helped inspire a generation of baby boomers to look to India for enlightenment.[6] By 1970, American writer John M Steadman determined that the image of a 'spiritual East' was well established.[7] Where the West was condemned as a mechanised culture of 'cold conformity' and 'nine-to-five living', the East was portrayed as its opposite, 'gnawing away at reason and common sense', and 'a world that has not yet turned plastic'.[8] The West's capitalist rat race was contrasted to an idealised Eastern artisanship, by which it was imagined that in Asia, 'cultured people shy from materialism', and 'craftsmanship is the rule and not the exception'.[9] Similarly, the West's greyness and dullness were contrasted to the colour and chaos of the East, and the complex system of social rules that bound conduct in the West was contrasted to the 'simple life and uncomplicated pleasures' that Asians were believed to enjoy.[10]

The link was reinforced by a common association between Asia and hallucinogenic drugs, which were thought to offer a pathway to a deeper and more authentic experience. Imagined associations between hallucinogens and the East stretched back several centuries, as Coleridge's *Kublai Khan* testifies. Again, key countercultural figures reinterpreted these older ideas for a self-conciously new generation. *The Psychedelic Experience* by radical academics Timothy Leary, Ralph Metzner and Richard Alpert traced the similarities between Tibetan Buddhism and psychedelic drugs.[11] The links between drugs, spirituality and Asia were strengthened by Alpert's departure for India, his conversion to Hinduism and the subsequent publication of his popular 'spiritual guidebook', *Be Here Now, Remember*.[12] Leary also went to Asia, and went on to claim that 'the impact of a visit to India is psychedelic'. Linking Asia with psychedelic drugs and the kind of deeper experiences they promised increased its appeal to young people dissatisfied with the conformity and greyness of life in the West.[13]

India was at the heart of the countercultural image of the 'East'. As musicologist David Reck has found, during the 1960s and 1970s 'India took on the aura of a land of dreams, a magical and mysterious place, colourful and exotic beyond hallucination, where drugs were inexpensive and plentiful'.[14] India was rumoured to be 'a place where nothing was unacceptable, people were free, turned on, naturally wise, and understood the concepts of enlightenment'. One young baby boomer declared that he was going to India because 'you could live in the forest, eat berries, meditate in a cave, wander round naked or do whatever you felt like and no one would take a blind bit of notice because everyone innately understood what you were doing, and not only tolerated you but felt it meritorious to support such activities if you were sincere'.[15]

The idea that the 'East' was innately 'turned-on' lured a new generation to Asia. Raised in a period of relative prosperity, and coming of age as the tourism industry matured, baby boomers had unprecedented opportunities to travel for leisure, entertainment and education. Their desire to see the world – particularly the East – gave rise to the Hippie Trail, a route stretching from Europe through Turkey, Iran, Afghanistan and Pakistan to India and on to Nepal. European and North American travellers tended to turn back and retrace their steps from Nepal, but Australians often went on to Thailand, Malaysia and Indonesia and returned home via Darwin. Others travelled in the opposite direction, ending up in London, where they stayed on to study or work. Although exact numbers were never collected, many thousands of young Australians set off on the Hippie Trail between 1965 and 1979, with numbers peaking in the mid-1970s.[16] Some took their own vehicles, others hitchhiked or relied on public transport; others still bought tickets on the 'Magic Buses' that shuttled between London or Amsterdam and Kathmandu. The trip could take anywhere from six weeks to a number of years; most travellers went for six to twelve months. Away from home for such a long time, discovering the world and themselves, baby boomers often came to regard their travels as defining moments, which they would recall with fondness for the rest of their lives.

The counterculture's interest in Eastern spirituality turned ashrams, meditation retreats and monasteries throughout India, Nepal and Thailand into tourist destinations. Marie Obst and Nicholas Ribush were certainly not the only young Australians looking for a quiet ashram. Going to India, finding a guru and cultivating a spiritual practice became the height of fashion after The Beatles' well-publicised visit to Maharishi Mahesh Yogi's ashram in Rishikesh in 1968. Celebrities including Mia Farrow, Donovan and the Rolling Stones also visited the Maharishi, and inspired young people from across the West to follow in their footsteps by making the pilgrimage to India. Psychologist Hugh Veness' primary concern on setting out on the Hippie Trail was 'to get somewhere Buddhist' because 'at that stage I was very into Buddhism'.[17] Others looked beyond organised religion. Sydneysider Jeffrey Mellefont spent a month living 'hermit-style in a little shelter of palm leaves' on Ko Samui in Thailand. After this, he headed for India, persevering through the 'blinding heat of Bodhgaya in the dreadful state of Bihar' in search of the Bodhi tree under which the Buddha had found enlightenment. Not sated, he then 'spent a whole month living alone in an ancient stone riverside lodging-house in Benares on the sacred Ganges, going to the river every dawn and dusk to watch the pilgrims and the burning bodies, and reading about Indian history and philosophy'.[18]

The search for spiritual enlightenment had a range of outcomes. Obst and Ribush were obviously deeply affected. Now known as Yeshe Khadro, she stayed at the monastery outside Kathmandu for four years, and is still a practising Buddhist nun today. For the past 15 years, she has headed the Karuna Hospice, a Brisbane-based palliative care organisation run according to Buddhist principles.[19] Ribush became a key figure in the International Mahayana Institute, and although he is no longer a monk he remains active in the movement.[20] Pilgrims returning from India were also largely responsible for establishing a number of spiritual communities including the Hare Krishnas and Orange People, as well as several variants of Buddhism, in Australia. Others brought back yoga, meditation and a range of practices that found increasing popularity during the 1970s and 1980s, which extended the aesthetic of the counterculture's Asia to mainstream Australian society.

Yet, others did not find spiritual satisfaction. Like Alfred Deakin, who had been attracted to Buddhist philosophy but disappointed by the way it was practised in India, many travellers became disenchanted once confronted with the reality of Asian religion. Arriving in India, Sydney artist Ken Whisson was disappointed to find that, far from being naturally wise or inherently deep, Indians 'talked about Hinduism in very much the way that a western Baptist or Catholic would talk about his religion', so that it 'all seemed very superficial'. The experience of Eastern religion had not lived up to his expectations; Whisson thought Christopher Isherwood's *Ramakrishna and his Disciples* 'seemed more in contact with Indian religion than anyone I talked to on the way'.[21] He was not alone in preferring the version in books written by prominent interpreters of Eastern religions such as Richard Alpert, Allan Watts and Jiddu Krishnamurti. Despite his earnest search, Jeffrey Mellefont was ultimately disappointed 'that the Buddhism of the villages was not that of Allan Watts'.[22] Twenty-year-old Abigayle Carmody, who had made her way to India from Geelong, was similarly disenchanted. Her interest in Eastern spirituality had been sparked by Krishnamurti, the mystic once hailed as the Theosophist 'World Teacher', who had broken away to preach his own popular brand of mysticism. As Carmody understood them, Krishnamurti's writings were 'about personal freedom – complete psychological freedom'. Arriving with high expectations, she was disappointed by what she saw at a spiritual community she visited in Pondicherry. 'I didn't find it very accessible', she remembered, and 'I was more interested in what Krishnamurti was saying' than in the flesh-and-blood devotees she met. Unimpressed, she didn't stay in Pondicherry for long.[23]

The most popular gurus and interpreters taught adherents to seek personal growth and inner consciousness. Focussing inwards often meant removing oneself from the 'real' world, and so drew some travellers' attention away from the day-to-day life of Asia. Far from Peggy Warner's insistence that 'Asia is People', travellers on the Hippie Trail were often more interested in Asian ideas, rituals or crafts than the people themselves. Instead of imagining Asians in politically current terms as 'neighbours' or 'friends', the counterculture posited the region as mystical and otherworldly; by doing so it removed Asia from the contemporary political context. This is important in that it laid the groundwork for future tourists to enjoy Asia without necessarily taking account of its politics – a development that contrasted to the Cold War tourism of Chapter 4. This helped lay the groundwork for mass tourism as it boomed from the mid-1970s; as the next chapter explores in more detail, it could also lead to conflict between tourists and local communities across Asia.

Like Deakin and Byles before them, countercultural seekers were drawn to the sensory experience of Asia. Religion in Asia was a feast for the senses, and the tinkling of ceremonial bells and the taste of exotic ceremonial dishes made a distinct impression on many visitors. The rituals of religious practice – the sounds of chanting, the smells of incense and flower garlands, the physicality of yoga, the taste of dahl – were often just as appealing as the promise of spiritual enlightenment. Returned pilgrims came home practising the aesthetics of Asian spirituality as well as its rituals. Communes and spiritual centres became places where Anglo-Australians wore saris, ate curries and burnt incense. At the New Govardhana Hare Krishna commune outside Murwillumbah in northern New South Wales, which remains active today, devotees went by names such as Chandra Emma or Dhara DesFours, reflecting their hybrid Indian-Australian lifestyles. As Chandra Emma reflected in an ABC TV interview some 30 years later, 'it was a pretty amazing experience ... a lot of colour, a lot of music, a lot of festivity'.[24] Travellers often brought some of the sensual experience of Asia back home with them, and Asian influences increasingly infused Australian culture from the 1970s.

P RETTY GROOVY GEAR | While countercultural seekers were drawn to Asia by its spiritual depth, there was also a more material attraction. Asia was, quite literally, fashionable during the late 1960s and into the 1970s. The counterculture's interest in Asia made the Eastern aesthetic the height of fashion and returned travellers proudly flaunted the exotic clothes they had acquired on the Hippie Trail. According to Abigayle Carmody, it seemed that 'everyone was wearing those scarves with all the Sanskrit imprinted on them', or Tibetan fur boots, or 'groovy little caps'. Their visibility served as an advertisement for the Hippie Trail, drawing others to seek a similar experience. The clothes were laden with special meaning: 'they were saying, "I've travelled and I've had great experiences and I've got a bigger, broader view of the world than Australia"'. They also seemed to say: 'I've broken away and I've rebelled and I'm pretty cool'. Carmody read so much meaning into the clothes that she later spoke of her decision to go on the Hippie Trail as a desire to break free and 'just put the kaftan on'.[25]

Clothing was very important for travellers in Asia. Cultural theorist Roland Barthes wrote of the counterculture as a 'fashion system' in which complex messages were communicated through clothing.[26] Carmody spoke of the messages conveyed by returned travellers' clothes back in Australia. On the Hippie Trail, clothes were also a marker of status that spoke to claims of being a traveller, rather than a tourist. As academic James Buzard has noted, the perennial division between travellers and tourists has been used to denote status since at least the days of the Grand Tour in the 18th century.[27] It became particularly important on the Hippie Trail, and travellers signalled that they were 'seasoned, long-term Asia hands … by our clothes', dressing in items sourced 'from local bazaars' rather than Western-style clothing.[28]

Clothes were so important that tales of conversion – from tourist to traveller, from 'square' to 'turned on', from novice to initiate – were typically framed through sartorial metaphors. These were trips on which one got changed, both literally and figuratively. Richard Neville, the editor of *Oz* magazine and a leader of Australia's countercultural scene, related such a story in his 1970 manifesto, *Play Power*. Neville created the character of Alf to embody everything that he disliked about mainstream Australia; Alf was conservative, racist and boorish. He set off in 'school blazer and golfing shoes; flag sewn neatly to rucksack', but the Hippie Trail soon changed him, and by the time Alf returned home, he wore 'a Moroccan djellaba and Indian sandals, a gold earring through his left ear and … a Turkish carpet bag'. His attitudes had changed along with his clothes and, as a result of his Asian experiences, 'Alf will never be the same again'.[29] In a memoir written some 25 years later, Neville returned to this metaphor to represent the moment that he and his real-life travelling companion, the celebrated artist Martin Sharp, became travellers rather than tourists. Checking out of the colonial Raffles Hotel, the pair headed to a local market, where they traded their smart luggage for 'disintegrating army rucksacks'; from this time they began to 'merge with the overland drifters'. After six months on the Hippie Trail, he wore an ankle-length embroidered Kabul coat and was weighed down with ethnic jewellery.[30] The irony of a traveller's allegiance to the counterculture – marked by a stated opposition to Western consumerism – being signified by specific commodities was not typically recognised.[31] Instead, this was understood as a substitution from Western articles that had been mass-produced (and so were deemed inauthentic) to handmade (and thereby authentic) Eastern garb.

Asia became increasingly fashionable in Australia, and across the West, during the 1970s. The promise of a different, more colourful world that was also more spiritually attuned lured droves of young seekers to the East. The combination was appealing; Abigayle Carmody was drawn to Asia partly because of the promise of spiritual fulfilment, and partly because 'there was some pretty cool gear to wear'.[32] Finding themselves penniless at the end of their own travels, Tony and Maureen Wheeler published a guidebook to the Hippie Trail, *Across Asia on the Cheap,* in 1973. Even then, they described the trip as being so popular 'that there's almost a groove worn in the face of the map'.[33] This popularity was to soar over the coming years; the Wheelers' start-up publishing company Lonely Planet was one beneficiary of the Hippie Trail's extraordinary appeal. As more and more young Westerners descended on Asia, the earnest seekers were steadily outnumbered by those looking only for fun and adventure, to whose story we will return in the next chapter.

L OVERS | The Hippie Trail introduced many travellers to carnal, as well as spiritual, enlightenment. Like many others, 19-year old photographer's apprentice Max Pam had set off to Asia looking for enlightenment and adventure in 1969. He found both – but not in the same place. 'In India I was really always a very good boy, a very spiritually oriented kind of person', he remembered, 'but … by the time I got to Bangkok, I'd completely change'.[34] Western fantasies about a sensual East have long had an erotic edge. Frustrated with Christian morality, Western men found an imaginative outlet in fantasies of Asian harems since at least the 18th century.[35] Women, too, fantasised about the swarthy and mysterious men of the East. As historian Hsu-Ming Teo has shown, 'sheikh fever' gripped the Western world from the 1920s and millions of women fantasised about dark and powerful men who, like Rudolph Valentino in the film adaptation of *The Sheikh*, would steal them away to the exotic East.[36] While the undercurrent of dangerous sexuality appealed to some women, other preferred to imagine Asian men as considerate and gentle. Rosa Praed's 1899 novel *Madame Izan: a tourist story* saw the heroine fall for a quiet Japanese count, rather than a brawny Australian. His gentle introduction to Japan's rich history and beguiling culture captured her intellect in a way that the empty bravado of the Queenslander could not, and the count's polite ways spoke to a respect that seemed to be beyond Western men.[37] Sexual fantasies often followed broader racial and cultural stereotypes. Darker-skinned men, such as *The Sheikh*, were often portrayed as driven by their primal urges, whereas East Asians were imagined to be gentle and respectful lovers. Regardless of the variant, women's sexual desire tended to be more covert than that of white men's lust for Asian women, which was expressed in a broad canon of literary and artistic works as well as in more straight-forward pornography. Borrowing from the Oriental harem and *Madama Butterfly*, these depictions encouraged what diplomat and writer Alison Broinowski has dubbed the 'Butterfly Phenomenon', by which Western men came to think of Asian women as 'a fragile art object, but also a cheap, replaceable commodity'.[38]

The fantasy image of the Erotic East drew Australians to Asia from the early years of the 20th century. As historian Adrian Vickers has shown, Bali came to be regarded as the archetypal Oriental paradise. From the 1920s, its image was fixed as 'the most exotic of exotic locations, a fantasy of all the splendours of the Orient and the beauties of the Pacific'.[39] The fact that Balinese women tradition-ally wore nothing but a sarong slung low around the waist was not insignificant. In the 1940s, Frank Clune wrote that 'the Balinese beauties are a great tourist attraction. Visitors come from every-where to look at them'. Clune had tittered over the visitors' com-ments in the famous Complaints Book of the Hotel Denpasar, in which amateur poets competed to cram as many puns and double entendres as possible into verses purportedly describing Bali's natu-ral or cultural attractions. The results, such as this 1932 poem about the island's volcanoes, suggest the extent of tourists' preoccupation:

> 'Oh noble breasts of Bali,
> Erect and proud you stand,
> A bronzed and rhythmic setting,
> To green and fertile land'.[40]

Bali's tourism promotional material was also unusually preoc-cupied with the Asian female form, even for a time when tourist advertising was habitually directed at a male consumer. But the fantasy image was not confined to Bali alone. In the 1940s, Qantas Empire Airlines advertised its routes to 'the East' with scenes of alluring female bathers posing bare-breasted in front of an aeroplane. Depicted in this way, Asia became a place of erotic fantasy; moreover, it was a fantasy that the tourist could leave behind at any time, borne away on the wings of the latest flying boat.

L OVE AND WAR | As we saw in Chapter 2, war introduced hundreds of thousands of Australian men to Asia. The notion that Asian women were submissive and sexually available took on a new significance in the heightened intensity of military conflict, which exaggerated the power divide between men and women, soldiers and civilians, occupiers and occupied. The original Anzacs had developed a taste for 'Oriental' women in brothels across the Middle East during the Great War and their sons were no different.[41] Girls were certainly on many diggers' minds as they landed in Asia at the outbreak of the Pacific War. As we saw in Chapter 2, many of the soldiers stationed in Singapore before the Japanese attack sought the company of taxi-girls and prostitutes. Those heading towards Europe or Middle East often spent their brief refuelling stops in Singapore, Bombay or Colombo touring the red light districts and, like Ivor White, many ended up paying for sex with 'a little dark sheila'.[42]

While the Pacific War introduced Australian men to Asian 'butterflies', it was the Vietnam War that institutionalised sex as part of the Asian experience. Nearly 60 000 Australian soldiers served in Vietnam between 1962 and 1973. More than one-quarter of them were conscripts, which lowered the average age of the deployment to 20 years.[43] Contacts with Vietnamese civilians were often marred by suspicion and fear as Australians found themselves unable to differentiate between allies and enemies. Allegedly 'friendly' villages could harbour Viet Cong fighters, and stories of trusted Vietnamese informants and friends who had turned out to be Viet Cong thrived. Even the most earnest soldiers could see that the mistrust was mutual, that many Vietnamese were 'not pleased about our presence', and were 'obviously not too happy about being saved from Communism'.[44] This only further strained relations between Australians and Vietnamese and helped establish what one former soldier called the 'consensus opinion that this was the arsehole of the earth'.[45]

For many, the only contact with civilians outside of this tense operational atmosphere came during brief periods of Rest and Recreation (R & R) leave. Longer breaks were typically spent in Bangkok, Hong Kong or Australia, but short spells of leave were taken at Vung Tau on the South Vietnamese coast. Previously known as Cap St. Jacques, Vung Tau had once been a well-known seaside resort patronised by French colonists. Despite the Army's best efforts to revive a carefree atmosphere, the fact that they were holidaying in a war zone was never far from soldiers' minds.[46] As an active war zone, the cordoned-off section of 'Australian' beach was protected on all sides by thick rolls of barbed wire. Soldiers on active duty patrolled the beach and although those arriving for leave were asked to check in their weapons on arrival, the streets were crawling with guns. Official Army photographers captured the tense and bizarre situation, depicting soldiers playing Australian Rules football while their guns hang at the ready on the goal posts, and others waxing their surfboards against a backdrop of barbed wire.[47]

Even so, Vung Tau provided a temporary respite from the war and soldiers tried to get the most out of two or three days' leave by packing in as many of its estimated 178 bars and 3000 bar girls as possible.[48] In the popular parlance, 'rest and recreation' became 'rooting and intoxication': a time to 'make a real animal of yourself'.[49] Private Mike Fernando remembered the bars 'becoming like a second home', and Trevor Pleace wrote of 'boozing and screwing, not stopping to breathe'.[50] Although it represented a fraction of their time, R & R loomed large in soldiers' letters and subsequent recollections. The Australian War Memorial holds a manuscript collection of diggers' poetry, and poems such as 'Two days rest in the city of sin' are particularly evocative:

> Two days rest in the city of sin
> Always makes a young digger grin
>
> Spend some piaster, get rotten drunk
> Take a lady and crawl to her bunk
>
> Love her hard and like its your last
> Pay her some money and wash up fast.
>
> Then its off to the street of bars
> Drunkenly weaving and dodging cars
>
> The ladies of Vung Tau are OK alright
> Ask any digger, who's spent a night
>
> He'll tell you a tale that will make you blush
> Of two days and a night, spent in a rush
>
> To screw the most and drink your share
> To fight the yanks with never a care
>
> After two days it's back to camp,
> To visit the medic, he's a champ
>
> He greets us all with a needle and a grin
> Welcome back grunts, from the city of sin.'[51]

After months of continuous service, many Australian soldiers found the attentions of Vietnamese bar girls a welcome distraction. As Private John S Gibson remembered, 'the war was terminated by the girls in the bars, if only for a day, a night or a week'.[52] Those less inclined to romance reflected that 'it was simply a question of financial negotiation'.[53] Negotiations are always revealing; in this situation, they point to the perceived value of Vietnamese women. Some soldiers, especially those on leave for the first time, were only too happy to buy every bar girl a drink and were overjoyed to secure a night at any price. But many Australians thought Vietnamese women were worth far less, and they complained about the high prices charged by prostitutes, bar girls and pimps. Some even took to haggling, and the most jaded revealed their contempt by offering 'a packet of soap powder', for 'a week of love with one of the bar girls'.[54]

The seedy atmosphere of Vung Tau only strengthened some soldiers' disdain for the Vietnamese as a people. Bombardier Peter Groves had had enough after only a few days, deciding 'I'm not really wanting to go to Vung-Tau again. Everything there is terribly dirty; I was nearly sick when I walked down the streets'.[55] Others were turned off by the local conmen and pickpockets who were always 'trying to rip round-eyes (Europeans) off'.[56] Engineer Sandy MacGregor remembered the paranoia that came with knowing that Vung Tau 'wasn't only used by us, it was also used by the Viet Cong'.[57] Corporal Phil Baxter was disturbed by the thought that 'the people you were drinking next to ... could be the people that you're firing out at ... the next day'.[58] Others wondered whether the barmen at Vung Tau's bars were actually VC, and a sip of stale beer could provoke anxiety about whether it 'was just the dregs or whether it was poisonous'.[59] The combination of bad smells, dirt and danger meant that many soldiers bypassed the town altogether, heading directly for the relative safety of the Australian Army's Peter Badcoe Club, where Vietnamese were not allowed to enter without official permission.

Like other travellers before them, Australian soldiers extrapolated from their contingent personal experiences to make broader claims about the nature of all Vietnamese, or even of all Asians.

Literary historian Robin Gerster has argued that the seediness of Vung Tau shaped soldiers' attitudes to 'Vietnamese' and 'Asians' in general.[60] Barry Wright, who had served in Vietnam, remembered that many soldiers came to think of the entire country as 'a vast brothel, the women whores, and the men either pimps or soldiers'.[61] Corporal Stan Sutherland thought it was 'a modern day Sodom or Gomorrah, full of black marketers, prostitutes, pimps, racketeers, scammers and beggars'.[62] Gunner Jason Neville wrote that all Vietnamese women were 'sex maniacks all they want is to have sexual intercorse they ask any soldier and they always say a price'.[63] As with so many travellers, these soldiers generalised outwards from their own personal experience, and came to think that all of Vietnam was like the Sodom and Gomorrah they experienced at Vung Tau.

R & R had another effect. On duty, soldiers were taught to enter villages and, if they suspected VC influence, take whatever action they thought necessary. The dictates of this war gave them the authority to impose themselves on local people and environments at will. At Vung Tau, this sense of dominance over a subordinate Vietnamese population was brought out of the battlefield and into civilian interaction. While it cannot be said of all soldiers, some Australians acted with a sense of impunity. Innumerable stories of diggers getting drunk and stealing from bars, beating up bar girls or getting into fights with barmen, hawkers and each other are backed up by official records. Bridging war and peace, R & R encouraged some soldiers to transfer the extraordinary behaviours of wartime to a civilian context.

# TOURING THE RED LIGHT DISTRICTS |

While most Australians took R & R in Vung Tau, Singapore or Hong Kong, the US Army built its major leave centres in Manila, Bangkok and Pattaya on the Gulf of Thailand. R & R left a legacy that lingered long after the withdrawal of Australian and American military personnel in 1973. The military's withdrawal left purpose-built R & R hotels empty and threatened the livelihoods of the many locals who had become economically dependent on the soldiers' insatiable appetite for sex. Military hotels in Bangkok and Pattaya were sold to private interests and quickly redeveloped for package tourism; prostitutes, pimps and touts also turned their attention to civilian tourists. Visitors to Pattaya in the mid-1970s found a throng of bars, nightclubs, massage parlours and coffee shops, all overflowing with bar girls: just like R & R, but during peacetime. In the coming years, long-standing fantasies about Oriental harems could finally be realised thanks to a sex industry and infrastructure that were largely the legacy of Vietnam-era R & R.

The Hippie Trail intersected with R & R in Bangkok, where civilian tourists occasionally interacted with soldiers on leave from Vietnam. At this time – the highpoint of the US Army's R & R program – the Bangkok bar scene was so renowned that Max Pam, a 'good boy' in India, 'saved my transgression up for Southeast Asia'.[64] As we have seen, the counterculture's image of India shaped the tourist experience, encouraging travellers to adopt the role of earnest pilgrim. The tourist culture of Thailand, Singapore and the Philippines was very different, and this also influenced visitors. Where the passages describing India in Richard Neville's *Play Power* focussed on drugs and religion, his depiction of the iconic Hippie Trail experience in Southeast Asia involved nibbling 'aphrodisiac chocolate in a South Thailand teenage brothel'.[65] Hippie Trail guidebooks were also upfront about sex in Southeast Asia in a way they were not in sections about India or Nepal. David Jenkins' student guidebook recommended Singapore's transvestite and transgender prostitutes as 'a must', and a 'good way to finish up an evening'.[66] Bill Dalton's *Traveller's Notes: Indonesia* also brimmed with advice about finding and soliciting prostitutes.[67] Tony Wheeler's first-ever Lonely Planet guides went so far as to advise female readers that they stood to make 'easy money' working for escort services in Singapore.[68]

Countercultural travellers were not the only ones seeking sex in Asia. By the 1970s, sex was becoming a mainstream tourist attraction. In Chapter 4, we met Colin Simpson, who wrote the most successful Asian travelogue of the Cold War period. Alongside its political sections, *The Country Upstairs* was saturated with sex: so much so that historian Richard White thinks it 'can retrospectively be seen as promoting Asia as a site for sex tourism'.[69] Indeed, the very first chapter took readers to the Bar Lido, with Simpson explaining that part of 'the research I had in mind' was to find out about sex in post-war Japan. And the research was painstaking. Alongside photographs of brothels and topless revue girls, Simpson catalogued the range of sexual services available to Westerners in Japan. He noted that a tourist could manoeuvre a bar girl into bed for ¥7000 (although 'she could probably be had for five'), and went on to carefully list the going rates for prostitutes, massage therapists and 'geisha-style girls'. When it came to genuine geisha, Simpson was so engrossed he devoted an entire chapter to their training, habits and tasks, as well as the services they would (and wouldn't) provide.[70]

Simpson became even more explicit in his later Asian travelogues. *Asia's Bright Balconies* (1962) saw him make a thorough inspection of 'enchantments for the roving male'.[71] *Off to Asia* (1973) included so many details about Asia's 'libido circuit' and the range and price of the pleasures and 'perversions' on offer that it really does read like a guide for the budding sex tourist. It seems that Simpson saw his books in this light, at one point complaining that 'there is virtually no mention in the general tourist literature ... of a whole area of sexual services'. Seeking to fill this gap, he recommended the most 'eyeworthy' revue shows, noted which barber shops offered more than haircuts and promoted the transvestite, transsexual and intersex prostitutes conducting their trade on Bugis Street as a 'distinctively Singapore' attraction. In fact, Bugis Street was so enticing that Simpson went out on a special mission to meet one of the 'panthers'. He had hoped to take a topless photograph, but the excitement got to him: he fumbled with the camera and the photo failed. Instead, Simpson had to make do with photographs taken by others – including some that had recently appeared in another mainstream Australian travel book, Ronald McKie's *Singapore*.[72] Like Simpson, McKie had described Singapore's sexual services in some detail and assured tourists that it was easy to 'hire an attractive Chinese girl from one of the many social escort services that advertise in the *Straits Times*'.[73] By listing this catalogue of sexual services, Simpson and McKie continued the long tradition of portraying Asian women as commodities to be purchased and enjoyed by the Western man – exotic 'lilies' who could be enjoyed at bargain rates. However, their practical instructions detailing where to look and how much to pay made it clear that the erotic East was now attainable by anyone with a passport and a few dollars in their pocket.

Sex tourism has drawn widespread criticism, both in the West and in Asia. In the West, the resonances between sex tourism and colonialism have been the subject of lively debate.[74] As well as the personal and moral questions it raises, it has been argued that part of the reason why sex tourism provokes such strong responses is because it crystallises the unequal power politics of tourism in general. As academic Nelson Graburn has it, mass tourism subjects developing nations to 'the "female" role of servitude, of being "penetrated" for money, often against their will; whereas the outgoing, pleasure seeking, "penetrating" tourists of powerful nations are cast into the "male" role'.[75] As a result, sex tourism forces tourists – whether they had come to Asia looking for sex or not – to consider the extent to which they are implicated in perpetuating colonial-era inequalities into the present day.

In Australia, the power dynamics of sex tourism were vigorously debated following the 1991 release of Denis O'Rourke's controversial documentary, *The Good Woman of Bangkok*. O'Rourke had spent months living with and filming Aoi, a Thai prostitute, and his documentary made for confronting viewing. Australian audiences were shocked by images of Australian men paying for sex with Thai women. The film was heckled and booed when it premiered at the 1991 Sydney Film Festival and at several later screenings. O'Rourke's relationship with Aoi, interspersed by interviews with other sex tourists (including a group of young Australians), confronted viewers with the fact that sex was eagerly sought out by a wide range of visitors to the neighbourhood. At least part of the discomfort stemmed from the broader political resonances of the film. By the late 1980s, prime ministers Bob Hawke and Paul Keating had begun a concerted push for Asian engagement, encouraging closer contacts at social and cultural as well as economic and diplomatic levels. As film scholar Chris Berry put it, *The Good Woman of Bangkok* gave viewers pause to wonder, 'is this what they mean by "Australia in Asia"?'[76] The intersection of sex and politics provoked intense debate, but the controversy did nothing to stem the tide of Australians heading north in search of sex.

The lure of sex attracted ever-growing numbers of Australian men to the region from the 1980s. In an in-depth report, Craig Scutt estimated that almost 100 000 Australians travelled to Thailand for sex in 2008, accounting for roughly 9 per cent of all sex tourists to Southeast Asia.[77] The arrest of a growing number of Australians on child sex tourism offences in Southeast Asia suggests that the 'libido circuit' has expanded to take in new carnal, as well as geographic, territory. As an industry, civilian sex tourism to Thailand and the Philippines largely grew out of military R & R. In recent years, Vung Tau has again become a site for sex tourism, and attained a measure of notoriety following the 2005 arrest of British pop star Gary Glitter on child sexual abuse offences. Australians will be among the many seeking its attractions this year.

EAT, PRAY, MAKE LOVE | Of course, not all relation-
ships were so utterly transactional. The famed sensuousness
of the Orient, along with the willingness to try new experiences
that can come with being away from home, gave rise to countless
holiday romances between Australians and Asians. Stories of love
blossoming across cultural divides became increasingly common as
tourism to Asia boomed from the 1970s. Reflecting a popular discomfort with the racial and gender dynamics of sex tourism rather
than a statistical reality, many of the better-known stories involve an
Australian woman falling in love with an Asian man.

As we have seen, Bali has long been associated with erotic sensuality and it is remarkably prominent in the real-life love stories
that have found a ready audience in recent years. The lush inland
town of Ubud had gained a special reputation for cross-cultural
romance even before the release of American writer Elizabeth Gilbert's best-selling memoir *Eat, Pray, Love* and the 2010 film of the
same name. One of the princesses of the royal house of Ubud, Jero
Asri Kerthyasa, was born Jane Gillespie and grew up in Sydney
before meeting her future husband on holiday in 1977. The couple
had three children, all of whom now regularly commute between
Indonesia and Australia. Another member of the Ubud nobility,
Catherine Ellen Putri Westhoff, is also originally Australian, as is
Janet de Neefe, the well-known proprietor of the Casa Luna restaurant and founder of the Ubud Writers and Readers Festival. In
her memoir, *Fragrant Rice*, De Neefe recounts arriving in Bali in
1974 and being immediately enchanted by a 'fragrant paradise …
saturated with sensuality and beauty'. She met her future husband,
Ketut Suardana, after the memory of 'exotic flavours, fragrances
and pervading beauty' drew her back to Bali some ten years later.
As a text, *Fragrant Rice* is unusually preoccupied with the sensory aspects of Balinese life, and its exotic flavours are particularly
prominent. De Neefe writes that Bali's 'seductive spices' arouse a
'passion for … this sensual cuisine', which 'runs hot through my

blood'. She carefully depicts sights, sounds and smells as well as tastes in sensuous passages evoking 'the haze and scent of steaming rice and smoky coconut oil … piles of aromatic rhizomes, smelling of earth and eucalyptus, sun-bleached fragrant seeds, creamy waxy nuts and dark shiny leaves'.[78] As she recounts it, the sensual attractions of Bali played an important role in her seduction, and continue to fuel her passions.

Of course, not every woman who has fallen in love with an Asian man has done so with a pure heart; neither was the love always reciprocated. Travel narratives, especially romanticised ones such as De Neefe's, cannot be taken as representative of the reality of Australian-Asian relationships. The lack of same-sex relationships in popular representations of cross-cultural romance, despite a long history of homosexual contact between Australians and Asians, is one glaring omission that speaks to a broader silence on relationships that do not comfortably fit within mainstream societal norms. In 2009, the documentary *Cowboys in Paradise* exposed the female sex tourism that had long been part of the Balinese economy. Although couched in euphemisms, by which Balinese men accepted 'gifts' in return for 'romance', it was evident that, apart from the gender reversal, the situation in Bali was not entirely different from that in Pattaya or Bangkok.

While the documentary aroused a good deal of controversy in Indonesia, female sex tourism was not a recent development. In the 1970s the *Indonesia Do-It-Yourself* guide openly reported that 'hundreds of visiting Australian single girls live with Balinese boys', and it even advised other 'wallflowers and the curious' to head to Bali so they could take advantage of this situation. Australian women as well as men have travelled to Asia seeking the full gamut of sensory experience. They were pilgrims and lovers; seekers of the carnal as well as the spiritual. As *Cowboys in Paradise* put it, many had gone to Asia looking to 'Eat, Pray, Make Love'.[79]

Asia's promise of deep spirituality and unbounded sensuality has appealed to Australians for well over a century. The body politics of conversion to an Asian religion or adoption of Eastern spiritual practices can situate Australians as inferiors in knowledge or wisdom and, at its extreme, has seen them take on the role of novices learning at the feet of Asian masters. However, visitors most often retained a critical perspective, and following the example set by Alfred Deakin, selected the most appealing elements of Asian spiritual traditions while leaving the rest behind. This selective approach helped introduce a range of Asian aesthetics and cultural practices into Australian life from the 1960s. The fact that Australians were eager to adopt Asian ways can appear significant in light of a history of racism and imperial condescension. However, Westerners have been appropriating decorative Oriental arts and traditions for centuries; indeed, the arrogation of Asian culture has drawn criticism as an act of imperial power. This ambiguity was reproduced by those who went to Asia looking to satisfy the demands of the flesh, especially as sex became commercialised in the wake of Vietnam War-era R & R. The Orientalist fantasy of submissive Asian butterflies became a reality through industrialised sex tourism. The body politics of sex tourism are contentious, reflecting longstanding Orientalist fantasies as well as gender inequalities, economic disparities and wider geopolitical power dynamics. Yet its inexorable spread also speaks to the continuing lure of Asia's sensual and sexual palette. This sensory attraction contributed to the rise of mass tourism in subsequent decades, which forms the subject of the following two chapters.

# 7: ADVENTURERS AND TROUBLEMAKERS

In 1894, a fair-haired, blue-eyed boy from Geelong pinned a black pigtail to his cap and set off to walk from Shanghai to Burma. It was an epic journey of over 4800 kilometres, but with dramatic understatement, George Ernest Morrison claimed to have done it to show 'how easily and pleasantly this journey, which a few years ago would have been regarded as a formidable undertaking, can now be done'. Morrison may have set out looking for a thrill, but the journey had more serious outcomes; his ideas about China and the Chinese crystallised with every step. Morrison was met by 'uniform kindness and hospitality, and the most charming courtesy', and this led him to develop increasingly warm sentiments. His previous aversion softened, so where 'I went to China possessed with the strong racial antipathy to the Chinese common to my countrymen … that feeling has long since given way to one of lively sympathy and gratitude'. Yet this sympathy extended only as far as China's borders; having seen them at close range, Morrison was even more convinced that 'we cannot compete with Chinese; we cannot inter-mix or marry with them; they are aliens in language, thought and customs'. Where it had previously been an abstract concept, Morrison now saw a real need for a White Australia Policy: 'admitted into Australia, the Chinese would starve out the Englishman', he claimed, and so their entry must be prevented 'at all hazards'.[1] Like his contemporary Alfred Deakin, who was engrossed by India but opposed to Indian immigration, Morrison's visit to Asia made him more determined to keep the Chinese out of Australia.

Morrison's claims to adventure, and the larrikin streak that propelled him, gave him access to a popular audience. He wrote a lively account of his journey, and *An Australian in China, Being the Narrative of a Quiet Journey across China to Burma* was well received. The length and breadth of his personal experience lent authority to his claims about the Chinese and his subsequent role as a correspondent for the London *Times* placed him in a position of direct influence. His views on the Chinese question helped inform public opinion at a time when Federation was being established, with the race question at the forefront of discussion. Addressing political debates under the guise of popular culture, his adventure narrative contributed to a public climate that was receptive to the Immigration Restriction Act.

A BOYS' OWN ADVENTURE | The steaming jungles and foetid fleshpots of the Orient were a temptation to generations of Australians who grew up reading tales of colonial adventure. From Rider Haggard to Rudyard Kipling, tales of derring-do taught young Australians that Asia was a place for high adventure. As scholar Robert Dixon has shown, colonial adventure novels emphasised both race and masculinity to portray the blueprint for the kind of British manhood that helped build an Empire. The heroes were strapping men: strong, resourceful and clever, with a practical intelligence rather than dusty book learning. This was a white man's masculinity and it shone most brightly in contrast not only to irrational white women but to Asian men, who appeared either as nameless, passive 'natives' or as menacing, scheming despots in the pages of boys' own fiction.[2] Girls were not addressed as an intended audience. However the lessons about racial fitness applied equally to both sexes.

The colonial adventure genre peaked in England during the period of High Imperialism, from roughly the 1870s to the 1910s. Although this period saw the British Empire extend to its broadest scale, it was also a time of great anxiety. A number of rebellions, most notably the Indian 'Mutiny' of 1857, had threatened European power in Asia. It was increasingly clear that Europeans would have to fight if they were to hold onto their tropical territories; unfortunately, it was widely believed that the standard of British manhood was in decline. In Australia, a widespread concern that city life was physically degrading Australian manhood was taken up by the urban reform movement. Social scientists published inquiries and convened civic meetings to address whether city living and 'brain work' made adult men weaker, and whether these traits were passed on to their sons.

The colonial adventure novel sprang out of these anxieties. In the pages of Kipling, British boys were provided with a model for the kind of rugged masculinity that could defend a nation and an Empire. Australians were voracious readers. Over one-quarter of all English books made their way to Australia at this time, and boys' own fiction made up a considerable proportion of book imports.[3] They were supplemented by a home-grown adventure fiction industry. Rather than India or Burma, antipodean adventure stories were typically set in untamed wildernesses closer to home: the Australian outback, the South Seas, or Southeast Asia. Yet, the heroes were invariably 'British' rather than Australian and said to uphold European or white civilisation rather than a regional or national variant. In doing so, they helped Australian boys imagine themselves as part of the British Empire; moreover, they were invited to regard themselves as colonisers rather than colonised.

These stories remained wildly popular in Australia long after the genre began to decline in England. Where a wave of modernist nihilism swept Europe after World War I, Australian readers continued to relish tales of high adventure in the South Seas into the 1950s and beyond. They also devoured a new genre of non-fiction adventure, in which the Australian 'taming' of Papua and New Guinea was portrayed as the real-life incarnation of boys' own stories. Popular titles included Charles Monckton's *Taming New Guinea* and *Last Days in New Guinea* (both published in 1922), Frank Hurley's *Pearls and Savages* (1924), Beatrice Grimshaw's *Isles of Adventure* (1930), Ion Idriess' *Gold Dust and Ashes* (1933), Jack Hides' *Through Wildest Papua* (1935) and *Papuan Wonderland* (1936), Frank Clune's *Prowling through Papua* (1942) and *Somewhere in New Guinea* (1951) and Colin Simpson's *Adam with Arrows* (1953) and *Adam in Plumes* (1954).

Children reared on these stories often grew up longing for adventures of their own. The role of rugged Australian adventurer established by 'Chinese' Morrison was taken up during the interwar years by Frank Hurley, Francis Birtles and Errol Flynn, among dozens of others who set off to make their fortunes in the South Pacific and Southeast Asia. Their swashbuckling exploits became legendary, creating a new image of Australians as devil-may-care adventurers and of Asia as the natural backdrop for their adventures.

A DVENTURES ON THE HIPPIE TRAIL | The tourism industry made high adventure an increasingly attainable commodity from the 1950s. In the previous chapter, we met those baby boomers who set off on the Hippie Trail in search of enlightenment and new sensations. Others were lured by its promise of adventure. Like their parents before them, baby boomers were raised on colonial adventure stories, and Kipling was a perennial favourite. References to *Kim, The Jungle Book* and his other titles peppered diaries and letters written along the Hippie Trail. Kipling was also prominent in travellers' recollections. Looking back, photographer Max Pam thought Kipling had played a part in inspiring his departure for the Hippie Trail: having read the books as a child, he now 'wanted a bit of that adventure' for himself.[4] Many baby boomers had come to think of Australia as safe but dull – the kind of place where nothing ever seemed to happen – and they left home looking for excitement. Setting off from Fremantle in 1965, the young Peter Jeans was attracted to Asia because it seemed 'extraordinarily dangerous and adventurous'.[5] Having recently graduated from university in Armidale, Frances Letters 'longed to be where the action was', and Asia seemed 'the obvious place to go' when one was in search of adventure.[6] Also just out of university, Sydneysider Jeffrey Mellefont left home 'with a very strong sense that I was setting myself on a journey that had no itinerary and could take me anywhere', but he also gravitated towards Asia.[7]

By the 1960s, the combination of a stable domestic economy and increasingly affordable transport meant that even young people could afford an overseas trip, especially if they adopted the latest trend of travelling 'on the cheap'. Pam found that six months' work as a labourer or dishwasher in Australia could fund six months' travel through Asia, and others found that they could travel overland for several months for the same price as a direct airfare to London.[8] Adventure was becoming increasingly accessible.

The Hippie Trail brought Asian adventure to the mainstream. Although many travellers liked to think they were pioneers, the Hippie Trail was in fact increasingly integrated into the tourist industry. Hippie Trail travellers shared transport, infrastructure and many of the same experiences as mainstream tourists, who were discovering Asia around the same time. Moreover, an 'alternative' travel industry, specially targeted towards young budget travellers, flourished along the Hippie Trail. Specialist companies including Penn Overland and Magic Bus, along with mainstream outfits such as Contiki, began to offer all-inclusive packages with accommodation, meals and overland transport from London or Amsterdam to

Kathmandu. *The Australian*'s travel classifieds section was peppered with advertisements for Asian overland tours in the early 1970s.[9] By 1976, Top Deck Travel offered an all-inclusive package deal from London all the way through to Sydney.[10] Even Tony and Maureen Wheeler, whose Lonely Planet guidebooks helped popularise an image of the Hippie Trail as an authentic adventure, later admitted that 'overland companies were shuttling back and forth across Asia like city buses'.[11] Although many travellers would have baulked at the comparison, the standardised route and timetabled stops of the Magic Buses were not entirely removed from the standard package tour, which had recently been satirised in the popular 1969 film, *If it's Tuesday, This must be Belgium.*

The Hippie Trail was abuzz with commerce. Guesthouses, restaurants and cafés catering to Western tastes opened along the length of the Trail; some became so popular they were destinations in their own right. Some of the most powerful travel and tourism corporations of subsequent years, including guidebook publishers Lonely Planet and Moon Guides as well as the travel agency franchise Trailfinders, all began on the Hippie Trail. Although originally offering tours of Europe, Top Deck Travel (later rebranded as Flight Centre) flourished by offering Asian overland tours during the 1970s. The Hippie Trail's countercultural cool was also co-opted by mainstream corporations. From the mid-1960s, Qantas ran advertising campaigns featuring psychedelic imagery, and it soon introduced a 'Pacesetters' program aimed at the under-26 market. It even developed a subsidiary brand, Qantastic Holidays, which borrowed the language and imagery of the counterculture in an attempt to build credibility in the youth market. Qantastic produced a series of entertaining booklets, *The How, Why, When and Where of Here, There and Everywhere*, and *A Second Attempt to get you out of the Country*, and published an 'Alternative Lifestyle Magazine' called *Detours*, which featured articles by countercultural stalwarts including *Oz* magazine contributor Peter Olszewski and

Phil Jarratt (editor of the surfing magazine *Tracks*). Other major travel companies, including Jetset, also co-opted the counterculture to promote its products to the increasingly important youth market.[12]

Even so, the Hippie Trail's appeal lay in its image as an authentic adventure, rather than a typical tourist vacation. David Jenkins' *Asia Traveller's Guide*, which was so popular that it ran to a new edition every year in the mid-1970s, was typical in pitching itself at travellers who wanted to get 'off the beaten track and into the real Asia'.[13] The spectacular success of the Lonely Planet franchise was largely predicated on its 'authentic' reputation and sneering disdain of mainstream tourists. Ironically, this contempt helped shape the culture of tourism, and the tourism industry, in Asia. From the 1960s, the claim that travel to Asia was an authentic adventure spurred the rise of many tourism companies. The claim to adventure has also animated countless Hippie Trail stories that have been spun from Kathmandu to Melbourne.

**HIPPIE SAHIBS** | Young people in Asia were out for adventure and in the 1960s and 1970s this often meant drugs. The Hippie Trail was also known as the pot trail or the bhang trail and the quality, price and availability of marijuana, hash and opium were favourite topics for travellers. The section on 'dope' in Lonely Planet's first-ever guidebook, *Across Asia on the Cheap*, was longer than the section on food and it promised that 'in Afghanistan … you can get stoned just taking a deep breath in the streets'.[14] It was largely for this reason that Tony Wheeler deemed Kabul (along with Kathmandu and Kuta) to be a hippie 'shrine'. And it lured a good many worshippers; indeed, so many young people came to worship that Wheeler later referred to these destinations as 'bottlenecks'.[15]

Drugs were the main event, so that many visitors to Hippie Trail bottlenecks did not feel as if they needed to visit any attractions, or even see any sights. Just being there (and being stoned) was enough – in fact the Lonely Planet guide insisted that travellers who dashed from one attraction to the next missed 'the whole lazy point of going'.[16] Tony and Maureen Wheeler preferred to while away their time. In Kathmandu, they spent days sitting in Sigi's café, sipping mint tea and 'occasionally repairing to the courtyard to shift the giant chess pieces around the giant chessboard'.[17] Frances Letters also stayed in Kathmandu for some weeks, where 'the weird, dreamy world of hashish ... dominated most of our days and nights'.[18] In 1974, a reporter with the *Sydney Morning Herald* asked one traveller how he spent his days in Kathmandu. The reply: 'I just live'.[19]

Sitting at Sigi's, or its equivalents in Delhi, Kabul and Bangkok, travellers could meet like-minded young people from around the world. This cosmopolitanism was a major attraction but if, as Australian countercultural figurehead Richard Neville liked to put it, the Hippie Trail was 'a turned-on league of nations', the delegates were almost exclusively Western.[20] Locals did not typically frequent the same hotels and cafés as travellers and cross-cultural contact rarely moved beyond the demands of commerce. As political scientist Dennis Altman observed at the time, travellers on the Hippie Trail mostly interacted with like-minded Westerners and so 'avoided for the most part any genuine confrontation with the reality of Asian society'.[21] Furthermore, travellers' hubs were firmly plugged in to the scene back home: Wheeler remembered that 'the rumour was that if Pink Floyd released a record in London on Monday it would be in Kabul by Friday'.[22] The most popular travellers' hubs could feel like Western outcrops within an Asian setting, so much so that Neville satirised those young Australians who 'escaped' to Asia only to recreate the atmosphere of the 'King George on a Saturday night' within the pages of *Oz* magazine.[23]

The division between locals and tourists could appear so stark that a number of observers drew the comparison between the

Hippie Trail and colonialism. The *Asia Travellers' Guide*, for example, bluntly referred to Kabul and Kathmandu as travellers' 'colonies'.[24] Although few travellers would have relished the comparison, the travel culture that developed along the Hippie Trail did indeed carry the imprint of Empire. Every country along the Hippie Trail had either been colonised by a European power, or fell within the United States' Cold War sphere of influence, or both. Furthermore, most travellers came from nations that had once been colonisers. In this context, the strong in-group identification between travellers could appear less like cosmopolitan internationalism than a reproduction of colonial-era divisions between 'European' and 'native'. In his countercultural manifesto *Play Power*, Richard Neville referred to his fellow travellers as 'hippie sahibs', and the description is truly fitting.[25]

The strong bonds made between travellers, and their lack of connections with locals, meant that travellers looked to each other to gauge the boundaries of acceptable conduct. The countercultural creed encouraged hippies to retain their sense of adventure and rebellion while travelling and they were no more disposed towards authority in Asia than at home. Drugs may have been ubiquitous in the travellers' hubs, but even those places that did not have narcotics legislation at the start of the Hippie Trail's popularity, such as Nepal and Laos, imposed strict anti-drug laws by the early-1970s. Moreover, some travellers paid their way by smuggling jeans, radios or alcohol for sale on the black market, or even by trafficking drugs. Police, immigration and customs officials came to be regarded as obstacles to be overcome rather than as legitimate figures enforcing local regulations. The strong military presence in many Asian countries was also regarded with contempt, and stories of travellers tricking officials by sneaking drugs or people through checkpoints and border crossings were a favourite at Sigi's and in subsequent retellings.

Many travellers also maintained their cultural rebellion in Asia. Unwilling to let go of the freedoms they had won through political protest and the sexual revolution, or simply eager to play up far from home, many young people pushed the boundaries. Legendary tales of travellers' experiments with drugs and sex circulated, and they accounted for at least some of the Hippie Trail's seemingly magnetic attraction. Travellers had come for an adventure and, as we saw in the previous chapter, India was thought to be 'a place where nothing was unacceptable'.[26] Of course, the reality was very different. Although the 1960s and 1970s saw dynamic political and cultural change across Asia, many people's lives continued to be structured by religion, family, gender and, in India, caste. In this context, countercultural rebellion often clashed with local mores and cultures. In hindsight, young traveller Abigayle Carmody acknowledged that 'there wasn't really ... a great consideration for the locals'.[27]

The hippies' exploits with drugs and sex aroused widespread disapproval that occasionally flared into open conflict. Rumours about travellers' debauchery spread the length of the Hippie Trail. Western 'decadence' was considered a serious problem in Iran and historians have noted that Afghans were also 'deeply shocked' at what they regarded as nihilism, a lack of responsibility and 'loose morals' amongst Westerner travellers in Kabul.[28] The threat was taken particularly seriously in India. Widespread concern led sociologist Tribhuwan Kapur to spend a decade observing Western travellers to determine whether they posed a danger to Indian society, and he published his findings in 1981 as *Hippies: a study of their drug habits and sexual customs*. Although he didn't think they posed a political threat, Kapur was concerned that hippies threatened social and cultural degradation. Rather than an earnest search for freedom and self-expression, he regarded the counterculture as a juvenile form of rebellion by which young Westerners set themselves 'against each and every culture'. He singled out hippies' drug use and sexual mores as ones that 'violate all ideas of "normality"', and he was concerned that this rebellion might infect Indian youth.[29]

The beaches of Goa on India's southwest coast became home to a legendary hippie scene from the late 1960s, and simmering tensions between travellers and locals frequently came to a head. Fuelled by hallucinogenic drugs and an intoxicating feeling of freedom, travellers hung out on the beach, stoned and naked; they had sex in the water and on the sand dunes as the mood took them. As the *Times of India* reported in 1969, 'it is safe to say that everyone here has swum naked in the pleasant surf, or ambled naked along the silent moonlit shore'.[30] This may have been part of Goa's attraction to visitors, but it conflicted with local mores and opposition to hippie 'orgies' was widespread.[31] By 1969 letters to Goa's *Navhind Times* complained that hippies were turning Calangute Beach into 'a den of depravity', and that these 'wrecks of humanity are posing an extremely dangerous challenge and threat to every home, family, society and nation'. The *Times of India* featured regular updates on how locals were faring against 'the Hippie Invasion'.[32] Occasionally, opposition boiled over. Abigayle Carmody was amongst one group of travellers who were attacked by Goan villagers in late 1976. Sitting in the sand, mostly naked and smoking dope, they were set upon by a mob brandishing sticks and shouting 'get out, get out!' Carmody, who had by this point begun to turn away from the hippie scene, was fully dressed and she escaped unhurt. Nonetheless, similar stories of small-scale retaliation abound. Another incident, in which a hippie was pelted with stones after urinating in a village well, illustrates a multitude of minor clashes.[33]

Local outrage grew as more and more hippies descended on Asia and citizens entreated their governments to take action. As early as 1967, letters demanding that India refuse entry visas to hippies began to appear in the *Times of India*.[34] Nepal introduced tougher visa restrictions that dramatically reduced the validity of tourist visas – from 30 years to just one week – in 1968. Laos, Malaysia, Singapore and Indonesia quickly followed. Indonesia introduced regulations that denied entry to travellers deemed 'improper' in dress, appearance or conduct, those suspected of attending 'abnormal' religious rituals or those without a fixed destination.[35] Thailand limited entry to 'bona fide tourists of sound financial means', and erected sharply worded signs demanding visitors dressed and acted appropriately at religious and cultural sites. Even tourist promotions materials had to add shade to their glistening portrait of the 'land of smiles'; in 1976, for example, Air Siam warned young travellers that they might face the consequences of 'negative stereotypes of the young Western traveller who carries a backpack, wears dirty or dishevelled clothing, has long hair, appears to use drugs or acts in ways that otherwise seem unacceptable to Asians who hold more conservative or traditional attitudes'.[36] As more and more countries shut their doors, Lonely Planet guides began to warn intending travellers that locals were becoming increasingly 'uptight'.[37]

Travellers on the Hippie Trail were not the first group to act without reference to local customs. Far from it: a general disregard for local mores characterised a good deal of tourism in Asia from the colonial period onwards. Neither was all bad behaviour punished; on the whole, locals were remarkably tolerant of outsiders' peculiarities – so much so that Tony Wheeler later claimed that many local communities actually began to expect bad behaviour from travellers.[38]

The hippies' behaviour aggravated simmering anti-Western sentiments along the length of the Trail. The 1960s and 1970s saw upheaval across much of the Middle East, South Asia and Southeast Asia. Rapid globalisation impacted on traditional ways of life and often led to political and social foment. In this context, travellers on the Hippie Trail could serve as symbols of Western decadence. Historians have argued that travellers' bad behaviour inflamed anti-Western resentment; as Martin Ewans noted, some Afghanis decided that, 'if this was how Westerners behaved, [they] wanted none of it'.[39] This could contribute to a growing belief that Westernisation was inextricably tied to a decline in Muslim practices, which according to historian Nikki Keddie, was linked to the rise of radical Islam in Iran during the 1970s.[40] Although the role played by the Hippie Trail in stirring anti-Western sentiment should not be over-played, it is worth noting that Tehran had been another famed trav-ellers' bottleneck in the years before the Islamic Revolution of 1979.

Of course, not all travellers were insensitive to local contexts. Frances Letters spent six weeks living with a local family in Kash-mir, and she went to great lengths to fit in with their way of life. She ate the same food, joined in the family's work during the day and helped care for the children at night. But although she was determined to fit in, she found she could not abide by all the local customs. 'For a month and a half I lived a Muslim woman's life for almost every minute of the day', she wrote, and 'for most of the time I alternated between violent resentment and a curious kind of submission'. She eventually rebelled against the strictures, and left the family for further adventures on the Hippie Trail. However, her sensitivity to local peoples' values, and her thoughtful reflec-tions about Indian ways, animate her personal travelogue, *People of Shiva*.[41]

By the 1970s, racist and imperialist language had come to seem increasingly objectionable, and many of the radical political move-ments arising out of the counterculture were avowedly anti-racist and anti-colonial. Travellers in Asia regularly found themselves con-fronting the same issues that were the subject of protest back home. Some politically progressive travellers railed against the enduring legacies of colonial-era power divisions. The rickshaw rides that had delighted Australians in the colonial period and during World War II aroused far more critical responses. Even before her conver-sion to Buddhism, Marie Obst was 'quite torn about whether to get in a rickshaw or not' in Calcutta. Her immediate response was to baulk against it, and she found it 'a real struggle to ask people to carry you like that'. But, at the same time, the drivers 'seemed to be so desperate to have the work' that she felt she should take up their offers. The ethical quandary accompanied her as she made her way north to Nepal.[42] With attitudes sharpened by the radical politics of the era, travellers' responses to the power dynamics of a rickshaw ride were often very different from their parents' and grandparents' before them.

The Hippie Trail was extremely significant in the history of Australian travel to Asia. It introduced the notion of Asian travel as a rite of passage for young Australians and established much of the infrastructure and culture of 'alternative' tourism in Asia. The baby boomers also helped expand the meaning of 'adventure' in Asia, to take in the modern-day thrills of drugs, sex and petty crime. Young Australians were eager to take part in this adventure, flocking to Asia until the Islamic Revolution in Iran and the outbreak of war in Afghanistan in 1979 effectively spelled the end of the Hippie Trail. Even after this time, the association between Asia and adventure remained strong. As the following chapter explores in more detail, Australians searching for fun and adventure increasingly flocked to Bali and Thailand, with the excesses of Kuta's nightclubs and Ko Phangan's Full Moon Parties forming one part of the complex legacy of the Hippie Trail.

TROUBLEMAKERS | Adventure could lead to trouble. The small-time smuggling that funded some hippies' travels matured into sophisticated drug trafficking operations during the 1970s and 1980s. Australians were involved from the early years. A 1976 crackdown in Indonesia saw 21 Australians arrested for drug offences. Among them was Donald Roy Tait, who was attempting to smuggle cannabis through Bali. Sentenced to 17 years in prison, Tait managed to escape, and in 1985 he was captured in Thailand and sentenced to death for drug smuggling, although the sentence was overturned on appeal. By this time, 23 other Australians were thought to be imprisoned in Thailand on drugs charges.[43] Despite regular arrests, the widespread belief that Southeast Asian police were so corrupt that tourists could bribe themselves out of trouble bred a sense of impunity, and Australians continued to use and smuggle drugs into the 21st century.

In recent years, Australian drug smugglers caught in Indonesia have become front-page news and their cases have even led to diplomatic tension between the two nations. Schapelle Corby was arrested in October 2004, after customs officials at Bali's Ngurah Rai International Airport discovered 4.1 kilograms of marijuana inside a bodyboard bag checked in under her name. She was charged with narcotics offences and taken to Bali's Kerobokan Prison to await trial. Corby vehemently pleaded her innocence, claiming that although the bodyboard bag was hers, the drugs were not. Elements of the media, particularly the *Gold Coast Bulletin* (Corby's hometown newspaper) and Channel 7 and Channel 9's national current affairs programs *Today Tonight* and *A Current Affair*, championed her cause. The public responded with a surge of support that surprised many social commentators, and in turn fuelled further media interest. As media scholar John Schwartz notes, by the time of her trial in May 2005 every major media outlet, with the exception of *The Australian* newspaper, presented Corby in an extremely sympathetic way.[44]

The case provoked an extraordinary public response. Many Australians came to feel deep, emotional connections with Corby and she was almost universally referred to by her first name alone. As academic Graeme MacRae noted, support for 'Schapelle' hinged on a broad recognition that she could be 'one of our daughters'.[45] Not only was she the archetypal girl-next-door but as a Gold Coast native who loved the beach, Corby reflected traditional conceptions of what it meant to be an ordinary Australian.[46] As one caller to Neil Mitchell's 3AW radio talkback show put it, she was 'the daughter of Australia'.[47] The intersection of personal identification and nationalism spurred many otherwise ordinary people to voice their opinions on talkback radio, in letters to newspapers and on the comments pages that were beginning to appear on news websites. The response was extraordinary at a time when widespread public engagement across Web 2.0 and social media platforms was still a recent innovation. The surge of public interest in Corby's case attracted further attention, instigating a cycle of media and popular fascination that seemed to feed on itself.

The fact that Corby had been captured in Bali, the heartland of Australia's pleasure periphery, was essential in facilitating this level of personal identification. Sympathetic media reports presented her as 'just another tourist' who was 'looking forward to just hanging out and doing some bodyboarding'.[48] As the *Gold Coast Bulletin* had it, Corby was an 'innocent abroad'.[49] This touched a chord with the millions of Australians who had been to Bali too, who began to fear that 'this could be any one of us travelling to Bali'.[50] Journalist Tony Wilson wrote a book about the Corby case that was unapologetically pitched at a popular market. He opened with the claim that 'one of the most frightening aspects is that it could happen to anyone'. Moreover, he directly appealed to his readers to 'place yourself in Schapelle's shoes', and suggested that they ask themselves questions such as 'What would I do now?' or 'how would I handle this situation?' as they weighed the evidence.[51] Literally millions of Australians had been to Bali by this time; moreover, as the next chapter explores in more detail, many had begun to see the island in a sentimental light as a symbol of lost innocence after the Bali bombings of 2002.

Corby's captivity also evoked such an intense public response because it played into broader debates about national identity. Community fears that multiculturalism threatened social cohesion had become prevalent in the years since the White Australia Policy was dismantled in 1973. They resurfaced in the 1990s, finding expression through One Nation's Pauline Hanson, and again after the terrorist attacks of 11 September 2001 and 12 October 2002. The battle for 'Schapelle' took on a broader meaning in this context. Corby came to be seen as a symbol of traditional Anglo-Australianness: naive and unworldly, perhaps even a little insular, but good-natured, healthy and above all, innocent. Her Australian innocence, in the sense of unworldliness, led some to believe in her innocence in the case brought against her. As 'Brad' wrote on a *Gold Coast Bulletin* message board, Corby was 'aussie and innocent, 2 qualities that will see [her] home'.[52] Another comment, posted on a ninemsn.com message board, presented her as a 'girl from the Sunshine State, far from home, surrounded by strangers and a legal system beyond anything she knows'; innocent in both senses of the word.[53]

Representing Corby's home constituency, the *Gold Coast Bulletin* was host to some of the most vehement responses. Readers inundated the newspaper's letters column and its website's comments pages to an extent that was unprecedented in 2004–05. Many addressed Corby directly, assuring her that 'Australia unites' behind you, that 'the whole of Australia loves you', and that 'true Aussies are on your side'.[54] A significant number used nationalistic language, claiming that 'real aussies wont cop less' than Corby's immediate release, or that 'all real Aussies' should boycott Bali.[55] In turn, those who did not support her were branded 'UnAustralian': Channel 7 was 'UnAustralian' for broadcasting a report that was seen to be critical of Corby, and even the Australian government – the sovereign representative of the Australian nation – had betrayed itself as 'not true blue' after Prime Minister John Howard refused to lobby the Indonesian President for Corby's immediate release.[56]

Corby's captivity galvanised an assertive strand of Australian nationalism, which was still finding expression in the early years of the new millennium. Adopted as a symbol of embattled Anglo-Australia, her plight stirred the blood of patriots who claimed that 'I would go to war for Schapelle', and that 'people are ready 2 die for this girl'.[57] Others invoked the Anzac spirit, aligning her cause with 'wot our anzacs fought 4'.[58] Again, Corby's case acted as a lightning rod for broader concerns. The battle over what was 'really' Australian simmered throughout 2005 and exploded later the same year during the Cronulla riots in December. Corby's captivity provided an early rallying point for self-professed 'real' Australians and provided a rare opportunity for the open expression of Anglo-Australian cultural nationalism.

The public's assertive mood peaked after Corby's sentencing on 27 May 2005. Comments on news websites seethed with outrage at the perceived injustice of her 20-year sentence, and mainstream newspapers republished selections of readers' comments in both print and digital editions. A significant number of posts demanded action, calling for economic boycotts of Bali and Indonesia to 'show them what happens when you mess with Australia'.[59] Others proposed boycotts of 'all Muslim products' and, somewhat inexplicably, 'the Philippines and even Japan'.[60] Others still called for a boycott of Qantas in light of allegations that baggage handlers had tampered with Corby's luggage, or to punish the airline for failing to preserve video evidence that some thought would exonerate her.

Much of this anger was directed towards Indonesia. Having made the link between Australianness and innocence, many of Corby's supporters also linked Indonesia with guilt and corruption. Popular responses portrayed Indonesia's judiciary and legislature as incompetent, corrupt and a danger to both Corby and Australia more generally. Impassioned messages claimed that 'the Indonesian courts are incapable of distinguishing between guilty and innocent' and pointed to the fact that, while Corby received 20 years for drugs offences, Abu Bakar Bashir, the Muslim cleric widely linked to the Bali bombings of 2002, had received only 20 months.[61] Hinting at collusion between the judiciary and terrorists, some messages warned that 'these people don't play by normal rules'.[62] The fact that Bashir was never conclusively linked to the bombings, or that his conviction was for the minor charge of conspiracy rather than any terrorist offences, was typically overlooked. Instead, some Australians expressed outrage that Corby would spend much of her adult life behind bars, while Bashir would soon walk free despite 'killing hundreds of Australians'.[63] As a result, the Corby trial affected some Australians' ideas about Indonesia. Readers of the *Gold Coast Bulletin* referred to 'those corrupt Indos', that 'unsafe place' or that 'rat infested country'.[64]

Many Australians related Corby's captivity to broader international relations, reading her sentence as evidence of Indonesia's lack of gratitude for the humanitarian aid Australia had provided after the Asian tsunami that had struck some six months before. In a media interview, Corby's ex-boyfriend, Shannon McLure, demanded that Indonesians 'should give us something in return. They should give us Schapelle'.[65] The broader diffusion of these ideas is evident in comments that Indonesia was a 'jumped up, trumped up, never come down law of its own country that owes Australia more than it will ever appreciate'.[66] For some, the Corby case had shown that 'Australians are the leaders showing compassion & millions of dollars 4 the country & they repay us by giving an innocent oz girl 20yrs'.[67]

The negative view of Indonesia even led to demands for the Australian government to 'pull rank on the Justice System of Indonesia'.[68] John Howard was criticised for refusing to intervene even though, as he had tried to explain on numerous occasions, he was unable to interfere in a foreign jurisdiction. As one reader of the *Daily Telegraph* railed, it was 'time to get off your backside Mr. Howard … your intervention and firm action is very long overdue'.[69] Another post on the ninemsn.com news website went further, arguing that 'we as Australian citizens should unite and pull rank on our disgusting government, and let them know, that we know that they can make this go away'. To rally fellow-Australians, the comment urged readers to 'remember this girl is one of us'.[70]

Angry at Indonesia, dissatisfied with the Howard government and fuelled by aggressive nationalism, some of Corby's supporters threatened to take justice into their own hands. Some assured her they would free her 'by ANY MEANS NECESSARY'.[71] Messages promised that 'me and my mates will bust you out', or that Corby should prepare for an 'Aussie swat team coming in through the roof'.[72] Several readers of the *Gold Coast Bulletin* even tried to facilitate a meeting of ex-SAS soldiers, who could band together to 'bust her out of Indonesia'.[73] While the threatened attack on Kerobokan Prison never eventuated, Corby's continued captivity did result in vigilante action. The Indonesian Embassy and several Consulates reported receiving menacing phone calls and death threats. Most dramatically, several packages containing an unidentified white powder were posted to the Indonesian Embassy in Canberra. Coming in the wake of a string of anthrax scares in the United States, this was a serious matter and the Embassy was evacuated from fear of bioterrorism. As Andrew MacIntyre noted in *The Australian*, for Indonesians 'the underlying message ... is that Australian extremists have launched what amounts to a biological attack on Indonesian diplomatic staff'.[74] In Adrian Vickers' analysis, this incident, which received wide coverage in the Indonesian media and was labelled 'Jemaah Corbyah' by an influential Indonesian news magazine, represented 'a new low in Australian-Indonesian relations'.[75]

Even in the wake of the bioterrorism hoax, public opinion continued to urge Howard to raise the Corby case in Australian-Indonesian diplomatic relations. A Morgan poll conducted in June 2005 found a clear majority of 58 per cent believed that Howard should make a direct demand for clemency, although opinion was divided about whether Howard should take this step immediately or wait until Corby had launched an appeal herself.[76] Howard refused to cede to popular demands, and consistent communication with Indonesian President Susilo Bambang Yudhoyono helped contain the diplomatic impacts. Yudhoyono also worked to contain the fallout from the bioterrorism scare within Indonesia.[77] Nonetheless, the case remained an irritant in Australia-Indonesian relations for several years.

THE FALLOUT | The emotive response to Corby's arrest was so strong it skewed media coverage of subsequent cases in which Australians were arrested in Asia. Australian tourists were routinely portrayed as innocent, even as a string of drug convictions across Asia, culminating in the execution of Nguyen Tuong Van in Singapore in December 2005, shone a light on the extent of Australian involvement in drug trafficking in Asia. The arrest of the Bali Nine in April 2005 and model Michelle Leslie in August 2005 instantly evoked comparisons with Corby. As with Corby, coverage of Leslie's arrest conflated tourism to Bali with innocence, resulting in headlines such as 'Model of Innocence'.[78] Even the Bali Nine, some of whom were captured with heroin strapped to their bodies, attracted reports insisting that 'they too were tourists'.[79] Media reports also continued to portray Asia as a dangerous place of corrupt police, unfair justice systems and hellish conditions in jail.[80] Headlines positing Leslie as the 'new face of a Bali drug nightmare' hinted at a systemic threat rather than individual responsibility.[81] The inclination to exonerate tourists and accuse Asian authorities reached a highpoint in a *Sunday Telegraph* headline of August 2005: 'How dealers target Australians – Naive tourists fall prey to Bali's flourishing drug trade as police hunt their next prize trophy'.[82] Such reporting contributed to the view that Asian authorities were corrupt and unjust, leading to what Tim Lindsey of Melbourne's Asian Law Centre identified as a growing sense that 'Australians should be immune from [Asian] legal systems'.[83]

More subtle, but perhaps even more significant in the longer term, was the case's impact on long-term popular attitudes towards Indonesia. Anxieties about corruption and injustice continue to jaundice Australian perceptions of Indonesia. The Lowy Institute for International Policy conducts an annual survey of popular opinion about foreign countries. Overall attitudes towards foreign nations are distilled into a single measure of warmth, expressed in a temperature score between 0° and 100°. Attitudes towards

Indonesia were notably cool in 2006, in the immediate aftermath of the Corby trial and the 2005 Bali bombings, which had killed four Australians. At 50°, Indonesia scored just a few degrees above Iraq, North Korea and Iran; by way of comparison, the United Kingdom scored a much warmer 74°. The survey found respondents 'were suspicious of Indonesian governance and fearful that Indonesia presents a potential security threat'.[84] The effects were not only strong but also long-lasting. A more detailed study of Australian attitudes towards Indonesia was commissioned by the Department of Foreign Affairs and Trade and conducted by Newspoll in 2013. It found that, eight years after the Corby trial, a significant proportion of Australians continued to associate Indonesia with drugs and drug trafficking. Moreover, 70 per cent were still concerned about the treatment of Australians in the Indonesian justice system, although a large proportion did acknowledge that the Indonesian government had made some moves towards ensuring that Australians accused of crimes in Indonesia were treated justly.[85]

Corby's 20-year sentence was reduced to 15 in 2010 and she was released on parole in February 2014, at which point she had served just over nine years. The decade since her arrest, and damaging revelations of the Corby family's involvement in drug networks, had taken some of the fervour out of her supporters' rhetoric, but her release aroused a fresh round of media attention. Although it brought some sense of resolution to the case, its long-term impacts continue to resonate in popular perceptions of Indonesia, and in diplomatic relations.

The fact that an individual troublemaker can evoke such dramatic outcomes points to complex undercurrents in popular Australian attitudes to Asia, which can rise to the surface with even minor provocation. Just as importantly, it reveals the full impact that travellers can have on diplomatic relations. Australians have long thought of Asia as a place for adventure, and occasionally their search for thrills has brought them into conflict with local communities and authorities. At a time when literally millions of Australians head to the region every year this carries the potential to destabilise both person-to-person and diplomatic relations. Corby's case captivated a broad swath of the Australian public because so many Australians could imagine themselves in the role of a tourist venturing to Asia for fun and adventure. As the next chapter outlines, this widespread identification placed the tourist near the centre of the turbulent political climate that marked the early 21st century.

# 8: TOURISTS

Australia is a nation of tourists. Australians are uniquely eager travellers who spend more on international travel than any other people on earth, on a per capita basis. The rate of travel is truly staggering. In 2010, seven million Australians headed overseas, out of a total population of 23 million. Roughly half of those trips – approximately 3.5 million – were to Asia. Even accounting for repeat visits by individuals in a single year, this rate of contact, by which something like one in every six Australians visits Asia in any one year, means that most people know something about the neighbourhood through personal experience.

Shifting patterns of mobility illustrate Australia's changing relations with the world. More Australians travelled to Asia than Europe for the first time in 1968, and have done so every year since 1980. By 1998, more Australians travelled to Indonesia than to the United Kingdom.[1] What has been the effect of all this contact? How do tourist experiences shape the ways in which Australians think about their place in the world? And how do these images affect political and diplomatic relations, at the precipice of the Asian Century?

International travel is now part of the Australian way of life and Bali is a favourite playground. In 2014, it is expected that one million Australians will visit Bali. The vast majority will go for no other reason than their own pleasure. The extraordinary reach of this experience affects Australian perceptions of the island of Bali, the nation of Indonesia and the Asian region as a whole. This chapter largely focusses on Bali, but it has broader relevance across the region, illustrating the importance of tourism to Australia's relations with Asia. While it may appear frivolous at first glance, the role of tourist is certainly the most pervasive, and perhaps the most fitting, role played by Australians in Asia today.

O FF TO ASIA | Tourism to Asia became part of the Australian way of life from the 1970s. Singapore, Hong Kong and Japan exerted a steady attraction for tourists eager for sightseeing and shopping. Singapore's tourism promotions promised the exoticism of Asia in a relatively safe, clean and Western environment and discounted package holidays to Singapore were astoundingly popular in the early 1970s. Hong Kong also promised a mix of East and West: 'the Chinese younger set are as "mod" and "a-go-go" as the youngsters in London, New York, San Francisco and Sydney', travel advertisements enthused, but 'fragments of life as it existed in ancient times are still to be found'. Both destinations balanced the exoticism of the Orient with references to their British colonial heritage and luxurious hotels, offering a frisson of Oriental excitement with the assurance of safety and security.[2] Japan's promotions took a different approach by avoiding all mention of the recent past altogether. Holiday cruises to Japan were surprisingly popular from the late 1950s. Where in 1947 the *Australian Women's Weekly* had editorialised about an 'undying hatred of the Japanese people', 20 years later it was more likely to be advertising its 'Cherry Blossom Cruises'.[3] As its economy surged, Japan was portrayed as a unique and often bewildering clash of Oriental tradition and futuristic technology. The antique past crashed into the distant future – and in doing so circumnavigated any mention of Japan's recent history, and particularly its role in the Pacific War.

These tourism stalwarts were joined by the emerging destinations of Thailand, Vietnam and Cambodia. The 'alternative' travel culture of the Hippie Trail transmuted into backpacking during the 1980s and Thailand attracted an ever-growing number of budget travellers. The number of Australians heading to Thailand rose by more than 1200 per cent in just 20 years from the 1970s to the 1990s.[4] Taking their cues from the Hippie Trail, backpackers sought 'authenticity' (although a definitive explanation of what this entailed was never established). They made their way to grungy guesthouses on Khao San Road, rustic beach shacks on Ko Phangan and mountain huts in Pai rather than the hotels and resorts patronised by mainstream tourists in Chiang Mai or Phuket. This is not to say that backpackers didn't represent a new kind of mainstream. Many were devoted to their guidebooks – particularly the Lonely Planet guides, which came to be known as the 'backpackers' bible' – and the budget tourism industry in Thailand flourished.[5] But they were often the earliest visitors to the next 'undiscovered' destination, helping open up new areas of Asia for tourism.

By the early 2000s, backpacking in Southeast Asia had become institutionalised as a rite of passage for young Australians. Young people headed to Asia on the same flights as their parents and grandparents, colleagues and friends, representing a cross-section of Australian society. Australians visited Asia for business and leisure, and were part of almost every conceivable tourist trend from ecotourism and adventure travel to high-end resort vacations and flashpacking. In 2002, the number of Australians travelling to Asia was approximately double that heading to Europe.[6] The webs of connection tying Australia to the world had been redrawn.

PARADISE FOUND | While tourism boomed across all of Asia, Bali held a special place in Australians' hearts. The rumour that Bali was a tropical paradise gained currency from the 1920s. As we saw in Chapter 6, exotic images of barely-clad belles fed a fantasy image of Bali as Paradise that drew visitors from around the world. Already in 1939 Frank Clune complained that Bali's 'glamour has been so hectically publicised' that it was being overrun by 'hordes of tourists' – adding the injunction to 'hasten, hasten dear reader, and visit Bali' before it was spoiled by tourism.[7] By the 1950s, the fantasy was so firmly established that the fictional setting for Rodgers and Hammerstein's *South Pacific* was called Bali H'ai. Apart from its beautiful women, Bali's major attraction at this time was its fascinating and colourful traditional culture. Every day seemed to bring a festival, and visitors marvelled at the elegant dances, sophisticated visual arts and elaborate religious ceremonies of the Hindu population – all in a lush, tropical setting.

Both the Sukarno and Suharto governments backed tourism as Indonesia's ticket to modernisation and development. Supported by World Bank expertise and Japanese war reparations, President Suharto opened Ngurah Rai International Airport in 1969. The introduction of the jumbo jet democratised tourism around the world and it brought a new onslaught of visitors to Bali. The tourism industry went into overdrive. By the early 1970s, it wasn't unusual for travel agencies to charter whole aircraft and requisition entire hotels, using the economies of scale to pass on substantial savings to Australian consumers through all-inclusive package holidays. By 1971, the *Sydney Morning Herald* enthused that Bali was not only 'a multi-coloured landscape as seen in a dream', but just as importantly, going there had become 'a matter of economics'.[8] Paradise now came at a reasonable price and first-time tourists headed to Bali in droves.

Bali also lured young 'alternative' travellers. It was a popular jumping-off point for the Hippie Trail during the 1970s and the Southeast Asian backpacker circuit of the 1980s and beyond. Surfers also discovered its clean breaks and cheap beer. In the 1970s, middle-class families headed to Sanur, while younger travellers congregated around the surfing beaches of Kuta. Initially, they stayed at simple *losmen* accommodation and ate at Indonesian restaurants such as Made's Warung and Poppy's. They may have railed at the comparison, but alternative 'travellers' were often drawn by the same fantasies of paradise as mainstream 'tourists'. Founders of the Lonely Planet publishing empire Tony and Maureen Wheeler first visited the island in 1972, and they reflected that Bali seemed like 'a perfect dream of a tropical island'.[9] The first edition of their Hippie Trail guidebook, *Across Asia on the Cheap,* noted that 'one could hardly ask for a more pleasant introduction to the type of cheap living you'll get used to all the way to Europe'. Echoing Clune's injunctions of some 30 years before, they also advised travellers that they should 'go soon' as 'the charm of Bali shows every indication of being rapidly eroded by tourism'.[10]

The convergence of these two major travel trends – package tourism and the budget travel – heralded a new tourist age. Statistics reveal continuous and dramatic rises, with the number of Australian tourists to Indonesia doubling every five years from the early 1970s.[11] From this time, the focus moved away from cultural tourism and Bali became entrenched as a 'sun, surf and schooners' destination. Guidebooks in the 1950s and 1960s had been so captivated by Balinese culture that they often neglected to mention a single beach. By the 1990s, the relative advantages of Kuta's breaks and Nusa Dua's white sand were debated over many pages in mainstream guidebooks, while 'doing' the local culture could be relegated to a relatively short section on Ubud.

Uniquely, the tourist culture in Bali developed for Australian tastes. Balinese adopted Australian slang, fashions and mores to boost their tourism businesses and local kids integrated elements of Australian beach culture into their own modern youth subculture. The influence flowed in both directions and Australians tried to revive a bit of the holiday atmosphere back home by introducing Balinese design aesthetics to their homes and gardens, and satay or nasi goreng to their kitchens.

The Australian influence was most apparent after sunset.

Historian Adrian Vickers dates the emergence of what he calls a 'swinging singles' scene of 'loud music, drunkenness and commercialising' to the 1970s.[12] By 1992, Lonely Planet guides noted that this scene had become geared towards 'Aussie drinkers', with AFL and NRL games relayed live and organised pub crawls (featuring beer-drinking and vegemite-eating contests) putting a new spin on the traditional tourist daytrip. The influence was reflected in the names of the pubs that now mushroomed around Kuta, such as the Bali-Aussie and the Koala Blu (which Lonely Planet described as being 'like an Australian barnyard-pub'). According to the guidebook *Bali at Cost*, by the mid-1990s the strip of Jalan Legian around the Sari Club was 'always overflowing with Australian visitors'.[13] As the *Sunday Age* reported in 1998, Kuta had an 'Aussie heartland' in which 'Victoria Bitter is everywhere' and the 'street sellers … speak their English with an Aussie accent'.[14]

Again, the international tourist industry facilitated this spread. Qantas and Garuda International targeted the youth market, promoting Bali as a place where young people could cut loose. Qantas Holidays developed a 'Troppo Zone: Bali's fun club for 18–30s', and ran youthful campaigns that promoted 'an unreal holiday' with 'plenty of sun and beaches, parties where you can go wild' and 'heaps of action … with a crowd of people all after the same things as you'. Garuda Indonesia's Bali Ocean Blue Club promised that 'no kids or Boring Oldies' would get in the way of a good time.[15] Guidebooks continued to insist that 'to get any taste of the real Bali then you have to abandon the beaches', but the increasing desperation of these appeals suggests that not all visitors were taking heed.[16]

The blurred cultural space of Bali – at once Indonesian and Balinese, a Hindu island in a Muslim nation and increasingly dominated by Australians – led some tourists to assume that local mores were flexible and all kinds of behaviour would be tolerated. As early as 1977, Lonely Planet's *South East Asia on a Shoestring* claimed that in Kuta, 'even the most outrageous behaviour is tolerated, even found amusing'. Another guidebook published that same year, the *Indonesia Handbook*, reported that Kuta was becoming a real 'Sin Alley', overflowing with 'wine, women and dope'. In the evocative words of 'Gazza', a young Australian visiting from Port Hedland who was interviewed for the *Sunday Age* in 1998, 'this is Bali, my friend. Make a fuckwit of yourself, doesn't matter. What goes away stays away'.[17]

R ELAXED AND COMFORTABLE | Australians had obviously made themselves comfortable in Bali. David Walker has shown that, although stereotypes about Asians changed over time, the region was thought to be overwhelmingly foreign and 'Other' well into the 20th century.[18] Early Australian depictions of Bali had followed this script. In the 1940s, Frank Clune wrote of the Balinese as 'pagan primitives who mesmerically embrace the ecstacies of their jungle rituals'. In 1969, travel writer Ronald McKie could still portray the Balinese as 'so profoundly Asian ... they could be perceived, but were beyond the perimeter of understanding'.[19] This sense of Otherness all but disappeared with the advent of Australian-accented mass tourism; to the contrary, some people began to wonder whether Bali could still be considered 'Asian' at all. Travel writers began to portray Bali as a miniature of Australia, with the time zone of Perth, the climate of Darwin and the beaches of Queensland. Furthermore, visitors were increasingly choosing Bali precisely because it was not too dissimilar to the kind of beach holiday they had previously enjoyed at home. As surfer and editor of *Tracks* magazine Phil Jarratt wrote from Kuta in 1977, 'we could be in Surfers Paradise or Lorne, except for the charm of the ten-year-old kids serving us, the full moon above us and that beautiful, tropical night aroma'. He thought that this was the key to Bali's attraction: 'that blend of the strange and the familiar' which made it 'a foreign country where you can get a good Vegemite sandwich at the right price'.[20] By 1998, the Australian Consul in Denpasar reported that many Australians were choosing to come to Bali simply because it was the new 'Gold Coast holiday'.[21]

The very banality of the tourist experience masks something of profound importance: Australians could feel at ease – even at home – in Asia. Australia's proximity to Asia had evoked concern since at least the 1850s. Yet, rather than feeling anxious about being a Western outpost in the Asian region, many Australians were pleased that they were close enough to Bali to pop over whenever they liked. Alongside the Fortune hunters and Seekers of earlier chapters, Tourists produced an important counter-narrative to ongoing negative perceptions of Asia. Most importantly, this narrative had a wide reach, experienced by millions of Australians who found that they enjoyed, rather than feared, Asia. The mass tourist boom effectively turned what was once the 'Far East' into the 'Pleasure Periphery'. The sheer number of Australians, and the familiar atmosphere around Kuta, began to encourage casual references to Bali as Australia's 'favourite playground', 'a home away from home', or even 'another State of Australia' by the late 1990s.[22] This mental annexation, and the suggestion that Bali was just as Australian as Asian, challenged what had previously been a stark dichotomy dividing Asia from Australia, East from West.

Tourism to Bali also affected the ways in which some Australians reflected on their own nation and its international relations. As we have seen throughout this book, travel can shape political views by encouraging people to think about their place in the world, both literally and metaphorically. If there had been one truism of Australian nationhood, it was that it was tyrannised by distance: 'the land down under' was far from anywhere. Tourism encouraged a reassessment – on a mass scale – that Australia was actually part of an Asian region. This buttressed the political and diplomatic moves towards 'engagement', 'enmeshment' and 'integration' that characterised Australian international relations since the Hawke and Keating governments of the 1980s and 1990s.

This wasn't without its attendant anxieties. Situating Australia within the Asian region raised many questions, including some about its suitability for the neighbourhood. Australia's Western heritage and culture did not easily fit in with the 'Asian values' that were being defined (with some controversy) over the same period. Some Asian politicians, most notably the long-serving Prime Minister of Malaysia Mahathir Mohamad, repeatedly aired doubts about whether Australia really belonged in the region. The notion that Australians' lack of cultural refinement rendered it unsuitable for membership of the Asian region was a troubling one. Mass tourism provided a space for critical investigations of Australia's cultural suitability to the Asian region, with Australians' impact on Bali a recurring source of tension. The early 1990s saw the release of two major tourist novels, Inez Baranay's *The Edge of Bali* and Gerard Lee's *Troppo Man*. Tellingly, both were set in Bali and charted the horrified reactions of 'sensitive' travellers when faced with Australian tourists. The protagonist of Lee's novel, Matt, declared his disgust: 'what was happening here, to the Balinese ... was terrible'. After only a few years of contact with Australians, 'one of the world's most refined and spiritual cultures had been corrupted'.[23]

The nightclubs that overflowed with young Australians were singled out for particular disdain. The *Sunday Age* explained that 'this is the Bali that more sensitive travellers avoid', and held up the Sari Club as 'exactly what they hate about the new Bali'. Reporter Chris Johnston thought that 'the cultured Australian ... would deem it another pitstop on a holiday from hell'.[24] Evidently, many did. Interviewed at the height of her fame in the late 1990s, actress Lisa McCune admitted that she had been to the Sari Club during a recent Bali trip, but had 'felt a bit embarrassed standing near Australians' because their behaviour 'was a bit out of control' and she was concerned lest their reputation rubbed off on her.[25] The belief that Australians should project a more diplomatic image abroad revealed a continuing insecurity about how the region, and the world, viewed Australia. It also betrayed unease about Australia's capacity to successfully engage with the region, and intersected with debates about Australia's 'Asia literacy' at a time when political rhetoric focussed on Asia's diplomatic and economic importance.

Importantly, while mass tourism can be taken as evidence for Australians' increasing comfort in the region, this only extended as far as the tourist experience. Australians were comfortable in hotels and restaurants, on the beach and in nightclubs – but not necessarily in other parts of Indonesia, or even less touristy areas of Bali. Tourists felt comfortable in spaces that had been appropriated primarily for their use. Critics have long pointed to parallels between tourism and neo-imperialism. Tourism expert Mike Robinson has identified a 'deep-seated imperialistic assumption that large areas of the world exist solely for the benefit of tourists'.[26] This assumption encouraged some tourists to feel that, as tourist places existed solely for their enjoyment, they could act with impunity; an attitude that contributed to some of the cross-cultural conflict examined in the previous chapter. The experience of being in Bali encouraged Australians to feel increasingly comfortable in Asia, but this did not necessarily benefit cross-cultural relations and international diplomacy.

PARADISE LOST | Any comfort Australians had come to feel in Bali was threatened as bombs tore through the heart of Kuta late on the night of 12 October 2002. The terrorist attacks at the Sari Club and Paddy's Bar killed 202 people and injured a further 209. With 88 dead, Australia suffered the greatest number of casualties. A second, less deadly, bombing attack in 2005 confirmed popular associations between Bali and terrorism. Speaking at the Australian Consulate in Denpasar within a week of the first attack, Prime Minister John Howard expressed a widespread sentiment when he said the bombings had 'shocked our nation to the core'.[27]

Across the nation, millions of Australians reacted to the bombings through the prism of their own experiences in Bali, personalising the events and so increasing the emotional impact of the attack.

When I first heard about the bombings, my mind raced back to my Balinese holiday some four years before. I could remember the strip of Jalan Legian around the Sari Club: hot and crowded, and at night overwhelmed with beeping traffic and tourists drunkenly weaving through the narrow street. I began to think about the people I'd met, and wondered whether they had been there on the night the bombs went off. I hoped they were OK, but the thought made the horrorscape of blood and destruction on television more frightening. I had recently returned from my first backpacking trip to Thailand, where the bar scenes on Ko Samui and Ko Phangan had reminded me of Kuta. The sense that the bombings could have struck anywhere, and at any time – that this tragedy could have happened to me – increased the emotional blow of the attacks. Moreover, I was planning to head off to Southeast Asia again in only a couple more months, and I couldn't help but worry. Was this going to happen again?

In the shock following the Bali bombings, the tourists' image of Bali as a 'home away from home' took on a new emotional resonance. Media coverage borrowed the sentimental language pioneered by tourists, casually portraying Bali as an extension of Australia in reports of terrorism striking 'home', 'our doorstep', or 'our backdoor'. *The Australian* portrayed Bali as an 'exotic little northern state' of Australia'.[28] The *Gold Coast Bulletin* went even further, referring to Bali as Australia's symbolic 'heart'.[29] Political rhetoric was also informed by sentimental tourist imagery. Politicians from both major parties nostalgically recalled Bali as a place of innocent family holidays and rite-of-passage adventures. Liberal Bruce Baird, for example, claimed that this was 'the first time we have seen such a terrorist attack directly on the people of Australia', and that it represented 'the loss of innocence for Australia'. Then

Leader of the Labor Opposition Simon Crean also saw this as 'a loss of innocence'.[30]

Years of comfortable holiday-making had facilitated casual slippages that referred to Bali as a part of Australia. This in turn supported the interpretation that the terrorist attack had been targeted at Australia, rather than at Indonesia. This came despite early interviews with sources close to the perpetrators that suggested they had chosen to attack Bali because it was a symbol of the degradation of Indonesian mores rather than an Australian space; and that their targets were Westerners in general and Americans, rather than Australians, in particular.[31] Yet *The Australian*'s Foreign Editor Greg Sheridan was not alone in reporting that 'there can be little doubt that Australians were specifically targeted'.[32] Media scholars have found that the great majority – as much as 99 per cent – of 'soft' coverage focussed on Australians and that the tone of reporting was overwhelmingly sentimental.[33]

Such views had distinct political impacts. The sense that the bombings had struck 'home', were directed at Australians, or had taken away the nation's innocence bolstered domestic support for the United States' War on Terror. In the words of Labor MP Sid Sidebottom, the sense that 'terrorism has struck at our doorstep' meant that 'we do not have an option to be neutral'. This rhetoric affected policy considerations in the immediate aftermath. The Australian Federal Police adopted a viewpoint that the Bali bombings were 'Australia's September 11', rather than Indonesia's. In an official report, the Department of Foreign Affairs and Trade (DFAT) claimed that the attack 'brought home to Australia the global reach of terrorism'. It also released a paper called *Transnational Terrorism: The Threat to Australia*, which claimed that the Bali bombings were proof that terrorists were targeting Australia because 'we stand in the way of their ultimate goal … to establish an Islamic super-state'. Political scientists have noted that this language worked in support of military engagement in Iraq and Afghanistan. As Federal MP

Damien Hale was to say during a subsequent commemoration ceremony, because of the Bali bombings, 'no longer do Australians feel that terrorism is someone else's problem; no longer do we feel that these events happen somewhere else in the world'. The view that an attack on Bali was an attack on Australia – an interpretation that was supported by the decades of tourist experiences of the island – bolstered a conservative foreign policy response that involved police and military, as well as political and diplomatic, action.[34]

In the short term, the Bali bombings had a profound impact on the way Australians thought about their role in the region. We have seen that, increasingly, Australians had adopted the role of pleasure-seeking tourists, out to enjoy themselves without becoming involved in Asia's complex politics. The Bali bombings once again politicised the tourist role. In media reports and in political rhetoric, the tourist came to be portrayed as a symbol of national innocence lost. Almost immediately, Prime Minister John Howard portrayed tourists caught up in the tragedy as 'going about something that is quintessentially Australian'.[35] During his visit to Bali days after the bombing, Howard claimed that Australians 'had a birthright of freedom to explore the world'. At the National Memorial Service at Parliament House a few days later, he repeated that travel was an Australian 'birthright' and insisted that 'the young of Australia will not be deterred from travelling in the years ahead'. At the Memorial Service at the Australian Consulate in Denpasar, he again reiterated that, as Australians, 'we will never lose our openness, our sense of adventure. The young of Australia will always travel. They will always have fun in distant parts'.[36] This rhetoric effectively raised tourism to the status of national duty. Symbolising an optimistic openness to the world and conveying naive innocence, the role of the tourist came to be seen not only as befitting individual Australians abroad, but as expressing something of the national character. His words found an echo in media reports that used the language and imagery of Anzac to describe both victims and survivors, and presented tourists caught up in the Bali bombings as embodying the national ideals of mateship and innocence. Ordinary Australians' visits to the neighbourhood were once again coloured with broader political concerns.

TOURING THE ARC OF INSTABILITY | The Bali bombings were not the only crises to hit tourism to Asia in the early years of the 21st century. The use of passenger aircraft as weapons in the 11 September 2001 attacks in the United States lent a frightening undertone to leisure travel. The media focus on tourists during the Severe Acute Respiratory Syndrome (SARS) outbreak of 2002, the Asian tsunami of 2004 and the arrest and incarceration of Schapelle Corby in 2005 further confirmed the association between travel to Asia and danger. The relentless news coverage made Asia out to be a place 'where relatively few white people live and bombs seemingly go off like clockwork'.[37] The trope of the Asia-Pacific region as an 'arc of insecurity', which became prominent in security and diplomatic discussions, supported a growing popular sentiment that tourists were vulnerable the moment they left Australia.

Tourism also became an increasingly prominent issue in Australia's diplomatic relations. Questions about the extent of the government's responsibility for the safety of its citizens abroad led DFAT to review its system of travel advisories. The department had come under sustained criticism in the wake of the Bali bombings, with newspaper headlines demanding 'Why didn't they tell us what they knew?'[38] Largely in response, DFAT launched the 'Smartraveller' system in September 2003 with a $9.7 million publicity campaign. The public was bombarded with advertisements on television, radio, in print and on billboards, urging them to check DFAT's advisories before they headed overseas. With the launch of the Charter for Safe Travel – a partnership program between DFAT and the travel industry – travel agents also undertook to inform tourists of the latest travel advisories before they booked tickets.

The DFAT advisories regionalised the perception of terrorist threat. Within days of the first Bali blast, DFAT had amended travel advice not only for Indonesia but also for Brunei, Cambodia, Laos, Malaysia, the Philippines and Singapore. On 25 October 2002, Foreign Minister Alexander Downer warned that the Thai holiday resort of Phuket was a potential target and advised Australians to defer non-essential travel to Thailand, even though no specific threat had been identified. Terrorism warnings were soon posted for almost every Southeast Asian destination, including those with little or no previous known terrorist activity.[39] The nearness of Asia, which after decades of mass tourism had begun to lose its threatening connotations, once again aroused popular concern.

DFAT's regionalisation of the terrorist threat provoked a strong reaction from a number of Southeast Asian leaders. The leaders of all 10 states in the Association of Southeast Asian Nations (ASEAN) joined to voice their criticism in November 2002.[40] Bilateral relations were also affected, as regional leaders pointed to an apparent bias by which Asian nations with no known terrorist activity attracted higher-level warnings than Western countries with a long history of terrorist attacks. Singapore's government criticised DFAT's 'alarmist assessments', which the Prime Minister Goh Chok Tong branded 'totally unfair'.[41] The Philippines government questioned whether it was 'the right response to a friendly nation'.[42] Thai Prime Minister Thaksin Shinawatra repeatedly questioned the credibility of Australian intelligence.[43] Malaysian Prime Minister Mahathir Mohamad retaliated by warning his citizens that Australia was 'completely unsafe' for Muslims.[44] The most serious and lasting effect was on Australia's relations with Indonesia. President of Indonesia Megawati Sukarnoputri was an immediate and vocal critic, warning that any downturn in tourism revenues 'would in turn encourage the terrorists with their objectives and expand their activities'.[45] Once he became President in 2004, Susilo

Bambang Yudhoyono regularly protested Indonesia's consistently high advisory level; by 2008, *The Age*'s Indonesian correspondent Mark Forbes judged the travel advisory 'the biggest irritant in the Australia-Indonesia relationship', an analysis backed by the Lowy Institute for International Policy.[46] The criticism continued until the advisory was finally eased in 2012.

The idea that Australians were vulnerable in Asia was certainly prominent, but how did ordinary Australians respond to the new threats? The wave of cancellations in the immediate aftermath of each new crisis reveals that many were clearly shaken. Increased anxiety regarding Islamic terrorism saw Australian travel to all Muslim-majority countries in the Asian region fall by an average of 18 per cent in the year after the 11 September 2001 attacks.[47] The numbers travelling to Indonesia plummeted by one-third in the year after the 2002 attacks and Australians were increasingly ambivalent about the popular holiday destination of Thailand, home to a significant Muslim population in the southern provinces surrounding tourist destinations including Krabi and Ko Samui. By contrast, nations with no popular association with Islam enjoyed significant, and sometimes dramatic, growth in the number of Australian visitors in the years immediately following the 2001 attacks. Cambodia, Laos, Vietnam, China, South Korea and Japan all experienced a surge of Australian visitors.[48] Many Australians began to differentiate between what they considered to be 'safe' and 'dangerous' destinations, mostly by avoiding majority-Muslim destinations, but they did not stop travelling to Asia altogether.

Indeed, despite the string of crises and emotive political and media rhetoric, more Australians set off to visit their neighbours than ever before. Tourism numbers to Indonesia had already begun to creep back to pre-bombings levels when the second Bali bombing attacks in 2005 sent them plummeting again. Yet, numbers had recovered by 2007, and then began a dizzying rise to record highs: 380 600 in 2008, 667 100 in 2010, 877 900 in 2012. As a point of reference, the pre-bombings record had been less than 350 000, which means that almost three times as many Australians now travelled to Indonesia than at any point before the bombings. Thailand's rise was nearly as dramatic as Indonesia's; indeed the number of Australians travelling to every Asian nation has seen steep growth in the past decade.[49]

How can we explain this apparent paradox, by which more Australians went to Asia even as its image came to be associated with danger? There is no simple answer, but many factors encouraged Australians to reprise the role of tourist. Along with the prime minister's injunctions that Australians continue to exercise their 'birthright' of travel, a discourse of defiance encouraged the view that, by cancelling holidays or otherwise changing their plans, Australians would be 'letting the terrorists win'. Secondly, as we saw in Chapter 5, the tourist industry encouraged Australians to think that 'the Balinese need us' in the wake of the bombings, and many were well inclined to listen. Thirdly, a steady rise in the Australian dollar, along with the introduction of budget airlines, stimulated overseas travel to all destinations. Finally, and most importantly, the tourist industry responded to the bombings with an aggressive discounting strategy, so that a holiday to Bali soon became cheaper than ever. In June 2005, Flight Centre offered a 10-night package to Bali, including airfares from Sydney, accommodation, a tour, two massages and some meals for $895. In 2006, Jetset offered a four-night family package, including airfares for one adult and accompanying children, transfers, all children's meals, entry to the Waterbom park and nine tours, for $949 – less than the average weekly income of $1058. After the period of crisis, many Australians could enjoy a family holiday in Bali without any saving or sacrifice whatsoever.[50]

In effect, Australians continued to travel to Asia for the same reasons as before: because it was cheap, convenient and comfortable. The speed with which they reprised their habit of visiting the neighbours reveals the power of longer-term attitudes, developed over decades of travel images and tourism experiences. Enduring patterns, by which Australians had become increasingly comfortable in Asia, reasserted themselves despite growing anxiety regarding the safety of Australians abroad in the early 21st century.

T HE POLITICS OF TRAVEL | Both sides of Australian politics have recognised the political significance of tourism to Asia, and forwarded the argument that people-to-people contact helped improve the nation's official relations with the region. In the 2003 Foreign Affairs White Paper, the Howard Government argued that people-to-people contact added 'depth and stability to our relationships' with Asia, and the Tourism White Paper of the same year emphasised leisure travel as 'a positive force in developing and deepening Australia's relations with other countries'.[51] This rhetoric remained largely unchanged when the Gillard government released the *Australia in the Asian Century* White Paper in 2012. It claimed that 'improving people-to-people links can unlock large economic and social gains'.[52] The Howard, Rudd, Gillard and Abbott governments have all designated people-to-people programs as a policy priority. They have devoted government money to educational and cultural exchange programs (including Gillard's Asia Bound and Abbott's New Colombo Plan schemes) and although they do not directly subsidise leisure travel, they continue to speak positively about the contribution that tourism makes to cross-cultural understanding.

Yet, despite the government's hopeful rhetoric, more tourism did not automatically lead to smoother diplomatic relations. In 2010, the President of the Republic of Indonesia, Susilo Bambang Yudhoyono, travelled to Australia on a state visit. In wide-ranging discussions, he covered topics including terrorism, people smuggling and foreign aid, but when it came to addressing Parliament (the first time an Indonesian leader had been granted the honour),

Yudhoyono singled out the issue of popular misunderstanding between Australians and Indonesians. He claimed that stereotypes about Indonesia held by ordinary Australians, and stereotypes about Australia common amongst Indonesians, had taken a significant toll on bilateral relations. Yudhoyono said Australians needed to recognise that Indonesia was 'more than a beach playground with coconut trees'; in his analysis, an inability to move beyond such stereotypes was 'the most persistent problem in our relations'.[53] Yudhoyono's analysis has been widely echoed, particularly in Australian foreign policy circles. Far from contributing to a better understanding of Indonesian society and culture, experts such as the Indonesia Institute's Ross Taylor fear that the predominance of Bali in Australians' personal experience perpetuates a skewed and inaccurate image of the Indonesian nation.[54]

Moreover, the latest tourist boom has not eradicated the inequalities that pervaded previous visitors' experiences. In Bali, the economic disparities of travel and tourism were exaggerated in the post-bombings context and some Australians began to manipulate the downturn in tourism for their advantage. As the *Sun-Herald* reported in 2006, some Balinese had become so desperate they were willing to accept just about any price for their wares, and 'everyone at the roadside stalls and craft shops was desperate to bargain'.[55] Reports about the many things 'super-friendly' staff were willing to do for Australian visitors unselfconsciously celebrated the economic inequality.[56] A 2005 *Sydney Morning Herald* article insisted that 'staying in a luxury, five-star resort is nothing to be ashamed of', and it brushed off critics who thought that tourism perpetuated economic inequality with the statement that 'Colonialism is passé.'[57] Another *Sydney Morning Herald* article casually referred to Bali as 'a lucky country colony', and observed that Phuket in Thailand was fast becoming one, too.[58] Despite decades of development, contemporary tourism retained striking resonances with previous, imperialist modes of travel.

In the age of mass tourism, old fears about the 'Asian mind' began to be replaced by personal memories of the smiling people and obliging staff encountered on holidays. As the hundreds of thousands of personal experiences became millions, 'Asia' became a far more quotidian, almost banal entity, and was recast as Australia's 'pleasure periphery' rather than the threatening north. By the 21st century, this image had grown so strong that not even a series of terrorist attacks, pandemics and natural disasters could shake it. Yet, the fact that this shift took place in the context of the tourism industry, which at its extremes reinvigorated the body politics of imperialism, complicates any assumptions about tourism acting as an unequivocal force for good.

This has been the prevailing narrative, but there were other experiences that are at least as important. Among those Australians setting off to Asia was a specific group who tended to perceive the region in a very different way. Australians of Asian heritage often had a more complex perspective that reflected their dual ancestry. As the next and final chapter shows, their stories link Australia and Asia in an entirely different pattern of connections.

# 9: SONS AND DAUGHTERS

I wasn't in the mood for queuing after a long flight from Shanghai last year. At least the 'Australian Passports' queue should be short, I thought, scanning my fellow passengers as we headed towards the immigration counters. Most looked to be Chinese and many were speaking Mandarin, so they would be heading for the 'Foreign Passports' counters. I was wrong. The passports in their hands were not the dark red ones issued by the People's Republic of China, they were the same blue-black as mine. My lazy assumptions were mistaken; most of my fellow passengers were Australian. The end of the queue snaked all the way back into the Duty Free store. It was going to be a long wait.

This is the Asian Century, not least demographically. Of the world's 7 billion people, some 4.3 billion live in Asia. The world's two largest nations by population are China and India; Indonesia is the fourth most populous. The population of Australia has also changed. In the 2011 census, some 6 million Australians (27 per cent of the total population) indicated that they had been born overseas. Taking account of those with a parent born overseas, the number rose to over 50 per cent. Since the White Australia Policy was finally repealed in 1973, migrants have increasingly come from Asia; those from India and China alone have accounted for almost 25 per cent of the intake in recent years.[1] The population of Australia is shifting, and there is no way to overstate the implications of this demographic shift for Australia's relations with the world.

This shift complicates the binary distinction between the categories of 'Australia' and 'Asia', which was taken for granted for much of the 20th century. This chapter points to the fact that Australian travel to Asia was not just a white or Anglo-Australian undertaking. Asian-Australians have been part of the fabric of Australian life for many generations, and they have been particularly enthusiastic travellers. How does the meaning of a journey change when the 'Australian' travelling to Asia is of Asian heritage? How have Asian-Australians experienced the region? How have they felt about 'going back'? And what does 'going back' even mean for those second-, third- or fifth-generation Australians who aren't even sure where their ancestral homeland is, let alone speak a word of the native tongue?

There is no simple answer, just as there is no single 'Asian-Australian' story. Some journeys brought joyful reunions, as visitors rediscovered a homeland and family they had left behind, or never knew they had. For others, the experience was bittersweet, provoking a recognition that they no longer fit in 'back home'. Feeling like outsiders in both their native and adopted countries, some faced a profound identity crisis; others relished in their in-between status and took on the role of cultural mediator. Asian-Australians were never a homogenous group, but what they had in common was that most did not regard Asia as Australia's 'Other'. This alone sets their journeys apart from many of those charted in this book.

While Australians have roots in all parts of Asia, this chapter focusses on the experience of Australians with Chinese ancestry. This is not to say that Australians with roots in the Indian subcontinent, Vietnam or Japan (not to mention Korea, Indonesia, the Philippines or other places) are not 'sons and daughters' too. Rather, it is mostly because the Chinese have the longest and best-documented history of Asian migrant groups to Australia, allowing for a sustained analysis. This exploration of Asian-Australians' journeys is only the briefest scratch on the surface of a subject that requires a book of its own. Like so much Asian-Australian historiography, this is only the beginning of the story.

SOJOURNERS | The extent of the recent demographic shift makes it emphatically clear that the category 'Australians' includes many individuals of Asian descent, but this is by no means a recent phenomenon. Around 100 000 people came to Australia from China between 1840 and 1900, many of them drawn by the shimmering prospect of 'New Gold Mountain', as they called Australia in the Gold Rush period. The White Australia Policy prevented the entry of new migrants after Federation, so by 1939 the number of Chinese in Australia had dwindled to approximately 15 000. But those who remained were extremely mobile. Historical demographer Paul Jones has estimated that Chinese-Australians made 80 000 overseas journeys between 1901 and 1939. As historian John Fitzgerald notes, this means that Chinese-Australians probably travelled more frequently than white Australians. Their lives were marked by mobility between and within China and Australia that can appear cosmopolitan, with their lives lived between and across borders, societies and civilisations.[2]

Chinese-Australians were so peripatetic largely because of strong family ties. Maintaining close connections between Australia and China was important, and as the restrictive White Australia Policy prevented their families from joining them in Australia, Chinese-Australians were forced to commute between their two homelands in order to maintain relationships with parents, siblings and sometimes even wives and children. Others travelled for trade, using their contacts and capacity to operate across East and West to build vast, profitable merchant networks. For both personal and business reasons, regular travel was immensely important.

Many retained emotional links with China as a place and an idea. Just as second- or third-generation Anglo-Australians referred to England as 'home' (even if they had never been there), Chinese-Australians retained a sentimental bond to their ancestral lands. Places of origin were particularly important for Chinese-Australians who were born overseas. In Australia, those hailing from the See Yap district (around the Pearl River in Southern China) incorporated into mutual aid societies, as did those from Doong Goong (now Dongguan, near Hong Kong) or Heungshan (near Macao). Members of these organisations looked out for each other's wellbeing, and in the Gold Rush period also loaned money to cover the cost of passage for intending migrants. The fact that these organisations were based around regional allegiances only underscores the importance of ties between Australia and China. Maintaining those ties required regular contact and travel.

For all these reasons, regular travel between Australia and China was essential to many within the Chinese-Australian community. Its importance became apparent during World War I as a shipping shortage threatened to curtail civilian travel. Desperate to retain its mobility, the Chinese-Australian community raised enough capital to launch its own shipping line, the China-Australia Mail Steamship Line, with two ships purchased and another one leased from Hong Kong. The investment proved a disaster, largely because the Australian government requisitioned the Line's two ships for wartime service and its inexperienced 24-year-old Director, William Liu, was unable to turn around the resulting deficit. This did nothing to raise the warmth of interactions between the Commonwealth government and the Chinese-Australian community. What it did reveal was that travel to China was seen to be essential by those who lived between the two countries.

I N BETWEEN EAST AND WEST | Few Chinese-Australians were fully accepted into mainstream society under the White Australia Policy but many were shaped by Australian norms and values. Historian John Fitzgerald has shown that the Chinese-Australian community was influenced by the Australian values of democracy, egalitarianism and mateship in the early years of the 20th century.[3] The experience of arriving in China could reveal the extent of their acculturation by emphasising the difference between Chinese-Australians and the Chinese. In Australia, they were seen as Chinese, but in China, they were regarded as Australians, or Overseas Chinese. Their accents, habits and appearance marked them as different and set them apart from both Chinese and white Australians. They lived in between Australia and China, West and East.

The sense of being in between two cultures can provoke an identity crisis in those who come to feel as outsiders in both their ancestral and adopted homes. But it can also have a reverse effect: being fluent in two languages and capable of operating across two cultures can be empowering. Some Chinese-Australians pondered the relative benefits of the two societies they knew and offered advice on how Australian values could improve China, or how Chinese civilisation could contribute to Australia's development. China underwent vast changes after the collapse of the ancient imperial system in 1911 and Chinese-Australians were actively involved in shaping the new China. Vivian Chow was raised in Grafton in northern New South Wales and worked as a journalist for the *Northern Star* before heading to China in 1925, aged 19. In Shanghai, he founded the Chinese-Australian magazine, *United China*, which spoke in 'glowing terms of the Australian traditions of egalitarianism, fair play and rule of law while regretting that these traditions were not extended under restrictive immigration laws to families of Chinese descent'. As Fitzgerald has noted, Chow 'shared equal pride in his Australian working-man's heritage and his Chinese ancestry'.[4] Another Chinese-Australian, baptised James See in Sydney in 1872, was also confident that Chinese-Australians had a special role to play in the history of both nations. In colonial Hong Kong, he co-founded one of the first Chinese revolutionary organisations, the Furen Literary Society, as well as the English-language newspaper, *South China Morning Post*. Known to posterity as Tse Tsan Tai, he holds a prominent place in China's modern history. Chow and See leveraged their first-hand experience of life in Australia to contribute to China. They thought that their intimate understanding of the values and practices of egalitarian democracy could benefit the embryonic Chinese Republican movement. Their regular travel between Australia and China, which spoke to an intimate understanding of both civilisations and political systems, was the capital that increased their status and authority.

Moving between two homes could also be profitable in a financial sense. A number of Chinese-Australians became immensely wealthy by introducing the Western style of consumerism (which had only recently emerged in Australia) to China. They reshaped the commercial scene of Kuomintang China by introducing department stores to Nanking Road in Shanghai. By the mid-1930s, the street's skyline was dominated by four huge Art Deco department stores: the Wing On, Sincere, Sun Sun and Sun Company stores. Every one of them had been established by Chinese-Australians who modelled their Shanghai emporiums on Australian department stores like Anthony Horderns' in Sydney and the Myer Emporium in Melbourne.

While they may have initially based their stores on Australian models, the Shanghai emporiums were not carbon copies, nor did they merely ape Western developments. As historian Sophie Loy-Wilson has shown, 'every step of the design process was imbued with the self-conscious need to "Chinafy" the project, to negate rumours that Sincere and Wing On were really fronts for European neo-colonialism, homogenising and corrupting Asia's city dwellers with their decadent Western goods and rituals'.[5] The vast, cosmopolitan population of Shanghai also spurred on new developments, which sometimes found their way back to Australia's department stores. The circulation of people and ideas between Australia and China brought individual profits; it also helped contribute to the development of commercial and popular culture more broadly.

While going 'home' to China could bring profit, it could also lead to disappointment and distress. Some Australians found that the homeland of their imagination was peopled not by kin but by bandits, liars and corrupt officials, all of whom wanted to relieve them of the wealth accrued in New Gold Mountain. Chinese could be scornful of the 'Gold Mountain Males' who returned to visit their ancestral villages, and the shifting political and security contexts of Republican China meant that the authorities could not be relied upon for protection. As one Australian recalled, by the 1920s and 1930s a visit to China could be 'a most painful and heart rending experience for returning countrymen'. They may have looked forward to the trip with great anticipation, but 'no sooner do they return home than they are subjected to kidnapping and extortion by corrupt officials, local bullies and evil gentry'.[6]

As we saw in earlier chapters, the Australian nation and identity were largely constituted against the Asian 'Other'. Yet, many Australians of Asian heritage did not think that their two cultures were incompatible. Travel could serve to emphasise the fact that they were both Chinese and Australian; it was in negotiating between their two homelands that many Chinese-Australians made sense of the entirety of their existence. The process of moving between their two homes – of travel – was in this regard partly constitutive of the Chinese-Australian identity.

Regarding themselves as living proof that Australia and Asia could coexist in harmony, a number of Chinese-Australians took on the role of cultural interlocutors in the optimistic belief that it was only misunderstanding that divided Australians and Chinese. Sydneysider William Liu devoted his life to the cause of bridging East and West. Over more than 50 years, he tried to prove that Australian and Chinese cultures were mutually compatible. He also worked to change the restrictive legislation that kept the two apart. Liu was born in Australia to a Chinese father and an English mother and his childhood was evenly divided between Australia and Asia. He was fluent in Cantonese and English and equally confident operating within both societies. Liu did not see a conflict between his Chinese and Australian sides, but was proud that he had a 'dual outlook and thinking' that allowed him to 'react to most situations as a dinkum Aussie and/or as a peasant Chinese'. He thought this made him fully bi-cultural – a 'Sino-Aussie'.[7] Furthermore, he thought that China and Australia were not very different at all. Believing that miscomprehension was the only thing dividing his two homelands, Liu attempted to bridge the two cultures by translating the Chinese values of loyalty and obeisance into the Australian lexicon of egalitarianism, loyalty and the 'fair go'.

Travel gave Liu the cultural capital required to operate as an interlocutor between East and West. He reflected that the feeling of being 'quite "at home" in … the lands of both my parents' was 'on account of my up-bringing and re-visits to China'.[8] In 1932, he wrote to Fred Quinlan, a senior bureaucrat in the Department of External Affairs, that 'this trip to China has made me realise more that something should be done' with regards to the 'Sino-Australian question'.[9] He devoted himself to lobbying politicians, publishing several pamphlets and writing up to 500 letters a year to highly placed people including Minister for Immigration, Arthur Calwell. Some letters pressed the case of individual Chinese threatened with deportation but others argued against the White Australia Policy in principle, and pointed to his own ability to bridge East and West as evidence that the two societies were not incompatible.

CULTURAL REVOLUTIONS | Life for Chinese-Australians took a different shape from the 1950s. In Australia, the policy of assimilation encouraged ethnic minorities to break their ties with ancestral homelands and adopt Australian characteristics.[10] Millions of migrants from Southern and Eastern Europe were admitted after World War II. However, intermittent proposals for a quota system that would allow even a token number of educated and 'respectable' Asians to settle in Australia were repeatedly quashed, despite a growing recognition that the White Australia Policy was resented by the new post-colonial nations of Asia.

The cosmopolitanism and mobility that characterised Chinese-Australian life before the war became more difficult under the policy of Assimilation. William Liu may have been proud of his ability to fuse Chinese and Australian characteristics, but his long-time interlocutor (and one of the architects of Assimilation policy) Minister for Immigration Arthur Calwell, thought that 'the Chinese tradition of dual citizenship is a great stumbling block to assimilation', largely because it encouraged 'an adverse opinion among European Australians'. Where Liu considered travel between Australia and China to be essential, Calwell saw it as 'an unacceptable indicator of his attachment to China and not compatible with his Australian identity'.[11] Liu's regular shuttling between China and Australia slowed: his next visit, in 1959, was the first in over 20 years.

Children growing up in the 1940s and 1950s were particularly affected by the rhetoric of Assimilation. Their distinctive features made Asian-Australian children easy targets for bullies, who taunted them with cries of 'Ching Chong Chinaman' or other gibes. Headstrong youngsters such as Helene Chung retaliated by calling out 'White Trash', but even she came to consider her ethnic background a source of shame rather than pride, and 'if my mother suddenly changed from English into Chinese in front of my school friends ... I quivered with embarrassment'.[12] Sydneysider Angela Chan remembered that it was not just other children who made their lives difficult: teachers made it clear that speaking Chinese 'was just basically totally unacceptable' by repeating that 'you are in Australia and you must speak English'.[13] Other signs of Chineseness, such as eating with chopsticks, were also discouraged. Chung remembered that, although rice made an appearance on her family's dinner table, 'like other Tasmanian children I ate lamb chops, mashed potatoes, grilled tomatoes and green peas with a knife and fork'.[14] Sending children to ancestral villages for a Chinese education could appear less attractive in light of Anglo-Australian disapproval. Even had they wanted their children to acquire a Chinese education, some second- or third-generation Australian-born Chinese lacked the intimate connections with 'home' that were required for such an arrangement after years in Australia.

Even more crucially, the Communist Revolution of 1949 transformed conditions in China and maintaining relationships with Overseas Chinese became increasingly fraught under Mao's regime. The Australian government's severance of diplomatic relations with the People's Republic of China also made the maintenance of direct contact more difficult from the Australian side. Although it never reached the pitch of the United States, the fear of communism made popular discourse about China increasingly shrill throughout the 1950s and 1960s.

Travelling to China became more difficult. Australian passports were rendered invalid for entry to the People's Republic of China and those wishing to travel there had to seek special permission from the Department of External Affairs. Although permits were usually granted, any application could arouse the suspicion of intelligence agencies.[15] The logistics were even more difficult on the Chinese side. International visitors, including Overseas Chinese, had to be vetted by the government before entry was approved.[16] Conditions became even more trying under the Cultural Revolution. Any interaction with the West could be used as evidence of reactionary or bourgeois inclinations, so contact with overseas relatives was constrained. Visits became increasingly rare and even letters grew infrequent as Chinese became afraid that they would be used to denounce them. Political and social considerations began to impact on family ties and personal connections became increasingly strained as the years wore on.

The strong links and constant mobility that had once defined the lives of Chinese-Australians weakened under these conditions. Even so, some Chinese-Australians continued to inhabit the space between Australia and China. A significant number of both Anglo- and Chinese-Australians regarded developments in the People's Republic with optimism. While Anglo-Australians usually did this because they were politically sympathetic to socialism, for Chinese-Australians it was often a continuation of the longer-term desire to present China in a positive light to Australian audiences.[17] A significant number of Chinese-Australians continued the effort to make China palatable for Australians; although politics was important, counteracting racial prejudice was even more so. William Liu, for example, continued to make representations for China and the Chinese in much the same way after 1949 as he had during the Kuomintang period. In one pamphlet, he presented Maoism as a new manifestation of the Chinese tradition of mutual assistance. He presented a personal story, in which his 'Ah Por' (grandmother) 'taught me to be always alert and ready to help', before claiming that 'Mao Tse-tung had the same idea. "Wei yun fook moo" he called it – "Serve the People!"'[18]

Movement and exchange did not cease altogether. Pamela Tan was born in Australia, set off for China in 1950 and lived through the politically turbulent Maoist years before returning in 1979. While hers is an exceptional case in many ways, it points to the fact that Australians could and did have a range of experiences in China during the Cold War. Tan was determined to live in China not only because she was inspired by the communist cause, but also because she felt alienated from the White Australia of her birth. As recounted in a self-published memoir, she had been stung by the casual racism of Anglo-Australians in the 1930s and 1940s. All the little incidents – being taunted by children at school, or watching her father forced off a tram as 'we don't want Chinamen inside with the ladies' – left her feeling like an outsider in her own land. Although the jeers taught her to resent her Chineseness, Tan was simultaneously drawn to China's culture and politics. She began to study the Chinese language as a teenager, and 'read as many books as I could on China, because one day I knew I was going there'. Her cultural hybridity – both Western and Eastern – is reflected in the list of reasons she gave for her decision to set off for China: an abiding interest in classical Chinese culture inherited from her father, a budding friendship with an Anglo-Australian communist and his family, the American writer Edgar Snow's *Red Star Over China* and the words of a visitor from Hong Kong who prophesied that she would 'go back to the Motherland and help build a new China'.[19]

Arriving in the People's Republic in 1950, just one year after the revolution and in the midst of the land-reform movement, Tan thought it 'exciting to be part of such an historical and revolutionary event'.[20] Initially posted to the Asian Australasian Liaison Bureau in Beijing, she prepared books and pamphlets on Chinese trade unions for friendly organisations in Australia and New Zealand and translated extracts from the Australian press, including the *Sydney Morning Herald* and *The Age*, to inform Party leadership about developments in Australian trade unionism. Later, her skills were used for translation and language teaching. At this stage, her in-betweenness, as someone living between Australia and China and bridging East and West, was valued.

The value of Tan's dual origins decreased as the regime became increasingly radical. Although she stayed for 30 years, Tan's time in China was not always a happy one. The sense of belonging she craved continued to evade her; in China, as in Australia, she could not escape her hybridity. After only a few weeks Tan had been reduced to tears by the realisation that she was never going to fit in, that 'in Australia I am Chinese, here I am not Chinese'. The question 'What am I?' continued to haunt her, but internal struggles were overshadowed by the very tangible ways in which her Australianness became a liability in the increasingly strident political climate of the Cultural Revolution. Tan's Australian roots aroused accusations of bourgeois leanings, and *dazibao* posters denouncing her 'illicit relations with foreign countries' began to appear at her workplace. Tan was eventually accused of being an enemy of the people and, following numerous denunciations and a humiliating show-trial, was sent for 'ideological remoulding' through imprisonment in 1968. Although she was deemed as rehabilitated and allowed to resume normal life after several months, the insecurity of her position, alongside the broader instability of life in a nation lurching from one ideological upheaval to another, led her to seek a return to Australia. She arrived in Australia with her Chinese husband and their two children in 1979. After almost 30 years in China, Tan had the curious experience of reverse culture-shock in the country of her birth. Now Australia was like a foreign country, and 'my first impression was that all the young people – blond haired and blue eyed – looked alike'. Deeper cultural differences also manifested, and contributed to her husband's suicide after only two years in Australia. Her abiding feeling of alienation had led her on a long and painful journey but finally at its end Tan found some peace. In old age, she came to think that both China and Australia felt like home.[21]

THE CHINA CIPHER | Pamela Tan was unusual in that, in her role at the Asian Australasian Liaison Bureau, she acted as a conduit for Australia and China from the Chinese side. More typical were those who continued the tradition of translating Asia to Australians. Like William Liu, Helene Chung used travel and the eyewitness account to try and understand China, and interpret what she had seen for the Australian public. In her case, the role was institutionalised when she became the China correspondent for the ABC in 1983 – the first woman, and the first Chinese-Australian, to assume this role.

Chung knew she was taking on a difficult task. She saw herself as working not only against long-standing ignorance and prejudice, but also against the rose-tinted reports of boosters such as Myra Roper and Dymphna Cusack, whose distorted accounts of New China were explored in Chapter 4. In a memoir of her time as correspondent, Chung wrote of 'the problem of trying to discuss the People's Republic with westerners who had a romantic view of China which they had gained from a distance or during a fleeting visit'. She constructed her view in opposition to this, presenting China as a cipher that was impossible to understand in its totality. Even after living and working there for three years, and despite her Chinese heritage, 'I had only peered into a few cracks and crevices of Chinese society'.[22] In contrast with the determined optimism of Roper and Cusack's accounts, Chung also wrote of the negative aspects of life in China. Her first impressions of China had been so negative that she believed 'any sentimental attachment I may have had because of my ethnic origin was obliterated' by the dirt and inefficiency she saw around her.[23]

Nonetheless, Chung's story points to the ongoing connections between Australians of Chinese heritage and the land of their ancestors' birth. Chung was the model of assimilated Chinese – as we have seen, she grew up on roast lamb and peas in Tasmania – but she nonetheless went on to study Chinese history at university and made several attempts to learn Mandarin. Moreover, she 'assumed I would one day see the land of my forebears'.[24] Once in China, she explored her Chinese heritage, travelling to the Guangdong counties from which many Chinese-Australians were descended as well as her own ancestral village in Taishan. There, she felt an emotional tug that was so strong she almost made a large donation to the Overseas Chinese Reception Bureau. Yet, the fact that she stopped herself from doing so points to the fact that her responses were always ambiguous. Chung's journalistic instincts told her that she was being taken advantage of, that a government eager to milk Overseas Chinese for foreign exchange was manipulating her emotions. She later reflected on her caution with some satisfaction, as on returning to Australia she discovered that the 'ancestral' village she had visited was not even in the same county as the one her ancestors had actually set out from over a century before.

With commuting patterns interrupted and China altered by 30 years of communism, many Chinese-Australians approached China as a foreign country by the 1980s. Clearly, Chung did not find adapting to Chinese ways as easy as William Liu had, half a century before. This was partly because she had not been habituated to Chinese customs in Assimilation-era Australia, and partly because China had undergone such dramatic internal change. Instead of mixing with Chinese, or with other Chinese-Australians, Chung's social and professional networks were made up of Westerners. Working as a foreign correspondent, she fell under the same government regulations as all other foreigners and her social life revolved around dinner parties and receptions with Australians, Americans and Europeans. Even her Southern Chinese genes did not seem suited to Beijing's northern climate and she thought that her skin and hair suffered as much as any other foreigner's.[25]

Chung came to think that her experience of China did not differ greatly from that of other Westerners; rather, being in China only seemed to reinforce her Australianness. She developed cravings for Western food along with Western ways: in her memoir, she recounted eating her first-ever Mars Bar in Beijing, after a sudden craving for Western junk food overcame her in a way it never had back home. Most of all, she reflected on the distance between herself and the local people, which precluded any close associations. She was scathing of the government regulations that kept foreigners 'segregated from Chinese for fear of a corrosive influence upon

China's higher Marxist morality'. With some disappointment, she concluded that 'in no other country have I raised my glass in a toast to "friendship" as often as in China … yet in no other country have I made so few friends among the local people'. Chung's experiences spoke to the sometimes alienating experience of being both Chinese and Australian, both Eastern and Western, in a rapidly changing and modernising Asia. In her apt words, this is what it felt like to be an 'Alien in the Motherland'.[26]

CONSUMING MULTICULTURALISM | After the mid-century hiatus, travel between Australia and China became easier than ever from the 1980s. Multiculturalism in Australia, the diplomatic recognition of the People's Republic in 1972 and the open-door policies implemented by General Secretaries of the Communist Party of China, Jiang Zemin, Hu Jintao and Xi Jinping, all facilitated the resumption of mobility between China and Australia. Shuttling between Australia and Asia became so common it earned a nickname: commuters were 'Astronauts' (because they lived in orbit). This group was not composed exlusively of Australians of Chinese ancestry. In the late 1970s, a large number of migrants came as 'boat people' from Vietnam; during the 1980s the Japanese came both as tourists and as settlers; from the 1990s an increasing proportion of new arrivals have come from India and Southeast Asia. Contemporary Australians have roots in all parts of the world, including every corner of Asia.

The path to multiculturalism has not been easy, nor is it complete. Voices of opposition have persisted and the sense that 'they' must adapt to 'our' way of life – which is inimical to the philosophy and policy of *multi*culturalism – continues to mark public discussion. Anxieties about the number of migrants, and Australians' willingness to tolerate ethnic and cultural differences, resurface in debates about a 'Big Australia' or about asylum seekers. Yet, while the politics remain contentious, Australian culture and the 'way of life' have become increasingly globalised. Nowhere is this reflected more clearly than in the nation's eating habits, which have come to reflect the cosmopolitan and multicultural reality of Australia's population. Chinese restaurants had burst the confines of Melbourne's Little Bourke Street by the 1970s and Thai restaurants mushroomed across Sydney from the 1980s. By the early 2000s, 'Modern Australian' cuisine came to be defined as a creative fusion of European, Asian and Mediterranean ingredients and techniques.

Cultural theorists warn against taking Australia's culinary promiscuity as a sign that it is genuinely multicultural, arguing that consuming foreign food does not necessarily mean a population will accept the less appetising aspects of other cultures.[27] But the nation's interest in food, and willingness to try different cuisines, has opened a door for non-Anglo-Australians to enter the cultural mainstream. Charmaine Solomon, born of Sri Lankan burgher parents, was one of the nation's first celebrity chefs: her *Complete Asian Cookbook*, first published in 1976, has sold over one million copies. In 2007, her contribution was recognised with a Medal of the Order of Australia. The recent outcrop of celebrity chefs has also brought a number of Australians of Asian heritage to prominence and even fame. Geoff Jansz, Kylie Kwong, Luke Nguyen and Cheong Liew, among others, have built careers introducing Asian cuisines to Australian palates.

The key to their mainstream success has lain in their hybridity and capacity to be both Asian and Australian. Their links 'back' to Asia are immensely important in lending credibility, and a number of prominent chefs have used travel and personal connection with Asia as cultural capital that enhances their authenticity and authority. Chef and author Kylie Kwong trades on her cultural hybridity, plating up contemporary Chinese cuisine from locally sourced ingredients. Her role as cultural interlocutor is premised on her being equally Australian and Chinese; in many ways she is the fulfilment of William Liu's hopes. Yet, Kwong's great-grandfather Kwong Sue Duk came to Australia in 1875; with Australian-born parents who never learnt Chinese, her cultural ties to China are far from direct when compared to more recent migrants. In an interesting reversal to Chinese children performing their Australianness during the era of Assimilation, Kwong has had to insist on her Chineseness in order to present her dishes as authentic. In promotional photographs, at book signings and on television, Kwong often wears traditional Chinese garments, such as silk robes with Mandarin collars, which are rarely worn in contemporary China. Even the chef's uniform she wears has been tailored to appear more Chinese, with a Mandarin collar and white piping sewn on a black jacket.[28] Kwong also refers to her 'full Chinese blood' in interviews, although she also insists that, in language and habits, she is more Australian.[29]

Travel is especially important as a marker of Kwong's cultural credibility. Pointing to a direct connection with China, she tells her travel stories to diners, readers and increasingly, television viewers. On her website, Kwong recounts that the inspiration for her signature restaurant Billy Kwong came during a 'life-changing trip to China' in 1999. Visiting a Shanghai-style tea-house 'really moved me' and she decided to open her own eatery 'then and there'. Since that time, she writes, she has returned many times, 'covering the length and breadth of this vast country'.[30]

As well as helping establish her credibility, Kwong's exotic blend of food and travel is an attractive product in an era of lifestyle programming. The 2007 television series *My China: A Feast for the Senses* and accompanying book was popular when it screened on ABC TV, and has won a number of publishing and industry awards since. The series followed Kwong on a journey through China, emphasising personal connections with the country she referred to as her 'homeland'. The first episode was titled 'home-coming', and in it Kwong 'returns' to her great-grandfather's village of Toishan. The psychology of returning 'home' to a place one has never been is fascinating in itself, but the popularity of Kwong's books and programs (along with those of other Asian-Australian celebrities who speak of going 'home' for inspiration, such as Luke Nguyen and Geoff Jansz) speaks to a broader context. In the cultural politics of contemporary Australia, Asia is increasingly regarded less as an unassimilable 'Other', but as a cultural influence that can enrich the Australian lifestyle.

THE IN-BETWEENERS | Travel to Asia is clearly important for those who, like Kylie Kwong, make a living by trading on their hybrid Asian-Australian identities. But what about 'ordinary' Australians of Asian heritage? What does travel to Asia mean for the many thousands of Australians, from all walks of life, who have some family connection to Asia?

As with most 'ordinary' people, few Asian-Australians look to broadcast their stories. Many simply don't think they're worth telling because they seem so ordinary. But that does not mean they're not important. Throughout this book, we have seen that individual experiences and their impact on individuals' thoughts can have a tangible impact on international relations. They shape the stories that nations tell about themselves, which have to resonate with 'ordinary' people in order to be meaningful. Those stories that are untold simply because they seem too 'ordinary' are often the most important.

I met Willa Zheng in a café in inner-city Sydney on a rainy day in November 2013. Over a couple of coffees, Willa told me her story. Born in Shanghai, she had come to Australia aged seven, in 1991. Her father had arrived as a student two years before and had been granted permanent residency in the wake of the Tiananmen Square crackdown. Two days after arriving she started at Glebe Public School in Sydney, then went on to St George Girls High School in the southern Sydney suburb of Kogarah. Her parents were determined that she should improve her English and before long her English was better than her Chinese; at home she spoke a mélange of both languages. At school Zheng didn't feel as if she belonged to any of the close-knit cliques that grouped together based on ethnic as well as cultural similarities. She didn't fit in with the Anglo kids who went out drinking on the weekends, nor the Hong Kong Chinese who spoke rapid-fire Cantonese and followed Asian pop groups, nor the Southeast Asian groups who mostly kept to themselves. As she put it, she was one of the 'in-betweeners' who floated between groups and categories.

It was nine years before Willa returned to Shanghai, but to her, 'it felt like going home'. The memory of China was still fresh, and even though she was now sixteen, she slotted easily into the carefree life she'd had before coming to Australia. She loved living with her grandparents again and visited her old primary school. A construction boom had begun and Shanghai was clearly changing – but the smell was still familiar and all the foods she had known as she was growing up were there, waiting to be rediscovered. Walking the streets with her father, it felt like she was 'reconnecting with the old version of me'. On a small television in her grandfather's Shanghai kitchen she watched the Millennium fireworks that lit up Sydney Harbour, and although it felt a bit strange to see a place so familiar from so far away, the sense of disconnection didn't worry her too much. She went to bed and woke up with the comforting feeling that, although she was beginning to feel quite Australian, she was also Chinese.

Another nine years elapsed before she returned again. This time Zheng was on her own, stopping in Shanghai on the way to a semester-long university exchange in Scotland. Although it was the height of summer, inside she wasn't feeling particularly warm. Her grandparents didn't understand English and she found she could no longer fully express herself with the vocabulary of a seven year old. Even worse, she 'just felt like the outsider'. It began the moment she walked in the door and heard her grandmother exclaim, 'the foreigner's arrived!' Her grandmother had meant it as a term of endearment, but as the days turned into weeks and the constant comments about her foreign habits and eccentric ways lost their novelty, she began to feel more and more alienated. She wanted to go out and explore the neighbourhood, but her family couldn't understand what was so interesting about suburban streets. She wanted to eat at the street stalls, but they thought she would do better to stick to a clean, air-conditioned restaurant. Things got worse when she returned on the way home from Scotland. Now it was the middle of a bitterly cold winter and, worried that she would get sick, her aunt and uncle tried to keep her at home as much as possible. Like many Chinese, they were careful about the cost of heating and showered only once a week to save on hot water. As Zheng has it, she was 'holed up in my auntie's apartment, just cold, and when you're cold your body goes into a kind of hibernation'.

It wasn't a good time, but at least she had Chinese New Year to look forward to. Zheng wanted 'the kind of fantasy New Year experience they depict in commercial ads' – vibrant street parades, sumptuous banquets, gifts and glutinous *Nian Gao* cakes. But again she was disappointed. China was not the place she thought she'd remembered, where people pulled together to create a good time. Now, Shanghai was all about money and the old sense of community didn't seem to exist any more. To tell the truth, Chinese New Year was dull and nothing like what she had hoped for, or what she remembered from her childhood. In fact, after 18 years away, she didn't really recognise much about Shanghai at all and definitely didn't feel much sense of belonging. The sense of loss was quite emotional. As Zheng reflected, 'I just felt like I wasn't Chinese at all now ... I felt like the Chinese side of me had just died'.

Zheng came back to Australia thinking that she had put China behind her, but there was one more trip to come. Her parents and grandparents became concerned that she remained unmarried despite being in her late 20s. In China, unmarried women over 27 are referred to as 'leftover women', so her family decided to take action by posting her photo and vital statistics alongside thousands of others in the matchmaking market at Shanghai's People's Park. Eventually, a suitable boy was found and in late 2012 Zheng found herself on the plane to Shanghai once again. She met her intended and after a few unexceptional dates both families seemed to think the match would work. But Zheng had begun to feel sick about the whole thing. Feeling boxed-in by the pressure to be a 'dutiful Chinese girl', she let her Australian side take over. She told her father that, given the choice, she'd rather spend her life in jail than go through with this arranged marriage. She went out every night, stumbling home reeking of alcohol at 3 am. Word trickled back to her prospective mother-in-law that she was seeing other men. Needless to say, Zheng returned to Sydney happily unmarried and with no plans to return to Shanghai anytime soon. 'My old China's gone', she says, but now without the sadness she had once felt.

You might have seen Willa Zheng on the street. She is not famous, or influential; despite her lively way of speaking and the twinkle in her eye, she doesn't stand out in a crowd. But, like many other 'ordinary' Asian-Australians her story is distinctly extraordinary. Her life has been shaped by mobility between Australia and China and she defines its meaning by her experiences of travel. The first trip 'back' was one of rediscovery and reaffirmation, which made her feel more connected to her Chinese side. The second one dramatically severed those sentimental bonds and she came back to Australia grieving for a China – and a Chinese self – that she had once known but had since lost. The third one served to confirm her choices. She couldn't be a Chinese woman any more than she could be a Chinese girl; her Western ways would reassert themselves whether she liked it or not. Not quite Chinese, but not quite Australian either, Zheng is entirely self-assured when she states that 'I'm an in-betweener'.[31]

AUSTRALIANS | A first-generation migrant, Willa Zheng must negotiate a personal connection with two places at once. Sounding, acting and feeling Australian, second- or third-generation Asian-Australians may not feel many pangs of sentiment towards the birthplace of their parents or grandparents. Many Australians of Asian heritage have not thought of Asia as 'home' but, like Australians of any ethnic background, they travel there for work or leisure. Travelling to Asia is, after all, now a normal part of being Australian.

What does this tell us about Australia and Asia? Firstly, it reveals that Asian-Australians' experiences are not always defined by their ethnicity. Being Asian in Australia is increasingly commonplace and the identities adopted by individuals become exponentially more complex. In this chapter, I have retold the experiences of people as different as William Liu, Helene Chung, Kylie Kwong and Willa Zheng under the racially determined category of 'Sons and daughters', but I could just as easily have written of them elsewhere. William Liu and Kylie Kwong's entrepreneurial connections with China fit in with other 'Fortune hunters', and Pamela Tan and Helene Chung's concerted efforts to bridge cultural misapprehension would surely qualify them as 'Good neighbours'. Willa Zheng's search for her Chinese past, and her romantic adventures, could fit in with other 'Seekers'; others were simply 'Tourists'. Individual experiences are always complex and often bridge several categories and this is no less true for Australians of Asian descent than it is for others.

Being 'Sons and daughters' of both Australia and Asia will be increasingly common in the future. Friendships, marriages and a host of other relationships will mean that those who are not 'Sons and daughters' themselves may be step-fathers or daughters-in-law, or godmothers or nephews. It will be increasingly difficult to make sense of these personal ties within a political culture that speaks of Australia's 'engagement' with Asia as if it were an entirely foreign place. As Australia moves into this future, it is important to look to 'Sons and daughters', to see how they have managed to balance East and West, and how they combined Australian values with Chinese (or Indian, or Indonesian) ones. We can also look to the roles they have adopted in Australia and abroad to see how they made sense of an identity bridging East and West, which was often crystallised in the act of travelling between the two. Australia's future is as a nation of in-betweeners; we would do well to look at how those in the same position have managed living between two nations, languages and civilisations.

# PEOPLE'S DIPLOMATS

The past few years have seen another iteration of the seemingly endless attempt to define Australia's place in the world. A common theme is the nation's lack of preparedness at the precipice of the Asian Century. Although it cuts across both parties and many media outlets, Prime Minister Julia Gillard put it most clearly when, launching the *Australia in the Asian Century* White Paper in Melbourne in 2011, she claimed that 'Australia hasn't been here before'.[1]

This book testifies that Australians *have* been here before; indeed, they have been visiting their neighbours for well over a century. Some visitors touched down for only a few hours, but other Australians have lived their entire lives in-between the two continents. Men and women, from country and city, they have come from all social and ethnic backgrounds and from every age group. They have gone there for a range of reasons – for business and pleasure, out of military or moral duty, to visit family or simply to get away from it all. Their stories can provide an insight into how a broad array of 'ordinary' Australians have approached the question of their nation's place in the world.

Travel to Asia not only reflected broader attitudes but was a catalyst that helped shift mainstream perceptions. Taken together, the chapters of this book chart a long-term process of negotiation between preconceptions, experiences and representations. Australians inevitably left home with expectations about what they would find in Asia. Many had their expectations confirmed; indeed travel could be a self-fulfilling prophecy. Those who thought of 'Asia' in strategic terms sought out political hotspots and kept an eye out for signs of political stirring, whereas those who were seeking religion, or sex, or just a place they could forget about the world found an entirely different 'Asia' in ashrams, bar strips or beach resorts. Even so, direct contact could act as a circuit breaker. First-hand experience forced some visitors to reconsider their assumptions about Asia, and about Australia's place in the region and the world. If preconceptions were challenged often enough, or if they were represented to a wide enough audience, they could generate new images and influence the preconceptions of the next wave of visitors.

Perhaps the most important single change came in the way Australians conceived of the relative distance between themselves and Asia. As the prolific Frank Clune enthused, 'there is no doubt about the aeroplane making short work of long distances' and air travel was particularly important in bringing the 'completely different world from which we have hitherto been isolated … within easy reach'. This forced a reconsideration of Australia's geographical and political place in the world, and Clune's voice was part of a growing chorus claiming that, 'thanks to air travel, the Far East has now become the Near North'.[2]

Clune was a professional travel writer, but many ordinary travellers came to a similar conclusion over the course of their own visits. In previous chapters we met William Wade, who thought of 'the East' as both geographically and mentally distant before setting off on his first visit in 1962. The experience of arriving in Asia on the same day as he had departed from home was shocking and it forced an epiphany: 'the world is sort of coming closer together in so many ways'. The logic of shrinking distances suggested that Australia could not escape more and closer contact with its regional neighbours and this made establishing good relations crucial. Seeing himself as an agent in international relations – a people's diplomat – Wade began by revising his own attitudes to the White Australia Policy as well as turning his mind to the question of broader Australian diplomatic relations with Asia.[3]

By the late 20th century, travelling to Asia had become a routine part of Australian life and sustained contact helped challenge some deeply entrenched stereotypes. In the late 1940s, journalists Robert Gilmore and Denis Warner thought that Australians would have to do lots of serious reading if they were to ever overcome their mistaken views of the 'mysterious Orient' as a place of 'snake-charmers and rope tricks, dusky maidens, Dr Fu Manchu, opium and the rest'.[4] Few Australians were voracious readers of diplomatic tomes, but decades of tourist contact had a similar effect. Images of Fu Manchu 'and the rest' became increasingly difficult to sustain as Australians came face-to-face with their neighbours. The more they travelled, the more comfortable they felt in the neighbourhood, and this drew them back again. In this feedback loop, tourism underpinned a conceptual leap that supported diplomatic engagement with Asia. At the same time, the constant mobility of Asian-Australians suggested the need to reappraise the binary categories of 'Australia' and 'Asia'.

This is not to suggest that travel was an unequivocally positive force driving towards cross-cultural understanding. The recognition of Asia's proximity could provoke anxiety and even fear, whether of falling dominoes or terrorist bombs. Moreover, while encouraging a broad logic of connection and engagement, travel and tourism have not been a one-way ticket to closer relations. As politicians and diplomats have admitted in the context of Australia and Indonesia, increased tourist contact can perpetuate mutual misperceptions, and even hamper diplomatic relations at the highest level.

Tourism can also keep colonial-era assumptions and body politics alive long after their use-by date has passed. The tourism industry is structured on the presumption of inequality: almost by definition, tourists have a surplus of cash and locals work to earn some of it. The low cost of labour in Asia and tourists' relatively high disposable income (exaggerated by holiday-time extravagance) often dramatised the gulf. The fact that so much Australian knowledge about Asia was shaped within this context could subtly extend imperial attitudes and neo-colonial assumptions. There are, of course, striking exceptions. Some well-meaning volunteers inverted colonial structures by living at a 'local' standard. Asian-Australians also experienced an entirely different power dynamic. But for many, the culture of travel worked to separate visitors from locals, and some Australians began to think of themselves as 'Europeans' or 'Westerners' in a way they may not have back home. Travel could increase the mental distance between Australia and Asia, even as it annihilated physical distance.

# AUSTRALIA'S PLACE IN ASIA | The roles assumed by Australians overseas, as covered in preceding chapters, have ranged from imperialists to sons and daughters. Each of these performances articulated an answer to the wider problem of Australia's role in relation to Asia. While we can identify some broad trends, it is impossible to reconcile all the roles adopted by travellers in Asia; indeed some of them are directly contradictory. Where some Australians attempted to project an air of imperial or cultural superiority as representatives of the white race or Western civilisation, others went as supplicants seeking to learn the wisdom of the East. Some went to try and make peace, others stirred up conflict; some went to help Asia's needy, others were interested only in securing their own advantage. Individuals could straddle two or more categories, and some changed their roles and behaviour after finding themselves in unexpected situations, or as their ideas about Asia changed. The confusion about Australia's role in the region, which saw individuals assume roles with contrasting body politics and meanings, points to the fact that Australian attitudes were never straightforward.

This is important in itself: the changeable nature of Australians' roles reflects the true complexity of the nation's international relations. Politicians, and even some historians, have cast Australian relations with Asia as a teleology, leading from fear to friendship. While it has long been assumed that Australia's destiny lies in Asia, there is no agreed endpoint towards which diplomatic policies or popular attitudes are progressing, and the intersections and contradictions that mark personal contacts reflect this basic fact. Australians have experimented with a range of roles in Asia. Recognising which roles appear appropriate to present circumstances, and understanding the political and cultural dynamics underpinning these roles, can help articulate contemporary aspirations. But the very profusion of roles and experiences should serve as a warning that Australia's relations with Asia cannot be distilled into a single catchphrase, statement or role. Any attempt to do so is bound to lack depth and authenticity and, like so many attempts to define an 'official' Australian outlook in the past, fail to convince either domestic or international audiences.

This is one reason why recognising the often-neglected history of Australian contact with Asia is so important. While Julia Gillard's 2011 statement that Australia had 'not been here before' is particularly illustrative, it stands for a much longer tradition in which past contacts and relations between Australia and Asia were ignored or elided. The myth that Australia has yet to confront the reality of its geographical position in Asia is firmly entrenched. Forgetting that many *have* been there before leaves Australians prone to yet another round of exhortations to 'Wake Up!' While there is nothing wrong with rejuvenation, this rhetoric suggests that there is no foundation from which to build future relations. The result has been a political culture that periodically attempts to face up to Asia from scratch, only to find the task so daunting that it rarely extends beyond the navel-gazing stage. While the history of Australian contact with Asia is too complex to be reduced to a simple good news (or bad news) story, or a useable past that can be applied for diplomatic purposes, recognising the rich store of previous connections is useful in that it reveals a foundation on which future discussions and policies can build.

Historians have also largely elided the extent of Australia's Asian contacts. Although there are signs that this is finally changing, mainstream Australian history is still largely written without reference to Asia; work tracing Australia's connections with its region tends to be regarded as niche and overly specialised. While this has helped produce a clean narrative of relatively self-contained national development (with a little help from England and the United States), the fact is that, at a time when more than half of all Australians are born overseas or have a parent born overseas, and almost a third of the nation heads abroad every year, this story no longer reflects the reality of the Australian nation – if it ever did. Ignoring the transnational and international connections that have helped constitute the Australian nation results in an overly simplistic and ultimately unsatisfying narrative, which fails to capture the complex reality of Australian life, and so risks irrelevance in an increasingly globalised world.

Far from being strangers to the region, Australians have been a growing presence in Asia for many years. Millions of Australians have headed to Asia and the diversity of their experiences indicates the complexity of diplomatic relations within the neighbourhood. It also points to the fact that diplomacy doesn't only take place between the official representatives of nation states; but that Australia's relations with Asia were shaped by the uncountable, and often unrecorded, experiences of ordinary Australians as they visited the neighbours.

# NOTES

## VISITING THE NEIGHBOURS

1   Richard Neville 1970, *Play Power*, Jonathan Cape, London, pp. 216–18; Richard Neville 1995, *Hippie Hippie Shake: The dreams, the trips, the trials, the love-ins, the screw ups…The Sixties*, William Heinemann, Melbourne, pp. 57–67; Tony Wheeler 1973, *Across Asia on the Cheap: A complete guide to making the overland trip with minimum cost and hassles*, Lonely Planet, Sydney, unpaginated foreword; National Union of Australian University Students 1969, *Student Travel Handbook*, NUAUS, Melbourne.
2   Data is for 2012. Australian Bureau of Statistics, *Overseas Arrivals and Departures, November 2013*, www.abs.gov.au/AUSSTATS/absé.nsf/DetailsPage/3401.0Nov%20 2013?OpenDocument, accessed 15 January 2014.
3   Department of Foreign Affairs and Trade/Newspoll 2013, *Australian attitudes towards Indonesia*, Newspoll, Sydney.
4    Edward W Said 1978, *Orientalism*, Routledge, London.
5   Edward W Said 1994, *Culture and Imperialism*, Vintage Books, New York; Arjun Appadurai 1996, *Modernity at Large: Cultural Dimensions of Globalization*, University of Minnesota Press, Minneapolis.
6   See, for example, Christopher Endy, 'Travel and world power: Americans in Europe, 1890–1917', *Diplomatic History* 22, no. 4, 1998; Christopher Endy 2004, *Cold War Holidays: American Tourism in France*, The University of North Carolina Press, Chapel Hill and London; Christina Klein 2003, *Cold War Orientalism: Asia in the Middlebrow Imagination, 1945–1961*, University of California Press, Berkeley; Richard Ivan Jobs, 'Youth Movements: Travel, Protest, and Europe in 1968', *American Historical Review* 114, no. 2, 2009.
7   David Walker 1999, *Anxious Nation: Australia and the rise of Asia, 1850–1939*, University of Queensland Press, St. Lucia. See also Alison Broinowski 1992, *The Yellow Lady: Australian Impressions of Asia*, Oxford University Press, Melbourne; Adrian Vickers, 'Australian Novels and South-East Asia, 1895–1945', *Australian Cultural History*, no. 9, 1990; Lachlan Strahan 1996, *Australia's China: Changing Perceptions from the 1930s to the 1990s*, Cambridge University Press, Cambridge.
8   Audio letters of William Wade, copy in author's possession. My thanks to Edward Duyker for the Wade recordings.
9   Mary Louise Pratt 1992, *Imperial Eyes: Travel Writing and Transculturation*, Routledge, London.
10  John Hutnyk 1996, *The Rumour of Calcutta: Tourism, Charity and the Poverty of Representation*, Zed Books, London.
11  Pratt, *Imperial Eyes*; Ann Laura Stoler, 'Rethinking Colonial Categories: European

communities and the boundaries of rule', *Comparative Studies in Society and History* 31, no. 1, 1989; Ann Laura Stoler 2002, *Carnal Knowledge and Imperial Power: Race and the Intimate in Colonial Rule*, University of California Press, Berkeley; Tony Ballantyne and Antoinette Burton (eds) 2005, *Bodies in Contact: Rethinking colonial encounters in world history*, Duke University Press, Durham and London.

12   Richard White 1981, *Inventing Australia: Images and Identity, 1688–1980*, George Allen & Unwin, Sydney.

13   Julia Gillard, 'Speech to the AsiaLink and Asia Society Lunch, Melbourne', 28 September 2011, www.pm.gov.au/press-office/speech-asialink-and-asia-society-lunch-melbourne, accessed 12 May 2012.

14   Tony Abbott, 'Address to the 2013 Sir Edward 'Weary' Dunlop Lecture', 5 December 2013, www.pm.gov.au/media/2013-12-05/address-2013-sir-edward-weary-dunlop-lecture-asialinks-chairman-dinner, accessed 3 January 2014.

15   Marilyn Lake and Henry Reynolds have recently demonstrated the transnational basis for much Australian racial thinking about Asia in the 19th and early 20th centuries. See Marilyn Lake and Henry Reynolds 2008, *Drawing the Global Colour Line: White Men's Countries and the Question of Racial Equality*, Melbourne University Press, Melbourne.

## 1:   IMPERIALISTS

1   Lake and Reynolds, *Drawing the Global Colour Line*.
2   Cindy McCreery and Kirsten McKenzie, 'Colonial Lives in a Connected Maritime World', in Alison Bashford and Stuart Macintyre (eds) 2013, *The New Cambridge History of Australia*, Cambridge University Press, Cambridge.
3   Angela Woollacott 2001, *To try her fortune in London: Australian Women, Colonialism, and Modernity*, Oxford University Press, New York; Carl Bridge, Robert Crawford, and David Dunstan (eds) 2009, *Australians in Britain: The twentieth-century experience*, Monash University ePress, Melbourne ; Richard White 1986, 'Bluebells and Fogtown: Australians' First Impressions of England, 1860–1940', *Australian Cultural History*, no. 5.
4   KS Inglis 1992, 'Going Home: Australians in England, 1870–1900', in David Fitzpatrick (ed.) *Home or Away? Immigrants in Colonial Australia: Visible Immigrants*, Division of Historical Studies, Australian National University, Canberra, pp. 105–106.
5   Agnieszka Sobocinska and Richard White, 'Travel and Connections', in Alison Bashford and Stuart Macintyre (eds) 2013, *The New Cambridge History of Australia*, Cambridge University Press, Canberra.
6   Walker, *Anxious Nation*, especially pp. 98–112; 168–180.
7   John M Mackenzie, (ed.) 2011, *European empires and the people: Popular responses to imperialism in France, Britain, the Netherlands, Belgium, Germany and Italy*, Manchester University Press, Manchester and New York, pp. 1–2; 57–89.
8   Robert Dixon 1995, *Writing the Colonial Adventure: Race, Gender and Nation in Anglo-Australian Popular Fiction, 1875–1914*, Cambridge University Press, Cambridge; Martyn Lyons and Lucy Taksa 1992, *Australian Readers Remember: An Oral History of Reading 1890–1930*, Oxford University Press, Melbourne.
9   Vickers, 'Australian Novels and South-East Asia'.
10   13 February 1929, Papers of Una Falkiner, ML MSS 423/14.
11   28 April 1928, Papers of Mabel Dowding, ML MSS 4249/8/710/c.
12   Ena Lilley cited in Ros Pesman 1998, 'Australian women encounter the East: the boat stops at Colombo', *Journal of the Royal Australian Historical Society* 84, no. 1.
13   Frank Clune 1944, *To the Isles of Spice: A Vagabond Journey by Air from Botany Bay to*

*Darwin, Bathurst Island, Timor, Java, Borneo, Celebes and French Indo-China*, Angus & Robertson, Sydney, pp. 74, 99.

14    Janey Rowe cited in Pesman, 'Australian women encounter the East'.

15    Winifred James cited in Pesman, 'Australian women encounter the East'.

16    Clune, *To the Isles of Spice*, p. 162.

17    13 February 1929, Papers of Una Falkiner, ML MSS 423/14.

18    May Tilton, cited in Walker, *Anxious Nation*; Pesman, 'Australian women encounter the East'.

19    28 April 1928, Papers of Mabel Dowding.

20    Frank Clune 1941, *All Aboard for Singapore: A Trip by Qantas Flying Boat from Sydney to Malaya*, Angus & Robertson, Sydney, p. 133.

21    28 April 1928, Papers of Mabel Dowding.

22    13 February 1929, Papers of Una Falkiner.

23    8 June 1929, Papers of Una Falkiner.

24    28 April 1928, Papers of Mabel Dowding.

25    Louise Mack 1902, *An Australian Girl in London*, T. Fisher Unwin, London.

26    James Hingston 1885, *The Australian Abroad*. William Inglis & Co., Sydney, p. viii.

27    28 April 1928, Papers of Mabel Dowding.

28    Srilata Ravi 2008, 'Modernity, Imperialism and the Pleasures of Travel: The Continental Hotel in Saigon', *Asian Studies Review* 32, no. 4.

29    Clune, *All Aboard for Singapore*, p. 134.

30    BW Higman 2002, *Domestic Service in Australia*, Melbourne University Press, Carlton, p. 45.

31    Clune, *All Aboard for Singapore*, p. 126.

32    Helen Rutledge (ed.) 1976, *A Season in India: Letters of Ruby Madden*, Fontana/Collins, Netley, South Australia, p. 67.

33    Angela Woollacott 1997, '"All This is Empire, I Told Myself": Australian Women's Voyages "Home" and the Articulation of Colonial Whiteness', *The American Historical Review* 102, no. 4.

34    Mack, *An Australian Girl in London*.

35    Rutledge, *A Season in India*, p. 51.

36    Hingston, *The Australian Abroad*, pp. 4, 16.

37    Clune, *To the Isles of Spice*, p. 187.

38    Vera Scantlebury Brown cited in Woollacott, 'All This is Empire', p. 1019;

39    Said, *Orientalism*.

40    Woollacott, 'All This is Empire'; Pesman, 'Australian women encounter the East'.

41    Clune, *To the Isles of Spice*, pp. 186–67.

42    10 June 1929, Papers of Una Falkiner.

43    Stoler, 'Rethinking Colonial Categories', Stoler, *Carnal Knowledge and Imperial Power*.

44    9 July 1929, Diary of Phillip M Chancellor, Chancellor-Stuart Field Museum Expedition to Oceania and Malaysia, 1929–1930, ML MSS 2824/0/8/522C.

45    Clune, *All Aboard for Singapore*, p. 126.

46    Clune, *To the Isles of Spice*, p. 172.

47    Before the collapse of European imperialism in Asia, only relatively marginal groups such as the Communist Party of Australia and the Theosophists provided an institutional critique of colonialism in Asia. See LC Rodd 1938, *Australian Imperialism*, Survey of Australia Series, no. 2, from material collected by the Australian Research Bureau, Modern Publishers and Importers, Sydney; Stuart Macintyre 1998, *The Reds: The Communist Party of Australia from Origins to Illegality*, Allen & Unwin, Sydney. For an account of Theosophy in Australia see Jill

Roe 1986, *Beyond Belief: Theosophy in Australia, 1879–1939*, UNSW Press, Sydney.
48  Laure Bruce Steer to Una Falkiner, 22 February 1946 and 19 February 1946; Jack Bruce Steer to Una Falkiner, 23 September 1946, Papers of Una Falkiner.
49  Hank Nelson 1982, *Taim Bilong Masta: The Australian Involvement with Papua New Guinea*, Australian Broadcasting Corporation, Sydney, p. 73.
50  Barbara Smythe Sherwood 2003, *Too long in the tropicals: a tale of Papua New Guinea in the fifteen years after World War II*, Parker Pattinson Publishing, Douglas Park, NSW, p. 33.
51  Peter Fitzpatrick 1980, 'Really rather like slavery: Law and labor in the colonial economy in Papua New Guinea', *Contemporary Crises* 4, p. 78.
52  Nelson, *Taim Bilong Masta*, p. 80.
53  Regis Tove Stella 2007, *Imagining the Other: The representation of the Papua New Guinean Subject*, University of Hawai'i Press, Honolulu, pp. 8, 90–110.
54  Frank Clune 1942, *Prowling Through Papua*, Angus & Robertson, Sydney, pp. 14–24.

## 2:  FORTUNE HUNTERS
1   Julia Gillard, 'Speech to the AsiaLink and Asia Society Lunch, Melbourne', 28 September 2011, www.pm.gov.au/press-office/speech-asialink-and-asia-society-lunch-melbourne, accessed 12 May 2012.
2   Australian Government 2012, *Australia in the Asian Century White Paper*, Government Publisher, Canberra, p. iii.
3   Campbell Macknight 1976, *The Voyage to Marege': Macassan trepangers in northern Australia*, Melbourne University Press, Melbourne; Regina Ganter 2006, *Mixed Relations: Asian-Aboriginal contact in north Australia*, UWA Publishing, Crawley, WA. Ganter's work shows that Aboriginal-Asian links were not only mercenary, but also personal and sexual.
4   McCreery and McKenzie, 'Colonial Lives in a Connected Maritime World'.
5   'Australia and the East', *Advertiser* (Adelaide), 1 May 1895, p. 5.
6   Simon Ville, 'The economy', in Alison Bashford and Stuart Macintyre (eds.) 2013, *The Cambridge History of Australia*, Cambridge University Press, Melbourne.
7   Stuart Ward, 'Sentiment and Self-Interest: The Imperial Ideal in Anglo-Australian Commercial Culture', *Australian Historical Studies* 32, no. 116 (2001).
8   'Trade with Japan', in *The Courier-Mail*, 4 January 1934, p. 10.
9   Clune, *To the Isles of Spice*, pp. 146, 226.
10  Frank Clune 1947, *Song of India*, Thacker & Co. Ltd, Bombay, p. 213.
11  Frank Clune 1939, *Sky High to Shanghai*, Angus & Robertson, Sydney; Commonwealth Bureau of Census and Statistics, *Commonwealth Year Book*, 1939, pp. 143–150.
12  Shannon L. Smith, 'Towards Diplomatic Representation', in David Goldsworthy (ed.) 2001, *Facing North: A Century of Australian Engagement with Asia, vol. 1: 1901 to the 1970s*, Department of Foreign Affairs and Trade with Melbourne University Press, Melbourne, p. 94.
13  'Australia's Future', *Geraldton Guardian and Express*, 11 July 1941, p. 5.
14  'Trade in Far East: Studebaker Official's Views', *Brisbane Courier*, 24 February 1931, p. 7.
15  'Eastern Conditions: Motor Man's Return', *Townsville Daily Bulletin*, 20 August 1932, p. 7.
16  'Dominant people: Japanese and the East', *Brisbane Courier*, 12 October 1932, p. 12.
17  'Japan and the Japanese: Some impressions of a Perth Business Man', *Sunday Times*

(Perth), 15 July 1934, p. 2.

18   'Progressive Japan, Senator Payne Impressed: China a contrast', *Advocate* (Burnie),
     7 September 1935, p. 7.
19   'Japan's remarkable progress', *Advocate* (Burnie), 13 October 1936, p. 2.
20   'East and West: Quaint contrasts in the Land of the Chrysanthemum', *Farmer and
     Settler*, 2 September 1932, p. 15.
21   'The Far East – Importance to Australia', *West Australian*, 1 November 1933, p. 17.
22   'Wool for the East, Population Wool-minded: Australia's 'Enormous Possibilities'',
     *Charleville Times*, 19 January 1934, p. 7.
23   'Trade with Japan: "Should be Increased", says Mr. Whitford', *Chronicle* (Adelaide),
     21 June 1934, p. 48.
24   'Trade with the East, Traveller's impressions: Mr. T.A. Stump's Observations',
     *Mercury* (Hobart), 11 September 1933, p. 2.
25   'East and West: Quaint contrasts in the Land of the Chrysanthemum', *Farmer and
     Settler*, 2 September 1932, p. 15.
26   'Japan and the Japanese: Some impressions of a Perth Business Man', *Sunday Times*
     (Perth), 15 July 1934, p. 2.
27   'East and West: Quaint contrasts in the Land of the Chrysanthemum', *Farmer and
     Settler*, 2 September 1932, p. 15.
28   'Eastern Conditions: Motor Man's Return', *Townsville Daily Bulletin*, 20 August
     1932, p. 7.
29   'Long hours for small pay: Conditions in the East', *Courier-Mail* (Brisbane),
     14 July 1934, p. 10.
30   'Tour of China and Japan, Mr. F.A. Wicks gives his impressions: Trade outlook',
     *Barrier Miner*, 16 May 1933, p. 2.
31   Clune, *Sky High to Shanghai*. See also Freda Barrymore, 'Books Received',
     *Townsville Daily Bulletin*, 29 September 1939, p. 9.
32   Clune, *To the Isles of Spice*, p. 149.
33   Clune, *Song of India*, pp. 252, 263.
34   Clune, *Song of India*, pp. 169–171.
35   'The varied experiences of Eastern travellers: Junk picnic', *Sydney Morning Herald*,
     22 July 1937, p. 18.
36   'Trade with the East, Traveller's impressions: Mr. T.A. Stump's Observations',
     *Mercury* (Hobart), 11 September 1933, p. 2.
37   Clune, *Sky High to Shanghai*. See also Freda Barrymore, 'Books Received',
     *Townsville Daily Bulletin*, 29 September 1939, p. 9.
38   Strahan, *Australia's China*, p. 108.
39   'Frank Clune Goes To the East', *Courier-Mail*, 23 September 1939, p. 10.
40   Clune, *Sky High to Shanghai*, pp. 348, 43.
41   Earl Albert Selle 1948, *Donald of China*, Invincible Press, Sydney, pp. 7–8.
42   Kate Bagnall, 'Crossing Oceans and Cultures', in David Walker and Agnieszka
     Sobocinska (eds) 2012, *Australia's Asia:*, pp. 121–144; Sophie Loy-Wilson, 'White
     Cargo: Australian residents, trade and colonialism in Shanghai between the wars',
     *History Australia* 9, no. 3, 2012, p. 159.
43   Loy-Wilson, 'The Smiling Professions: Salesmanship and promotional culture
     in Australia and China, 1920–1939', PhD thesis submitted to the Department of
     History, 2012, University of Sydney, p. 371.
44   Loy-Wilson, 'White Cargo', p. 155.
45   Loy-Wilson, 'The Smiling Professions', p. 363.
46   Loy-Wilson, 'White Cargo', p. 155.
47   Strahan, *Australia's China*, pp. 94–107.

48  'Tour of China and Japan: Mr. F.A. Wicks gives his impressions, Trade outlook', *Barrier Miner*, 16 May 1933, p. 2.

49  'Trade with Japan', *Australian Women's Weekly*, 5 July 1947, p. 10.

50  Tomoko Akami and Tony Milner, 'Australia in the Asia-Pacific region', in Alison Bashford  and Stuart Macintyre (eds) 2013, *The Cambridge History of Australia*, Cambridge University Press, Melbourne.

51  Roderic Pitty, 'The Postwar Expansion of Trade with East Asia', in David Goldsworthy (ed.) 2001, *Facing North: A Century of Australian Engagement with Asia*, Department of Foreign Affairs and Trade and Melbourne University Press, Melbourne, p. 220.

52  Commonwealth Bureau of Census and Statistics, *Year Book of the Commonwealth of Australia*, no. 50, 1964, p. 297.

53  Advertisement, 'Qantas to the Orient', *Australian Women's Weekly*, 30 January 1957, p. 24.

54  'Business in Japan: Green Tea and Politeness', *West Australian*, 24 November 1933, p. 4.

55  'Diary of a visit to Manila, Japan & Hong Kong, 27th October – 17th November 1963', Papers of Colin York Syme, NLA MS 6498, Box 2.

56  Audio letters of William Wade.

57  'Diary of a visit to Hong Kong, Taiwan and Tokyo 11–21 March 1970', Papers of Colin York Syme, Box 2.

58  Audio letters of William Wade.

59  Colin Simpson 1962, *The Country Upstairs*, revised and enlarged ed., Angus & Robertson, Sydney, p. 22.

60  'Japan's remarkable progress', *Advocate* (Burnie), 13 October 1936, p. 2.

61  'Dominant people: Japanese and the East', *Brisbane Courier*, 12 October 1932, p. 12.

62  'Diary of a visit to Manila, Japan & Hong Kong, 27th October – 17th November 1963', Papers of Colin York Syme, Box 2.

63  Audio letters of William Wade.

64  Colin Simpson 1962, *Asia's Bright Balconies*, Angus & Robertson, Sydney, unpaginated preface.

65  Cited in Stephen FitzGerald, 'Australia's China', *Australian Journal of Chinese Affairs*, no. 24, 1990, p. 317.

66  David Goldsworthy, 'Regional Relations', in Peter Edwards and David Goldsworthy (eds) 2003, *Facing North: A Century of Engagement with Asia; Volume 2: 1970s to 2000*, Department of Foreign Affairs and Trade/ Melbourne University Press, Melbourne, p. 141.

67  Goldsworthy, 'Regional Relations', p. 141.

68  Edmund Fung, 'Australia and China', in PJ Boyce and JR Angel (eds) 1992, *Diplomacy in the Marketplace: Australia in World Affairs, 1981–90*, Longman Cheshire, Melbourne, p. 283.

69  FitzGerald, 'Australia's China', p. 315; Strahan, *Australia's China*, pp. 304–306.

70  James Reilly and Jingdong Yuan, 'Australia's relations with China in a new era', in James Reilly and Jingdong Yuan (eds) 2012, *Australia and China at 40*, UNSW Press, Sydney, p. 6.

71  Michael Wesley 2011, *There goes the neighbourhood: Australia and the rise of Asia*, New South, Sydney, p. 8.

72  Graeme Hugo, Dianne Rudd, and Kevin Harris 2003, *Australia's Diaspora: Its size, nature and policy implications*, Committee for Economic Development of Australia, Canberra, p. 22.

73    Kevin Sinclair and Iris Wong Po-yee 1990, *Culture Shock! China*, Time Books International, Singapore, p. 5.

74    Harry Irwin 1996, *Communicating with Asia: Understanding people and customs*, Allen & Unwin, Sydney; National Centre for Language Training 2008, *Doing Business in China: A guide for Australians*, UNSW Press, Sydney; Coopers & Lybrand 1995, *Doing Business in North Asia*, Coopers & Lybrand, Sydney; Nick Dallas 2007, *How to do Business in China: 24 lessons in engaging the dragon* McGraw-Hill Australia, Sydney.

75    Gavin Crombie 2005, *The Way of the Dragon: A guide for Australians doing business in China*, Wrightbooks, Milton, p. vii.

76    Arthur Andersen & Co. 1986, *China Business Guide*, Longman, Hong Kong, foreword.

77    National Centre for Language Training, *Doing Business in China: A guide for Australians*, pp. 8–10; Crombie, *The Way of the Dragon*. See also Sophie Loy-Wilson, 'Commercial encounters: Business guidebooks and cross-cultural relations between Australia and China' in Chengxin Pan (ed.) 2014, Australia and China in the 21st century: Challenges and ideas in cross-cultural engagement, China Social Science Press, Beijing.

78    Crombie, *The Way of the Dragon*, p. 7.

79    Sinclair and Wong Po-yee, *Culture Shock! China*, pp. 8–9.

80    Sinclair and Wong Po-yee, *Culture Shock! China*, pp. 8–9.

81    Australian Government, *Australia in the Asian Century White Paper*, p. iii.

82    Reilly and Yuan, 'Australia's relations with China in a new era', p. 3.

83    Asialink, 'Developing an Asia capable workforce: a national strategy', www.asialink. unimelb.edu.au/__data/assets/pdf_file/0008/619793/Developing_an_Asia_Capable_ Workforce.pdf, September 2012, accessed 6 September 2013.

## 3:    WARRIORS

1    'Our real battle stations', *The Argus*, 28 July 1942, p. 2.

2    David Horner, Peter Londey, and Jean Bou (eds) 2009, *Australian Peacekeeping: Sixty Years in the Field*, Cambridge University Press, Cambridge, p. 7.

3    Peter Londey 2004, *Other people's wars: a history of Australian peacekeeping*, Allen & Unwin, Sydney; Christine de Matos 2008, *Imposing Peace and Prosperity: Australia, Social Justice and Labour Reform in Occupied Japan*, Australian Scholarly Publishing, Melbourne; Clinton Fernandes 2004, *Reluctant Saviour: Australia, Indonesia and the independence of East Timor*, Scribe, Melbourne.

4    Walker, *Anxious Nation*; Gregory Clarke 1967, *In Fear of China*, Lansdowne, Melbourne; Simon Philpott, 'Fear of the Dark: Indonesia and the Australian National Imagination', *Australian Journal of International Affairs* 55, no. 3, 2001; Anthony Burke 2008, *Fear of security: Australia's invasion anxiety*, Cambridge University Press, Melbourne.

5    David Dutton, 'A British Outpost in the Pacific', in David Goldsworthy (ed.) 2001, *Facing North: A Century of Australian Engagement with Asia*, DFAT/Melbourne University Press, Melbourne.

6    Antonia Finnane, 'Chinese in Australia', in Graeme Davison, John Hirst, and Stuart Macintyre (eds) 1998, *The Oxford Companion to Australian History*, Oxford University Press, Melbourne.

7    Strahan, *Australia's China*.

8    Charles Pearson (ed.) 1913, *National Life and Character: A Forecast*, Second Edition (1894, reprinted 1913) Macmillan and Co. London, p. 17.

9    Strahan, *Australia's China*.

10   David Walker, 'Shooting Mabel: Warrior masculinity and Asian invasion', *History Australia*, vol. 2, no. 3, 2005, pp. 89.1–89.11.
11   Neville Meaney 2009, *A History of Australian Defence and Foreign Policy, vol 1: The Search for Security in the Pacific,* University of Sydney Press, Sydney, pp. 1–14.
12   Robert Menzies, Transcript, www.aso.gov.au/titles/radio/menzies-speech-declaration-war/clip1/, accessed 17 June 2013.
13   'Prime Minister's Warning: Apathy to War', *Sydney Morning Herald*, 22 January 1940, p. 9.
14   'The gravest hour of our history', *Sydney Morning Herald*, 9 December 1941, p. 6.
15   Prue Torney-Parlicki, '"Fighting on the Front is Coldly Animal": Australian Press Representations of Japan during the Pacific War', in Vera Mackie and Paul Jones (eds) 2001, *Relationships: Japan and Australia, 1870s–1950s*, Department of History, University of Melbourne, Melbourne.
16   Gavin Long 1966, *The Final Campaign*, vol. 7, Australia in the war of 1939–1945, Canberra Australian War Memorial, p. 633.
17   John Barrett 1987, *We Were There: Australian Soldiers of World War II*, Viking, Ringwood, Vic., p. 53.
18   Reg Lavery, 21 October 1944, in Lavery Family Papers, Australian War Memorial, PR01487/1.
19   Barrett, *We were there*, p. 53.
20   EE Dunlop 1990, *The War Diaries of Weary Dunlop: Java and the Burma-Thailand Railway, 1943–1945,* Penguin Books, Ringwood, Victoria, p. xxv.
21   Brian Walpole and David Levell 2004, *My War: An Australian Commando in New Guinea and Borneo*, ABC Books, Sydney, p. 12; Barrett, *We were there*, p. 60.
22   Sean Brawley and Chris Dixon 2012, *Hollywood's South Seas and the Pacific War: Searching for Dorothy Lamour*, Palgrave Macmillan, New York. See also Lachlan Grant 2010, 'The AIF in Asia and the Pacific 1941–1945: a reorientation in attitudes towards Asia, Empire and Nation', PhD thesis, Department of History, Monash University.
23   Jack Lavery, 23 April 1944, in Lavery Family Papers.
24   Bob McIlree, 10 May 1941, cited in Grant, 'The AIF in Asia and the Pacific', p. 51.
25   See for example John Wyett 1996, *Staff Wallah at the fall of Singapore*, Allen & Unwin, Sydney, pp. 14–16.
26   Interview with Maxwell Venables, Australians at War film archive, Archive no. 2044, www.australiansatwarfilmarchive.gov.au/aawfa/interviews/1504.aspx, accessed 15 September 2009; Interview with Joseph Jameson, Australians at War film archive, Archive no. 1112, www.australiansatwarfilmarchive.gov.au/aawfa/interivews/1012. aspx, accessed 15 September 2009.
27   Christopher Dawson 1995, *To Sandakan: The Diaries of Charlie Johnstone, Prisoner of War, 1942–1945*, Allen & Unwin, Sydney, pp. 23–24. Dawson was one of a number of Australians who served with the RAF, rather than with Australian forces.
28   AJ Humphreys to Mrs EA Humphreys, 'Letters from the Boys', *Australian Women's Weekly*, Vol. 8, No. 25, November 23, 1940, p. 14.
29   Papers of Private Roy Maxwell Poy, Australian War Memorial: AWM PR02023, wallet 1, unpaginated memoir. All punctuation as in original.
30   Don McLaren 1998, *Mates In Hell: The Secret Diary of Don McLaren, Prisoner of War of the Japanese: Changi, Burma Railway, Japan, 1942–1945*, Seaview Press, Henley Beach, SA, p. 1.
31   Interview with Ivor White, 'Australians at War film archive', Archive no. 0144, www. australiansatwarfilmarchive.gov.au/aawfa/interviews/635.aspx, accessed 16 September 2009.

32    Wyett, *Staff Wallah at the fall of Singapore*, pp. 22, 29–30.
33    Interview with Lionel King, Australians at war film archive, Archive no. 0624, www.australiansatwarfilmarchive.gov.au/aawfa/interviews/720.aspx, accessed 15 September 2009.
34    The term 'coolies' was used in Interview with Maxwell Venables. The term 'dhobi' was used in Interview with Cyril Gilbert, Australians at War film archive, Archive no. 0821, www.australiansatwarfilmarchive.gov.au/aawfa/interviews/1939.aspx, accessed 15 September 2009.
35    Photograph, 'Calcutta, India. c. October 1945', Australian War Memorial, Negative SEA0281; 'Dhubalia, Bengal, India. 11 January 1945', Australian War Memorial, Negative SEA0110.
36    Margot Heale, 'Australia's Laughing Soldiers', *Australian Women's Weekly*, 8 March 1941, p. 9.
37    Joan Rodwell, 13 September 1945 and Howard George Barker, 1 April 1941, cited in Grant, 'The AIF in Asia and the Pacific', pp. 97–98.
38    Grant, 'The AIF in Asia and the Pacific', p. 95–98.
39    Reg Lavery, 21 October 1944, in Lavery Family Papers.
40    Adele Shelton Smith, 'Tour of Malaya: I go to curry tiffin with 400 AIF', *Australian Women's Weekly*, Vol. 8, No. 46, April 19, 1941, p. 7.
41    Adele Shelton Smith, 'Tip-Top Tucker in the Tropics', *Australian Women's Weekly*, Vol. 8, No. 47, April 26, 1941, p. 7.
42    Prue Torney-Parlicki 2000, *Somewhere in Asia: War, Journalism and Australia's Neighbours, 1941–75*, UNSW Press, Sydney, pp. 33–34; Interview with Maxwell Venables.
43    Russell Braddon 1974, *The Naked Island*, Pan Books, London.
44    Les Atkinson 2001, *My Side of the Kwai: Reminiscences of an Australian Prisoner of War of the Japanese*, Kangaroo Press, Sydney, p. 19.
45    Atkinson, *My Side of the Kwai*, p. 44.
46    Barbara Angell 2003, *A Woman's War: The Exceptional Life of Wilma Oram Young, AM*, New Holland, Sydney, p. 45.
47    Hugh V Clarke, 'Of elephants and men', in Gavan McCormack and Hank Nelson (eds) 1993, *The Burma-Thailand Railway: memory and history*, Allen & Unwin, Sydney, p. 38.
48    Agnieszka Sobocinska, 'The Language of Scars: Australian prisoners of war and the colonial order', *History Australia* 7, no. 3, 2010, pp. 59.1–59.20.
49    Cited in Christina Twomey, 'Emaciation or Emasculation: Photographic Images, White Masculinity and Captivity by the Japanese in World War Two', *Journal of Men's Studies* 15, no. 3, 2007, pp. 301–302.
50    Stan Arneil 2003 (1980), *One Man's War*, Pan Macmillan Australia, Sydney, p. 73.
51    Dawson, *To Sandakan*, p. 53.
52    Richard Lloyd Cahill in Michael Caulfield 2008, *War Behind the Wire: Australian Prisoners of War*, Hachette Australia, Sydney, p. 11.
53    Betty Jeffrey 1997, *White Coolies*, Angus & Robertson, Sydney, p. 107.
54    Angell, *A Woman's War*, p. 82.
55    John Balfe 1985, *...And Far from Home: Flying RAAF Transports in the Pacific War and After*, Macmillan, Melbourne, p. 120.
56    Braddon, *The Naked Island*, p. 283.
57    Creighton Burns (credited as Crayton Burns), 'Men of the 8th come home from Singapore', *Argus*, 20 September 1945, p. 3.
58    Twomey, 'Emaciation or Emasculation'.
59    Commonwealth of Australia Parliamentary Debates, 18 July 1945, pp. 4220–21.

60   Jeffrey, *White Coolies*.
61   Braddon, *The Naked Island*.
62   Roy Whitecross 2000 (1951), *Slaves of the Son of Heaven*, Kangaroo Press, Sydney.
63   Grant, 'The AIF in Asia and the Pacific', p. 157.
64   Reg Lavery, 6 November 1944, in Lavery Family Papers.
65   Hank Nelson, '"The Nips are Going for the Parker": the Prisoners Face Freedom', *War & Society* 3, no. 2, 1985, pp. 137–38.
66   Grant, 'The AIF in Asia and the Pacific', p. 171.
67   Dvr R Lewis (NX39104), *Salt*, vol. 11, no. 3, 8 October 1945, p. 50.
68   'O-Pip looks the world over', *Salt*, vol. 11, no. 4, 22 October 1945, pp. 18–22; see also letters from Pte PL Smith, QX44886, *Salt*, vol. 11, no. 7, 3 Dec 1945, p. 48; Sgt H Pottage, VX139386', *Salt*, vol. 11, no. 8, 17 Dec. 1945, p. 47.
69   Letters from Pte NL Rosser VX93408, *Salt*, vol. 11, no. 5, 5 Nov 1945, pp. 51–52; WO1 G Steele, VX101839, *Salt*, vol. 11, no. 5, 5 Nov 1945, p. 52.
70   Letters from Dvr M Smith, NX124188, *Salt*, vol. 11, no. 6, 19 Nov 1945, p. 51; Sgt J Ross, V215939, *Salt*, vol. 11, no. 9, 31 Dec. 1945, p. 48; Cpl FG Lynch, WX38152, *Salt*, vol. 11, no. 4, 22 October 1945, p. 48; WO1 G Steele, VX101839, *Salt*, Vol. 11, No. 5, 5 Nov. 1945, p. 52.
71   See for example, 'Letters from Our Boys', *Australian Women's Weekly*, Vol. 13, no. 12, 1 September 1945, p. 14.
72   Rupert Lockwood 1982, *Black Armada: Australia and the struggle for Indonesian Independence, 1942–49*, Hale & Iremonger, Sydney; Margaret George 1980, *Australia and the Indonesian revolution*, Melbourne University Press, Melbourne.
73   Neville Meaney 1985, *Australia and the World: A Documentary History from the 1870s to the 1970s*, Longman Cheshire Pty Ltd, Melbourne, p. 537.
74   John Thompson 1946, *Hubbub in Java*, Currawong Publishing Company, Sydney.
75   Menzies, cited in Meaney, *Australia and the World*, pp. 533–34.
76   Cited in Christopher Waters, 'War, Decolonisation and postwar security', in David Goldsworthy (ed.) 2001, *Facing North: A century of Australian engagement with Asia*, Department of Foreign Affairs and Trade and Melbourne University Press, Melbourne. p. 125.
77   See James Wood 1998, *The Forgotten Force: The Australian Military Contribution to the occupation of Japan, 1945–1952*, Allen & Unwin, Sydney; Carolyne Carter, 'Between War and Peace: the experience of occupation for members of the British Commonwealth Occupation Force, 1945–1952', PhD thesis, Australian Defence Force Academy/ University of New South Wales, 2002; Christine de Matos 2007, 'A Very Gendered Occupation: Australian women as "conquerors" and "liberators"', in *Faculty of Arts - Papers*, University of Wollongong, Wollongong; Robin Gerster 2008, *Travels in Atomic Sunshine: Australia and the Occupation of Japan*, Scribe, Melbourne.
78   John Dower 1999, *Embracing Defeat: Japan in the wake of World War II*, W. W. Norton & Company, New York, pp. 23, 203.
79   Dower, *Embracing Defeat*, pp. 73, 79, 222–23.
80   Mary Coles, 'To command Empire troops in Japan', *Australian Women's Weekly*, 4 May 1946, p. 18.
81   Cited in Wood, *The Forgotten Force*, p. 68.
82   'Personal instruction from Lt-Gen John Northcott, Commander-in-Chief BCOF', cited in Carter, 'Between War and Peace', p. 247.
83   James Wood, 'The Australian Military Contribution to the Occupation of Japan, 1945-1952', *Australian War Memorial*, Australians at War series, www.awm.gov.au/atwar/BCOF_history.pdf, accessed 20 February 2010; James Wood, *The Forgotten Force*, pp. 64–66.

84 Frank Clune 1950, *Ashes of Hiroshima*, Angus & Robertson, Sydney, pp. 27, 56.
85 de Matos, 'A Very Gendered Occupation'; Robin Gerster, 'Six Inch Rule: Revisiting the Australian Occupation of Japan, 1946–1952', *History Australia* 4, no. 2, 2007, p. 42.7.
86 Gerster, 'Six Inch Rule', p. 289.
87 Carter, 'Between War and Peace', pp. 305, 243, 229.
88 Although the exact figures of VD incidence are impossible to determine, most historians agree with Peter Bates that it was 'an extremely high rate'. Peter Bates 1993, *Japan and the British Commonwealth Occupation Force 1946–52*, Brassey's, London, pp. 103–104. For media reaction, see Wood, *The Forgotten Force*, pp. 69, 99–103.
89 Dorothy Drain, 'Air Force officers live in Jap viscount's house: Domestic staff in kimonos', *Australian Women's Weekly*, 18 May 1946, p. 17.
90 Keiko Tamura, 'Home away from Home: The entry of Japanese war brides into Australia', in Paul Jones and Vera Mackie (eds) 2001, *Relationships: Japan and Australia*, Department of History, University of Melbourne, Melbourne), p. 241.
91 Walter Hamilton 2012, *Children of the Occupation: Japan's Untold Story*, NewSouth Publishing, Sydney.
92 Allan S Clifton 1950, *Time of Fallen Blossoms*, Cassell & Company Ltd, London, Toronto, Melbourne.
93 RT Foster, 'Our Soldiers Like the Japanese', *Sunday Herald*, 20 January 1952, p. 2.
94 Colin Simpson 1956, *The Country Upstairs*, Angus & Robertson, Sydney, pp. 5–6.

## 4: GOOD NEIGHBOURS

1 Audio letters of William Wade.
2 Clune, *To the Isles of Spice*, p. 275.
3 George Johnston 1947, *Journey Through Tomorrow*, F.W. Cheshire Pty. Ltd, Melbourne, p. 6.
4 Clive Turnbull, 'White Australia: Policy and passion' in Robert J Gilmore and Denis Warner (eds) 1948, *Near North: Australia and a Thousand Million Neighbours*, Angus & Robertson, Sydney, p. 89.
5 Klein, *Cold War Orientalism*.
6 GGS Browne and ND Harper 1953, *Our Pacific Neighbours*, F.W. Cheshire, Melbourne; East Asia Christian Conference 1959, *Our Asian Neighbours: articles on the churches of East Asia*, Joint Committee of the Australian Council for World Churches and the National Missionary Council of Australia, Sydney; GT Roscoe 1959, *Our Neighbours in Netherlands New Guinea*, Jacaranda Press, Brisbane; Keith Shann 1968, *Our Indonesian Neighbours*, Syme Oration, Adelaide; Education Department of Western Australia 1970, *Northern Neighbours: a study of an Indonesian community*, Education Department of Western Australia, Perth; Gilmore and Warner, *Near North*; William Macmahon Ball 1949, *Our Thousand Million Neighbours*, Pioneers' Memorial Trust, Wangarratta.
7 Judith Brett, 'Menzies' Forgotten People', *Meanjin* 43, 1984, p. 259.
8 Publication details from PR Stephensen to Frank Clune, 17 September 1946, in Papers of PR Stephensen, ML MSS 1284, Box 3.
9 E.W. Tipping, 'Australians in the Near North', in Gilmore and Warner, *Near North*, pp. 45–46.
10 John Tebbutt, 'Frank Clune: Modernity and popular national history', *Australian Journal of Communication* 24, no. 3, 1997, p. 54; See also Tebbutt, 'The travel writer as foreign correspondent: Frank Clune and the ABC', *Journal of Australian Studies* 34, no. 1, 2010.

11   Tipping, 'Australians in the Near North', pp. 45–46.
12   Publishing figures are from Colin Simpson 1975, *This is Japan*, Angus & Robertson, Sydney, p. v; Claim is from Simpson to Isamu Igarashi, 1 April 1974, in Papers of Colin Simpson, NLA MS 5253, Folder 328. Simpson's claims are challenged by the publishing figures for Douglas Sladen's *The Japs at Home*, published in 1892, which according to David Walker, sold approximately 150 000 copies. See David Walker, 'Rising Suns', in David Walker and Agnieszka Sobocinska (eds.) 2012, *Australia's Asia*, p. 74.
13   Simpson, *Asia's Bright Balconies*; Colin Simpson 1972, *Bali and Beyond* Angus & Robertson, Sydney; Colin Simpson 1973, *Off to Asia*, Angus & Robertson, Sydney.
14   Peggy Warner 1961, *Asia is People*, F.W. Cheshire, Melbourne.
15   Klein, *Cold War Orientalism*.
16   Dymphna Cusack 1958, *Chinese Women Speak*, Angus & Robertson, Sydney; Maslyn Williams 1967, *The East is Red - The Chinese: A New Viewpoint*, Sun Books, Melbourne; Myra Roper 1966, *China: The Surprising Country*, Heinemann, London. See Agnieszka Sobocinska, 'Australian fellow-travellers to China: devotion and deceit in the People's Republic', *Journal of Australian Studies* 32, no. 3, 2008.
17   Frank Clune 1958, *Flight to Formosa*, Angus & Robertson, Sydney, p. vii.
18   Clune, *Song of India*, p. 213.
19   Angus & Robertson to Clune, 8 January 1958, Papers of PR Stephensen, Box 3.
20   'Gumleaf brought her home!' *Sydney Morning Herald*, 14 February 1963; 'She went to China for a chat', *Melbourne Herald*, 19 February 1958.
21   'Plea for more China contact,' *The Age*, 25 February 1964, p. 11.
22   Clune, *Ashes of Hiroshima*, p. pp. 37–39, 60–63, 298–99.
23   Clune, *Flight to Formosa*.
24   Strahan, *Australia's China*, p. 183. See also Eric Aarons, 'As I saw the Sixties', *Australian Left Review* no. 27, 1970, pp. 60–73.
25   'Ellen Dymphna Cusack', NAA, A6119: 1555.
26   Ailsa Zainu'ddin, 'Dragon Awakening', *Sydney Morning Herald*, 3 September 1966, p. 23.
27   Warner, *Asia is People*, p. 4.
28   Clune, *Sky High to Shanghai*, pp. 60, 167, 192, 234–35.
29   Cusack, *Chinese Women Speak*, pp. 5, 13, 48.
30   Walker, *Anxious Nation*.
31   Simpson, *The Country Upstairs*, pp. 245, 5, 8.
32   Warner, *Asia is People*, pp. 20–26.
33   Luxingshe (China International Travel Service) 1980, *The Official Guidebook of China*, Books New China, New York, p. 7.
34   Colin Mackerras and Neale Hunter 1967, *China Observed, 1964/1967*, Thomas Nelson (Australia), Sydney, p. 2.
35   John Jackson 1971, *Ping Pong to China*, Sun Books, Melbourne, p. 5.
36   Leslie Haylen 1959, *Chinese Journey: The Republic Revisited*, Angus and Robertson, Sydney, p. ix.
37   Jackson, *Ping Pong to China*, p. 7.
38   Roper, *China: The Surprising Country*, p. 2.
39   Anne-Marie Brady 2003, *Making the Foreign Serve China: Managing Foreigners in the People's Republic*, Rowman & Littlefield Publishers Inc, Lanham, Maryland.
40   Cusack, *Chinese Women Speak*, pp. 80–93.
41   'Programme', in Papers of Myra Roper, NLA MS 7711, Folder 4: Trip to China, 1974.

42    Simon Leys 1977, *Chinese Shadows*, The Viking Press, New York, p. x.
43    Meriel Wright and R Douglas Wright 1973, *China: The New Neighbour*, Tempo Books, Sydney, p. 71.
44    Cusack, *Chinese Women Speak*, p. 87.
45    Paul Fussell (ed.) 1987, *The Norton Book of Travel*, Norton, New York, pp. 15–16.
46    Clune, *Flight to Formosa*, pp. xvii–ix.
47    United Nations World Tourism Organization, *Yearbook of Tourism Statistics*, no. 41, 1988.
48    Australian Bureau of Statistics, *Year Book Australia, 1977–1978*, 702.
49    Commonwealth Bureau of Census and Statistics, *Demography Bulletin*, various editions.
50    Some of the rise in travel to Singapore can be attributed to travel by servicemen serving in the Vietnam War; however the numbers continued to rise according to trend even after the withdrawal of the last numerically significant contingent in December 1972.
51    The Australian Bureau of Statistics was restructured following the election of the Whitlam government in 1972 and data collection methods varied during this period. Data for entry to Singapore alone was collected in some years, and 'Singapore and Malaysia' in others.
52    Cited in Strahan, *Australia's China*, p. 296.
53    Jane Doulman and David Lee 2008, *Every Assistance & Protection: A History of the Australian Passport*, The Federation Press/Department of Foreign Affairs and Trade, Sydney, p. 145.
54    Interview with Kenneth Myer conducted by Heather Rusden, National Library of Australia: NLA ORAL TRC 2655.
55    'Tuesday 16th August 1955', *Travel Diary*, 1955, Papers of Joan Mavis Rosanove NLA MS 2414, Correspondence Folder.
56    Monday 24 November, 'Overseas Diary, 1958. Mr and Mrs CY Syme', in Papers of Sir Colin York Syme, 1946–1985, Box 1, 145–46.
57    Audio letters of William Wade.
58    Warner, *Asia is People*, p. 3.
59    Audio letters of William Wade.
60    Brochure, 'China and Beyond: 1979 Tours to China, USSR and Europe', Thomas Cook, Qantas, Ansett Joint Venture, 1979, Papers of Paddy Pallin, Mitchell Library, ML MSS 6016/2-4X.
61    Gordon Aldridge, 'There Are Plenty of Wongs!! But Very Little Wrong in the People's Republic of China', Unpublished manuscript, 1977, Papers of Paddy Pallin, Box 3
62    Audio letters of William Wade.
63    Tuesday 16 August 1955, *Travel Diary 1955*, Papers of Joan Mavis Rosanove, Correspondence Folder.
64    Clune, *Song of India*, p. 234.
65    'Visit Abroad (U.K. & Continent), 24 April to 20 November 1946', Papers of Colin York Syme, Box 1, 261–62.
66    Papers of Colin York Syme, Box 1, 376.
67    For a description of Wade's political views, see Edward Duyker, 'William Glen Wade (1911–1983): A biographical memoir', *Sutherland Shire Historical Society Quarterly Bulletin* 2(1995), pp. 209–13. The Democratic Labour Party had recently made support for non-European immigration a part of its platform.
68    Audio letters of William Wade.
69    Simpson, *The Country Upstairs*, p. 23.

70   25 March 1967, in 'Travel Diary 1967', Papers of Gordon Clive Bleeck, NLA MS 9149, Box 3.

71   GC Bleeck to Mr and Mrs DL Downs, 28 March 1967, in Papers of Gordon Clive Bleeck, Box 1.

72   Audio letters of William Wade.

73   Donald Horne 1964, *The Lucky Country: Australia in the Sixties*, Penguin, Melbourne, p. 100.

74   Robert C Hazell 1966, 'The Tourist Industry in Hong Kong, 1966', The Far Eastern Research Organisation for the Hong Kong Tourist Association, Hong Kong, pp. 58, 35.

75   Warner, *Asia is People*, pp. 3, 33.

76   Audio letters of William Wade.

77   6–8 November 1946, in 'Visit abroad (UK & Continent), 24 April to 20 November 1946', Papers of Colin York Syme, Box 1.

78   20 October 1968, 'Diary of Visit to New Delhi, Villa d'Este, London and Singapore', 19 October to 10 November 1968', Papers of Colin York Syme, Box 2.

79   Frank Clune 1948, *High-Ho to London: Incidents and Interviews on a Leisurely Journey by Air from Australia to Britain*, Angus & Robertson, Sydney, p. 113.

80   Mark McKenna 2011, *An Eye for Eternity: The Life of Manning Clark*, The Miegunyah Press, Melbourne, pp. 349–63; Mark McKenna, 'Turning Away from Britain: Manning Clark, History, Public Intellectuals and the End of Empire in Australia', paper presented to Sydney Sawyer Seminar: Varieties of Empire in the Antipodes', 30 October 2009, University of Sydney.

81   Horne, *The Lucky Country*, p. 7. The 18 000 copies of the first run sold out in nine days. Quote referring to the book as a publishing phenomenon from Donald Horne, 'Still lucky but getting smarter', *Age*, 28 August 2004, www.theage.com.au/articles/2004/08/27/1093518072356.html, accessed 20 May 2013.

82   Daniel A O'Brien 1958, *I Circle the Earth*, W.R. Smith & Paterson, Brisbane, p. 61.

83   Gwenda Tavan 2005, *The Long, Slow Death of White Australia*, Scribe, Melbourne, 121–28.

84   The period of 'reorientation' is identified as 'from the middle 1960s to the end of the 1970s' in David Goldsworthy et al., 'Reorientation', in David Goldsworthy (ed.) 2001, *Facing North: A Century of Australian Engagement with Asia, Volume 1: 1901 to the 1970s*, Department of Foreign Affairs and Trade/Melbourne University Press, Melbourne, pp. 310–71. See Agnieszka Sobocinska, 'Visiting the Neighbours: The political meanings of Australian travel to cold war Asia', *Australian Historical Studies*, vol. 44, no. 3, 2013, pp. 382–404.

## 5:  HUMANITARIANS

1   Meaney, *Australia and the World*, pp. 537–39.

2   Joan Hardjono and Charles Warner (eds) 1995, *In Love with a Nation: Molly Bondan and Indonesia*, Charles Warner, Picton, NSW, unpaginated preface.

3   Herb Feith, 'Molly Bondan: Pioneer, Mentor and Role Model', in Anton Lucas (ed.) 1996, *Half a Century of Indonesian-Australian Interaction*, Department of Asian Studies and Languages, Flinders University of South Australia, Adelaide, p. 8.

4   Ivan Southall 1964, *Indonesia face to face*, Lansdowne Press, Melbourne, p. 56.

5   Jemma Purdey 2011, *From Vienna to Yogyakarta: The Life of Herb Feith*: UNSW Press, Sydney, pp. 105, 172.

6   Volunteer Graduate Association for Indonesia 1962, *Living and Working in Indonesia*, Volunteer Graduate Association for Indonesia, Melbourne, p. 6.

7    Hardjono and Warner, *In Love with a Nation*, p. 109.
8    See, for example, Cliff Murray's photographs of Miss M Day, NAA: A1501, A597/1–5, and John Tanner's photographs of Miss Noela Motum and Miss Joan Minogue, NAA: A1501, A934/1.
9    Peter Russo, 'Behind the news: The students don't need advice', *The Argus*, 12 January 1956, p. 2.
10   Australian Volunteers International, www.australianvolunteers.com/index. asp?menuid=100.030 , accessed 13 November 2009.
11   Elizabeth Cobbs Hoffman 1998, *All you need is love: the Peace Corps and the spirit of the 1960s*, Harvard University Press, Cambridge, MA., p. 1.
12   Daniel Oakman 2004, *Facing Asia: A history of the Colombo Plan*, Pandanus Books, Canberra, pp. 3, 74.
13   Oakman, *Facing Asia*, pp. 74–78, 145.
14   Agnieszka Sobocinska, 'Hearts of Darkness, Hearts of Gold' in David Walker and Agnieszka Sobocinska (eds.) 2012, *Australia's Asia: From Yellow Peril to Asian Century*, UWA Publishing, Crawley, WA.
15   Paul Hasluck, 'Non-military aid to Vietnam – Decision 40, National Archives of Australia, NAA: A4940, C4641.
16   Rachel Stevens, '"Captured by Kindness": Australian press representations of the Vietnam War, 1965–1970', *History Australia* 3, no. 2, 2006, pp. 45.5–6.
17   For recent contributions to this body of criticism see Dambisa Moyo 2009, *Dead Aid: Why aid is not working and how there is another way for Africa*, Farrar, Straus and Giroux, New York and William Easterly 2006, *White Man's Burden: Why the West's efforts to aid the rest have done so little good*, Penguin Press, New York.
18   Rosemary Taylor 1988, *Orphans of War: Work with the Abandoned Children of Vietnam, 1967–1975*, William Collins Sons & Co. London.
19   CARE Australia, 'Our Mission', www.care.org.au/page.aspx?pid=1076, accessed May 2012.
20   Australian Youth Ambassadors for Development, 'What is AYAD?', www.ayad.com. au/about-ayad/what-is-ayad, accessed May 2012.
21   Ludmilla Kwitko and Diane McDonald, 'Australian Government Volunteer Program Review: Final Report', www.ausaid.gov.au/partner/pdf/volunteer_review. pdf, accessed May 2011.
22   Lillian McCombs, 'Give a little and learn a lot', *Sun-Herald*, Travel Supplement, 4 December 2005, p.14.
23   Louise Southerden, 'The Feelgood Factor', *Sun-Herald*, Travel Supplement, 11 March 2007, p. 20.
24   EM Raymond and CM Hall, 'The development of cross-cultural (mis) understanding through volunteer tourism', *Journal of Sustainable Tourism* 6, no. 5, 2008, p. 531.
25   Michael Gebicki in the *Sun-Herald*, cited in Emma Tom 2006, *Bali: Paradise Lost?*, Pluto Press, North Melbourne.
26   Michael Gebicki, 'After the wave, a battle for business', *Sun-Herald*, 30 January 2005, www.smh.com.au/news/Thailand/After-the-wave-a-battle-for-busine ss/2005/02/16/1108500134125.html, accessed 9 March 2005.
27   Paul Edwards, 'After the tsunami', *Sunday Age*, 23 January 2005, www.smh.com.au/ news/Asia/After-the-tsunami/2005/02/15/1108229995799.html, accessed 9 March 2005.
28   Tony Abbott, 'The Moral Imperative for Tourists', *Sydney Morning Herald*, 19 July 2006.
29   Rohan Geyser, cited in Marian Carroll, 'The buzz is back', *Sydney Morning*

*Herald*, 6 December 2004, www.smh.com.au/news/Indonesia/The-buzz-is-
back/2004/12/06/1107228687818.html, accessed 9 March 2005.

30   Andy Boucher, cited in Eric Unmacht, 'Kuta bounces back', *Sydney Morning Herald*, 10 July 2005, www.smh.com.au/news/indonesia/kuta-bounces-
back/2005/07/08/1120702555504.html, accessed 10 July 2005.

31   Kwitko and McDonald, *Australian Government Volunteer Program Review: Final Report.*

32   Hutnyk, *Rumour of Calcutta.*

## 6:   SEEKERS

1   Alfred Deakin 1893, *Temple and Tomb in India*, Melville, Mullen and Slade, Melbourne, pp. 77–84. See also p. 104.

2   Ipsita Sengupta, 'Entangled: Deakin in India', in David Walker and Agnieszka Sobocinska (eds) 2012, *Australia's Asia*, pp. 53, 57, 67.

3   Marie Beuzeville Byles 1962, *Journey into Burmese Silence*, George Allen & Unwin, London, pp. 9, 22, 50.

4   Theodore Roszak 1969, *The Making of a Counter Culture*, Faber and Faber, London; Julie Stephens 1998, *Anti-Disciplinary Protest: Sixties Radicalism and Postmodernism*, Cambridge University Press, Cambridge.

5   Interview with Kenneth Whisson, conducted by Barbara Blackman, 20 April 1984, Canberra. National Library of Australia: NLA ORAL TRC 1660, tape 3.

6   Jack Kerouac 1959, *The Dharma Bums*, Andre Deutsch Ltd, London; Allen Ginsberg 1970, *Indian Journals, March 1962–May 1963: notebooks, diary, blank pages, writings*, Dave Haselwood Books, San Francisco.

7   John M Steadman 1970, *The Myth of Asia*, Macmillan, London, p. 183.

8   David Jenkins 1975, *Asia Traveller's Guide*, Acme Books, Melbourne, p. 9;  David Jenkins 1976, *Asia: A Traveller's Guide*, Rigby Limited, Adelaide, p. 9.

9   Frank Palmos and Pat Price 1976, *Indonesia Do-It-Yourself*, Palmii, Melbourne, p. 4.

10   Jack Parkinson 2001, *Farewell Hippy Heaven: Rites of Way on the Overland Route*, Lothian Books, Melbourne, p. 19.

11   Timothy Leary, Ralph Metzner, and Richard Alpert 1964, *The psychedelic experience: a manual based on the Tibetan book of the dead*, Citadel Press, New Jersey.

12   Ram Dass 1971, *Be Here Now, Remember*, Lama Foundation, San Cristobal, New Mexico.

13   Cited in Stephens, *Anti-Disciplinary Protest*, pp. 49–50.

14   David Reck, 'Beatles Orientalis: Influences from Asia in a Popular Song Tradition', *Asian Music* 16, no. 1, 1985, p. 92.

15   David Tomory 1998, *A Season in Heaven: True Tales from the Road to Kathmandu*, Lonely Planet Publications, Melbourne, p. 13.

16   Australian Bureau of Statistics, 'Overseas Arrivals and Departures', various editions 1960–1976. Although the statistics do not differentiate between those travelling on the Hippie Trail and for other purposes, tourism arrival figures collected by the Indian government reveal that Australia's share as a percentage of all tourists peaked at 3.63 per cent during the early-mid 1970s, before sliding back to 1.64 per cent (roughly in keeping with the long-term average) in 1981. Many, although not all, of these would have been on the Hippie Trail. See Subas C Kumar, 'The Tourism Industry in India: Economic Significance and Emerging Issues' in Kartik C Roy and Clement A Tisdell (eds) 1998, *Tourism in India and India's Economic Development*, Nova Science Publishers Inc., Commack, N.Y., p. 28.

17    Interview with Hugh Veness conducted by Alex and Annette Hood, 15 November 2003, Canberra. National Library of Australia, NLA ORAL TRC 4864/35, tape 5.

18    Jeffrey Mellefont to Agnieszka Sobocinska, 9 August 2006.

19    Interview with Yeshe Khadro conducted by Sean O'Brien for ABC Radio, March 2009, copy in author's possession.

20    Nicholas Ribush, 'On Becoming a Monk', www.lamayeshe.com/about/articles/monk.shtml, accessed 6 October 2006.

21    Interview with Kenneth Whisson, tape 4.

22    Jeffrey Mellefont to Agnieszka Sobocinska, 9 August 2006.

23    Interview with Abigayle Carmody, conducted by Agnieszka Sobocinska, Melbourne, 11 May 2011, copy in author's possession.

24    Australian Broadcasting Corporation, Compass, 'Whatever happened to…the Hare Krishnas', www.abc.net.au/compass/s3795750.htm, accessed 13 November 2013.

25    Interview with Abigayle Carmody.

26    Roland Barthes 1983, *The Fashion System*, trans. Matthew Ward and Richard Howard,  Hill and Wang, New York, pp. 27–33.

27    James Buzard 1993, *The Beaten Track: European Tourism, Literature and the Ways to 'Culture' 1800–1918*, Oxford University Press, Oxford, pp. 1–17.

28    Jeffrey Mellefont to Agnieszka Sobocinska, 9 August 2006.

29    Neville, *Play Power*, p. 208.

30    Neville, *Hippie Hippie Shake*, p. 59.

31    This irony lay at the heart of the counterculture, which had a complex relationship with capitalism. Thomas Frank 1997, *The Conquest of Cool: Business Culture, Counterculture and the rise of hip consumerism*, University of Chicago Press, Chicago and London.

32    Interview with Abigayle Carmody.

33    Wheeler 1973, *Across Asia on the Cheap*, p. 2.

34    Interview with Max Pam conducted by Sean O'Brien for ABC Radio, March 2009, copy in author's possession.

35    Richard Bernstein 2009, *The East, the West, and Sex: A history of erotic encounters*, Alfred A. Knopf, New York; Ian Littlewood 2001, *Sultry Climates: Travel and Sex*, Da Capo Press, Cambridge, MA.

36    Hsu-Ming Teo 2012, *Desert Passions: Orientalism and Romance Novels*, University of Texas Press, Austin.

37    See Walker, 'Rising Suns', Walker, 'Shooting Mabel'.

38    Broinowski, *The Yellow Lady: Australian Impressions of Asia*, pp. 105–107.

39    Adrian Vickers 1989, *Bali: a paradise created*, Penguin Books, Melbourne, pp. 2–3.

40    Clune, *To the Isles of Spice*, p. 317.

41    Richard White, 'Sun, Sand and Syphilis: Australian Soldiers and the Orient: Egypt 1914', *Australian Cultural History*, no. 9, 1990, pp. 49–54.

42    Interview with Ivor White.

43    Ian Grant 1992, *A Dictionary of Australian Military History*, Random House, Sydney, p. 381.

44    'The Frontier of Freedom', unpublished manuscript in Papers of John S Gibson, AWM MSS 1045; Robin Harris, 'The New Breed', in Keith Maddock (ed.) 1991, *Memories of Vietnam*, Random House, Sydney, p. 38.

45    Robin Harris, 'The New Breed', in Maddock, *Memories of Vietnam*, p. 34.

46    Agnieszka Sobocinska, '"Two Days' Rest in the City of Sin": Australian Soldiers on R & R in Vietnam', in *Conference Proceedings: Resorting to the Coast: Tourism, Heritage and Cultures of the Seaside*, ed. Daniela Carl and Domenico Colasurdo (Leeds: Centre for Tourism and Cultural Change, 2009).

47    See, for example, 'Vietnam, 1966-05-26', AWM FOR/66/0421/VN and William
      Alexander Errington, 'Vung Tau, South Vietnam, 11/1968', AWM ERR/68/0998/VN.

48    Figures are from Gary McKay 1998, *In Good Company: One man's war in Vietnam*,
      Allen & Unwin, Sydney, p. 103.

49    McKay, *In Good Company*, p. 102; 'Bob' in Interview with Tom Molomby, Peter
      Hamilton and Others, 1 January 1971, NLA ORAL TRC 0245.

50    'National Service Experience in Vietnam', in Papers of Mike Fernando, AWM PR
      91/180; 'Vietnam 1962–71' in Papers of R Andrews and T Pleace, AWM MSS 1288.

51    'Vietnam 1962–71' in Papers of R Andrews and T Pleace, AWM MSS 1288.

52    'The Frontier of Freedom', unpublished manuscript in Papers of John S Gibson,
      AWM MSS 1045, p. 478.

53    Graeme Mann 2006, *The Vietnam War on a Tourist Visa*, Mini Publishing, Sydney,
      p. 17.

54    Incident recounted in 'The Frontier of Freedom', unpublished manuscript in Papers
      of John S Gibson.

55    Papers of Peter W Groves, AWM PR 86/248, Folder 3.

56    'National Service Experience in Vietnam', in Papers of Mike Fernando, AWM PR
      91/180.

57    Interview with Sandy MacGregor (Engineers 1 RAR): Archive 2584,
      www.australiansatwarfilmarchive.gov.au/aawfa/interviews/2044.aspx, accessed
      15 December 2008.

58    Interview with Phil Baxter (4RAR, 6RAR): Archive 2580, www.
      australiansatwarfilmarchive.gov.au/aawfa/interviews/2041.aspx, accessed
      15 December 2008.

59    Interview with Sandy MacGregor.

60    Robin Gerster, 'Asian Destinies/Destinations: The Vietnam Tour', *Australian Studies*
      10, 1996, pp. 61–69.

61    Cited in Gerster, 'Asian Destinies/Destinations' p. 65.

62    Stan Sutherland 2007, *In This Man's Army: A Vietnam War Memoir*, Self-published,
      Yackandandah, Victoria, p. 133.

63    Papers of Jason Neville (Gnr 105th Field Battery), AWM PR 91/069. All spelling
      and grammar as in the original.

64    Interview with Max Pam.

65    Neville, *Play Power*, pp. 208–209.

66    Jenkins, *Asia: A Traveller's Guide*, p. 288.

67    Bill Dalton 1974, *Travellers' Notes: Indonesia*, Moon Publications/ Tomato Press,
      Sydney, pp. 19–20.

68    Wheeler 1973, *Across Asia on the Cheap*, p. 43.

69    Richard White, 'The Retreat from Adventure: Popular Travel Writing in the 1950s',
      *Australian Historical Studies* 28, no. 109, 1997, p. 104.

70    Simpson, *The Country Upstairs*, pp. 25–35, 58–66, 137–39.

71    Simpson, *Asia's Bright Balconies*, pp. 87–94.

72    Simpson, *Off to Asia*, pp. 41–44, 153–58.

73    Ronald McKie 1972, *Singapore*, Angus & Robertson, Sydney, p. 112.

74    For example, see Rana Kabbani 1986, *Europe's Myths of Orient*, Indiana University
      Press, Bloomington; Martin Oppermann, 'Sex Tourism', *Annals of Tourism Research*
      26, no. 2, 1999; Erik Cohen, 'Lovelorn farangs: the correspondence between foreign
      men and Thai girls', *Anthropological Quarterly* 59, no. 3, 1986; Erik Cohen 1996,
      *Thai Tourism: Hill Tribes, Islands and Open-Ended Prostitution*, White Lotus Press,
      Bangkok; Thanh-Dam Truong 1990, *Sex, Money and Morality: Prostitution and
      Tourism in Southeast Asia*, Zed Books, London; David Leheny, 'A Political Economy

of Asian Sex Tourism', *Annals of Tourism Research* 22, no. 3, 1995.

75    Nelson Graburn 1983, 'Tourism and prostitution', *Annals of Tourism Research*, vol.10, no. 3, pp. 437–56.

76    Chris Berry, 'Denis O'Rourke's Original Sin: *The Good Woman of Bangkok*, or "Is this what they mean by 'Australia in Asia'?"', in Chris Berry, Annette Hamilton, and Laleen Jayamanne (eds) 1997, *The Filmmaker and the Prostitute: Denis O'Rourke's The Good Woman of Bangkok*, Power Institute of Fine Arts, Sydney.

77    Craig Scutt, 'Love thy neighbour: Australia's shameful fetish', *Griffith Review*, no. 22, 2008.

78    Janet De Neefe 2003, *Fragrant Rice: my continuing love affair with Bali*, Flamingo, Sydney, pp. 15–17, 24.

79    Cowboys in Paradise, www.cowboysinparadise.com/, accessed 14 November 2013.

## 7:   ADVENTURERS AND TROUBLEMAKERS

1    GE Morrison 1895, *An Australian in China: being the narrative of a quiet journey across China to British Burma*, Horace Cox, London, pp. 1–2; 223–28.

2    Dixon, *Writing the Colonial Adventure*.

3    Dixon, *Writing the Colonial Adventure*.

4    Interview with Max Pam.

5    Peter Jeans 1998, *Long Road to London*, Rawlhouse Publishing, Perth, p. xv.

6    Frances Letters 1968, *The Surprising Asians: A hitch-hike through Malaya, Thailand, Laos, Cambodia and South Vietnam*, Angus & Robertson, Sydney, p. v.

7    Jeffrey Mellefont to Agnieszka Sobocinska, 9 August 2006.

8    Interview with Max Pam.

9    *The Australian*, 5 August 1972, pp. 17–18.

10   Mandy Johnson 2005, *Family, Village, Tribe: The story of Flight Centre Limited*, Random House Australia, Sydney, p. 18.

11   Tony Wheeler and Maureen Wheeler 2005, *Once While Travelling: The Lonely Planet story*, Viking Press, Melbourne, p. 9.

12   'Options: a comprehensive range of new travel ideas for the under 35s', Jetset Tours Student Travel, 1st Edition, March 1981, in 'Ephemera – Tourism', (Mitchell Library), Box 29.

13   Jenkins, *Asia Traveller's Guide*, p. 9.

14   Wheeler 1973, *Across Asia on the Cheap*, p. 14.

15   Wheeler and Wheeler, *Once While Travelling*, p. 17.

16   Wheeler 1973, *Across Asia on the Cheap*, p. 16.

17   Wheeler and Wheeler, *Once While Travelling*, p. 16

18   Frances Letters 1971, *People of Shiva: Encounters in India*, Angus & Robertson, Sydney, p. 166.

19   See 'Easing the hippies out of their Himalayan haven', *Sydney Morning Herald*, 25 July 1974, p. 6.

20   Neville, *Play Power*, p. 210.

21   Dennis Altman 1979, *Coming Out in the Seventies*, Wild and Woolley, Sydney, p. 172.

22   Wheeler and Wheeler, *Once While Travelling*, p. 16.

23   Richard Neville, 'Go East Young Punk', *Oz*, July 1966, p. 10.

24   Jenkins, *Asia Traveller's Guide*, p. 9.

25   Neville, *Play Power*, pp. 305–306. See Agnieszka Sobocinska, 'Following the "hippie sahibs": Colonial cultures of travel and the Hippie Trail', *Journal of Colonialism and Colonial History*, vol. 15, no. 2, Summer 2014.

26   Tomory, *A Season in Heaven*, p. 13.

27 Interview with Abigayle Carmody.
28 Nikki Keddie 2006, *Modern Iran: Roots and Results of Revolution*, 3rd ed., Yale University Press, New Haven, esp. p. 223; Martin Ewans 2002, *Afghanistan: A short history of its people and politics*, HarperCollins Publishers, New York, p. 207.
29 Tribhuwan Kapur 1981, *Hippies: a study of their drug habits and sexual customs*, Vikas Publishing House, New Delhi, p. 3.
30 Bob Hobman, 'World Hippies find new Eastern paradise: Goa', *Times of India*, 9 March 1969.
31 Petri Hottola 2002, 'Amoral and Available? Western Women Travellers in South Asia', *Gender/Tourism/Fun*, p. 168.
32 Reported in Bob Hobman, 'World Hippies find new Eastern Paradise: Goa', *Times of India*, 9 March 1969.
33 Interview with Abigayle Carmody; Tomory, *A Season in Heaven*, p. 155.
34 Benarsi Das Kumar to *Times of India*, 24 November 1967, p. 8.
35 'Interim Notice No. 31: 19 November 1972', in *Qantas Travel Handbook*, Qantas Airways Ltd, Sydney, 1972.
36 'Interim Notice No. 3/72: 8 February 1972', in *Qantas Travel Handbook*; Richard Rawson, ed. 1976, *On Your Own: Air Siam's Student Guide to Asia*, Volunteers in Asia, Inc, Stanford, CA, pp. 7–8.
37 Tony Wheeler 1975, *Across Asia on the Cheap: A complete guide to making the overland trip with minimum cost and hassles*, 2nd ed., Lonely Planet, Melbourne, pp. 33–34.
38 Wheeler and Wheeler, *Once While Travelling*, p. 20.
39 Ewans, *Afghanistan*, p. 207.
40 Keddie, *Modern Iran*, p. 223.
41 Frances Letters 1971, *People of Shiva: Encounters in India*, Angus & Robertson, Sydney, pp. 10–60.
42 Interview with Yeshe Khadro.
43 Hamish McDonald, 'Tougher line by Indonesia over drugs', *Sydney Morning Herald*, 12 November 1976, p. 7; Neil Kelly, 'Australian drug trafficker faces death by machinegun', *Sydney Morning Herald*, 22 October 1985, p. 22.
44 John Schwartz, 'Pot and Prejudice: Australian media coverage of the Corby saga', *Metro*, no. 145, 2006.
45 Graeme MacRae, 'Fear and Loathing in our own holiday paradise: the strange tale of Schapelle Corby (et al.)', *Australian Journal of Anthropology* 17, no. 1, 2006, p. 80.
46 Stephen Crofts, 'Media Constructions of the Schapelle Corby trial: populism versus multiculturalism', *Australian Journal of Communications* 33, no. 2/3, 2006.
47 'Jackie' cited in Farah Farouque and Liz Gooch, 'The Bali Backlash', *Age*, 31 May 2005. See also 'The agony of a young woman and her family', *Canberra Times*, 5 February 2005; Bille Chatfield, 'Schapelle could be anyone's child, so support her', *Gold Coast Bulletin*, 10 March 2005, p. 56. All public submissions to radio, newspapers and websites cited are reproduced under the alias they were posted, and reproduced with original grammar and spelling.
48 See Philip Cornford, 'Weighing the evidence', *Sydney Morning Herald*, 5 March 2005; Nick Squires, 'Tourist's drug case plea', *Daily Telegraph*, 29 April 2005, p. 19; Cindy Wockner, 'Schapelle Corby's Holiday in Hell', *Herald-Sun*, 21 May 2005, p. 31; Tony Wilson, 'Waiting game weighing on Schapelle', *Gold Coast Bulletin*, 8 January 2005; Paul Weston, 'Going by the board: friend tells of dope-charge surfer's cleanskin lifestyle', *Sunday Mail*, 13 March 2005, p. 13.
49 Terry Wilson, 'Bali drug allegations just don't add up', *Gold Coast Bulletin*, 27 October 2004, p. 23.

50   Sharon Vogel, 'Do something to save Schapelle', *Gold Coast Bulletin*, 8 March 2005,
     p. 14.
51   Tony Wilson 2008, *Schapelle: the facts, the evidence, the truth*, New Holland, Sydney,
     p. 10.
52   Brad in 'Schapelle Corby – Messages of Support', *Gold Coast Bulletin*, 14 May 2005.
53   Lachlan McEachran, in *The Corby Trial: Have your say*, www.news.ninemsn.com.au/
     article.aspx?id=63349, accessed 8 February 2008.
54   Glen Hogan in 'Schapelle Corby – Messages of Support', *Gold Coast Bulletin*,
     14 May 2005; Anonymous in 'Schapelle Corby – Messages of Support', *Gold Coast
     Bulletin*, 14 May 2005; Catherine in 'Schapelle Corby: Your reaction to the verdict',
     *Gold Coast Bulletin*, 1 June 2005.
55   Brad, in 'Schapelle Corby: Your reaction to the verdict', *Gold Coast Bulletin*,
     30 May 2005; Anonymous in 'Schapelle Corby: Your reaction to the verdict', *Gold
     Coast Bulletin*, 30 May 2005.
56   M Howitt in 'Schapelle Corby: Your reaction to the verdict', *Gold Coast Bulletin*,
     30 May 2005; Anonymous in 'Schapelle Corby: Your reaction to the verdict', *Gold
     Coast Bulletin*, 1 June 2005.
57   Paul, in 'Schapelle Corby: your reaction to the verdict', *Gold Coast Bulletin*,
     30 May 2005; Anonymous, 'TXT: Schapelle Corby your reaction to the verdict',
     *Gold Coast Bulletin*, 1 June 2005.
58   Anonymous in 'Schapelle Corby: Your reaction to the verdict', *Gold Coast Bulletin*,
     30 May 2005. See also Adrian Vickers, 'A paradise bombed', *Griffith Review*, no. 1,
     2003.
59   Cited in 'Bali travel boycott threat', *Daily Telegraph*, 28 May 2005.
60   Anonymous in 'TXT Schapelle Corby: Your reaction to the verdict', *Gold Coast
     Bulletin*, 1 June 2005.
61   Sarah, in 'Schapelle Corby: Messages of Support', *Gold Coast Bulletin*, 14 May 2005.
62   Carmel S in 'Schapelle Corby: Messages of support', *Gold Coast Bulletin*, 14 May
     2005.
63   Lata Sharma in 'Schapelle Corby: your verdict', *Townsville Bulletin*, 21 May 2005.
64   The quotes 'those corrupt Indos' and 'unsafe place' come from two separate
     anonymous posts, and 'rat infested country' is from a post from 'Karin', published
     in 'Schapelle Corby: Messages of Support, *Gold Coast Bulletin*, 14 May 2005.
65   Shannon McLure in Greg Stoltz, 'Boycott Bali, says former boyfriend', *Hobart
     Mercury*, 30 May 2005.
66   John P Hannon in 'Schapelle Corby: your verdict', *Townsville Bulletin*, 31 May
     2005.
67   Musos & oz home4corby in 'Schapelle Corby: your reaction to the verdict', *Gold
     Coast Bulletin*, 20 May 2005.
68   Stephen Davies in 'Schapelle Corby: Messages of support', *Gold Coast Bulletin*,
     14 May 2005.
69   David in 'The People's Verdict: Schapelle Corby: Fight for justice', *Daily Telegraph*,
     30 May 2005.
70   Aileen Tattersall, in *The Corby Trial: Have Your Say*, www.news.ninemsn.com.au/
     article.aspx?id=63349, accessed 8 February 2008.
71   Chrispy in 'Schapelle Corby: Your reaction to the verdict', *Gold Coast Bulletin*,
     30 May 2005.
72   Anonymous, and Wil, in 'Schapelle Corby: Messages of Support', *Gold Coast
     Bulletin*, 14 May 2005.
73   Chris Brock, in 'TXT Schapelle Corby: Your reaction to the verdict', *Gold Coast
     Bulletin*, 31 May 2005.

74 Andrew MacIntyre, 'Powdered fear and hate', *Australian*, 3 June 2005.
75 Adrian Vickers, 'Jemaah Korbyah: Another low in Australian-Indonesian Relations', *Asian Currents* June 2005: www.coombs.anu.edu.au/SpecialProj/ASAA/asian-currents-archive/asian-currents-05-06.html, accessed 3 February 2008.
76 Cited in Derek McDougall and Kingsley Edney, 'Howard's Way? Public opinion as an influence on Australia's engagement with Asia, 1996–2007', *Australian Journal of International Affairs* 64, no. 2, 2010, p. 217.
77 Marianne Hanson, 'Issues in Australian Foreign Policy, January to June 2005', *Australian Journal of Politics and History* 51, no. 4, 2005, p. 571.
78 'Model of Innocence', *Cairns Post*, 23 August 2005, p. 10.
79 Stephen Fitzpatrick, 'Back to Bali', *Weekend Australian Magazine*, 7–8 February 2009, p. 13.
80 'Asia's deadly drug trap', *Hobart Mercury*, 27 August 2005, p. 25; Erin O'Dwyer, 'A hell away from home', *Sunday Age*, 9 October 2005, p. 11.
81 Sian Powell, 'New face of a Bali drug nightmare', *Australian*, 23 August 2005, p. 3.
82 Ellen Connolly, 'How dealers target Australians – Naive tourists fall prey to Bali's flourishing drug trade as police hunt their next prize trophy', *Sunday Telegraph*, 28 August 2005, p. 4.
83 Tim Lindsey, cited in Erin O'Dwyer, 'The truth behind bars', the *Sun-Herald*, 9 October 2005, p. 56.
84 Ivan Cook 2006, *Australia, Indonesia and the World: Public Opinion and Foreign Policy*, Lowy Institute for International Policy, Sydney.
85 Department of Foreign Affairs and Trade/Newspoll, *Australian attitudes towards Indonesia*, pp. 3–12.

## 8: TOURISTS

1 United Nations World Tourism Organization, *Tourism Highlights*, 2011 edition, www.mkt.unwto.org/sites/all/files/docpdf/unwtohighlights11enhr.pdf, accessed 12 November 2012; Sobocinska and White, 'Travel and Connections'.
2 Brochure, 'Hong Kong Adventure – Entertainments, Festivals, Shopping, Food, Fun', Hong Kong Tourist Association, 1969 in Mitchell Library Ephemera Collection – Tourism, Box 29.
3 Editorial, 'Trade with Japan', *Australian Women's Weekly*, 5 July 1947, p. 10.
4 ABS, 'Overseas Arrivals and Departures, Short-term movement, Resident departures, Selected Destinations – Original' dataset, January 2014 release, www.abs.gov.au/Ausstats/absé.nsf/0/C5717BACF2EA231ACA25751A0019DBB7?OpenDocument. accessed 3 April 2014.
5 Gillian Kenny, '"Our Travellers" out there on the Road: *Lonely Planet* and its Readers, 1973–1981', *Journal of Australian Studies*, no. 72, 2002; Peter Welk, 'The Lonely Planet Myth: "Backpacker Bible" and "Travel Survival Kit"', in Kevin Hannam and Irena Atelejevic (eds) 2008, *Backpacker tourism: concepts and profiles*, Channel View Publications, Clevedon; Jeff Jarvis, 'Yellow Bible Tourism: Backpackers in South East Asia', in Brad West (ed.) 2005, *Down the Road: Exploring backpacker and independent travel*, API Network, Perth.
6 ABS, *Overseas Arrivals and Departures*, dataset, January 2014 release.
7 Clune, *To the Isles of Spice*, pp. 308–313.
8 Alexander Macdonald, 'Bali revisited – still island of escape', *Sydney Morning Herald*, 17 May 1971, p. 27.
9 Wheeler and Wheeler, *Once While Travelling*, pp. 20–27.

10    Wheeler 1973, *Across Asia on the Cheap*, p. 35.

11    The numbers rose some 1200% from 1974 to 1994. ABS, *Overseas Arrivals and Departures and Australian Yearbooks*, various editions.

12    Vickers, *Bali: a paradise created*, p. 187.

13    Tony Wheeler and James Lyon 1992, *Bali & Lombok – a travel survival kit*, 4th ed., Lonely Planet, Melbourne, pp. 118, 145; Lynne Maree Smith 1995, *Bali at Cost*, Little Hills Press, Sydney, p. 128.

14    Chris Johnston, 'A Bar called BALI', *Sunday Age*, 17 May 1998, p. 6.

15    Qantas Holidays, 'Bali Troppo Zone 1993/1994', advertising brochure; Garuda Indonesia, 'Bali Ocean Blue Club, for 18–35s', 1988/89 and 1993/94. My thanks to Adrian Vickers for these sources.

16    Wheeler and Lyon, *Bali & Lombok – a travel survival kit*, p. 133.

17    Tony Wheeler 1977, *South-East Asia on a Shoestring*, Lonely Planet Publications, Melbourne, p. 209; Bill Dalton 1977, *Indonesia Handbook*, Moon Publications, Michigan, p. 209; 'Gazza' cited in Johnston, 'A bar called BALI', *Sunday Age*, 17 May 1998, p. 6.

18    Walker, *Anxious Nation*; Strahan, *Australia's China*; See also Philpott, 'Fear of the Dark: Indonesia and the Australian National Imagination'.

19    Clune, *To the Isles of Spice*, p. 316; Ronald McKie and Beryl Bernay 1969, *Bali*, Angus & Robertson, Sydney, p. 7. See also Vickers, *Bali: a paradise created*.

20    Phil Jarratt, 'Bali with a touch of Java', *Detours: the Qantastic alternative travel magazine*, no. 1, November 1977, p. 23.

21    Chris Johnston, 'A Bar called BALI', *Sunday Age*, 17 May 1998, p. 6.

22    Greg Lenthen, 'Bali highest on list of Australians' favourite playgrounds', *Sydney Morning Herald*, 1 October 1998, p. 3; 'home away from home' was a quote from one Australian tourist interviewed by Johnston, see 'A Bar called BALI', *Sunday Age*, 17 May 1998, p. 6; Academic Annette Hamilton declared Bali 'another State of Australia' in Annette Hamilton, 'Fear and Desire: Aborigines, Asians and the National Imaginary', *Australian Cultural History*, no. 9, 1990.

23    Gerard Lee 1990, *Troppo Man*, University of Queensland Press, St Lucia, Queensland, p. 3. See also Inez Baranay 1992, The edge of Bali, Angus & Robertson, Sydney; Graham Huggan 1997, 'The Australian Tourist Novel', in Maryanne Dever (ed.) *Australia and Asia: cultural transactions*, University of Hawai'i Press, Honolulu.

24    Chris Johnston, 'A Bar called BALI', *Sunday Age*, 17 May 1998, p. 6.

25    Cited in Deborah McIntosh, 'True Blue to Bali', *Sun-Herald*, Travel supplement, 19 January 1997, p. 78.

26    Mike Robinson 2001, 'Tourism Encounters: Inter and Intra-Cultural Conflicts and the World's Largest Industry', in Nezar AlSayyad (ed.) *Consuming Tradition, manufacturing heritage: global norms and urban forms in the age of tourism*, Routledge, London, p. 43.

27    John Howard, 'Transcript of the Prime Minister the Hon John Howard MP address to memorial service, Australian consulate, Bali', 17 October 2002, www.pandora.nla. gov.au/pan/10052/20021121-0000/www.pm.gov.au/news/speeches/2002/speecj1929. htm, accessed 14 July 2009.

28    E Ellis, 'Strangers who saw Paradise', *Australian*, 22 October 2002, cited in Robert Schutze, 'Terror in "our backyard": negotiating "home" in Australia after the Bali bombings', *Crossings*, vol. 8, no. 1, 2003.

29    'Aimed right at Australia's heart', *Gold Coast Bulletin*, 17 October 2002, p. 20.

30    Commonwealth of Australia, *Parliamentary Debates*, 22 October 2002, p 8327; Commonwealth of Australia, *Parliamentary Debates*, 14 October 2002, p. 7501.

31    Michael Hitchcock and I Nyoman Darma Putra 2007, *Tourism, Development and*

*Terrorism in Bali*, Ashgate, Hampshire, UK, pp. 141–45.

32  Martin Hirst and Robert Schutze, 'Duckspeak Crusader: Greg Sheridan's unique brand of seculo-Christian morality', *Overland*, no. 176, 2004, pp. 18–25.

33  Beate Josephi, 'Expressing concern: Australian press reporting of the Bali bomb blasts', *Australian Journalism Review* 26, no. 1, 2004, pp. 59–60; Jeff Lewis and Sonya de Masi, 'Unholy Wars: Media Representations of the First Bali Bombings and Their Aftermath', *Media International Australia*, no. 122, 2007, pp. 59–72.

34  Sid Sidebottom cited in Commonwealth of Australia, *Parliamentary Debates*, 22 October 2002, pp. 8332–3; Australian Federal Police, *Bali Bombings 2002*, www.afp. gov.au/international/operations/previous_operations/bali_bombings_2002, updated 2 May 2006, accessed 6 February 2008; Department of Foreign Affairs and Trade 2004, *Transnational Terrorism: The threat to Australia*, National Capital Printing, Canberra; Department of Foreign Affairs and Trade, *Transnational Terrorism: The Threat to Australia Information Sheet 2: Why Australia is a Terrorist Target*, www.dfat.gov.au/ publications.terrorism/is2.html, updated 15 July 2004, accessed 8 February 2008; Damien Hale, 'Anniversary of the Bali Bombing', 15 October 2008, www.damianhale. alp.org.au/news/1008/speeches15-01.php, accessed 30 July 2010.

35  Brad West, 'Collective memory and crisis: the 2002 Bali bombing, national heroic archetypes and the counter-narrative of cosmopolitan nationalism', *Journal of Sociology* 44, no. 4, 2008; Jeff Lewis, 'Paradise defiled: the Bali bombings and the terror of national identity', *European Journal of Cultural Studies* 9, no. 2, 2006; Vickers, 'A paradise bombed'; John Howard cited in Michael Gordon, '50 days beyond Bali', *Age*, Insight Section, 30 November 2002, p. 1.

36  John Howard cited in Alan Atkinson 2002, *Three weeks in Bali: A personal account of the Bali Bombing*, ABC Books, Sydney, p. 97; John Howard, 'Transcript of the Prime Minister the Hon John Howard MP, National Memorial Service Reflection, The Great Hall, Parliament House', 24 October 2002, www.pandora.nla.gov.au/ pan/10052/20021121-0000/www.pm.gov.au/news/speeches/2002/speech1941.htm, accessed 14 July 2009; John Howard, 'Transcript of the Prime Minister the Hon John Howard MP address to memorial service, Australian consulate, Bali', 17 October 2002.

37  Nick Bray, 'The round-the-clock television coverage', *Courier-Mail*, 19 October 2002.

38  Mark Riley, Tom Allard and Marian Wilkinson, 'Why didn't they tell us what they knew?' *Sydney Morning Herald*, 19 October 2002, p. 5.

39  See, for example, 'Terrorism "significant problem" in Asia-Pacific, Downer says', *Asian Political News*, 9 December 2002.

40  Mark Baker, 'Asian leaders scorn travel alerts', *Sydney Morning Herald*, 5 November 2002, p. 1; Mark Baker, 'Beyond the pale', *Sydney Morning Herald*, 9 November 2002, p. 34.

41  Jake Lloyd-Smith, 'Canberra slammed over travel warning', *South China Morning Post*, 1 November 2002, p. 14.

42  Mark Forbes, 'Terror warnings spark angry Asian backlash', *Age*, 23 October 2002, p. 8.

43  Mark Forbes, 'Dispute around new terror alert', *Age*, 17 May 2003, p. 4.

44  Jennifer Hewett, 'Familiar rants need not deter Australia', *Sydney Morning Herald*, 7 November 2002, p. 13.

45  Tom Allard and Mike Seccombe, 'Megawati pleads: tell Australians it's safe to come back', *Sydney Morning Herald*, 28 October 2002, p. 6.

46  Mark Forbes, 'Bali vulnerable to terrorist attack: general', *Age*, 14 June 2008, p. 5; Fergus Hanson 2010, *Indonesia and Australia: Time for a Step Change*, Lowy

Institute for International Policy, Sydney, p. 12.

47    ABS, *Overseas Arrivals and Departures*. These statistics do not include the Muslim-majority nations of Bangladesh, which attracted only marginal numbers of Australians, and Brunei, for which statistics aren't available.

48    ABS, *Overseas Arrivals and Departures*.

49    ABS, *Overseas Arrivals and Departures*.

50    Flight Centre, 'The Captain's Best Deals', and Air Paradise International, 'Paradise on Sale', advertisements in *Sun-Herald*, Travel supplement, 26 June 2005, pp. 6, 19; Jetset, 'Free kids airfare to Bali', advertisement in *Sun-Herald*, travel supplement, 28 May 2006, p. 4.

51    Department of Foreign Affairs and Trade 2003, *Advancing the National Interest: Australia's Foreign and Trade Policy White Paper*, Commonwealth of Australia, Canberra, pp. xv–xvi, 82; Department of Industry, Tourism and Resources 2003, *Tourism White Paper: A Medium to Long Term Strategy for Tourism* Canberra, p. 8.

52    Australian Government, *Australia in the Asian Century White Paper*, p. 3.

53    Phillip Coorey and Hamish McDonald, 'Time for a new spirit of trust', *Sydney Morning Herald*, 11 March 2010, www.smh.com.au/national/time-for-new-spirit-of-trust-20100310-pzdy.html, accessed 16 October 2013.

54    Bernard Lane, 'Chance to gain wisdom on Asia', *Australian*, 4 October 2013, www.theaustralian.com.au/news/features/chance-to-gain-wisdom-on-asia/story-e6frg6z6-1226732537081, accessed 8 October 2013.

55    Amanda Hooton, 'Name your price', *Sydney Morning Herald*, Forty-Eight Hours supplement, 20 December 2003, p. 13.

56    Kate Cox, 'Blissfully busy in paradise', *Sun-Herald*, Travel supplement, 25 June 2006, p. 12.

57    Lisa Brigid Mackey, 'The idyll rich', *Sydney Morning Herald*, Travel supplement, 22 January 2005, p. 7.

58    David Wilson, 'Undiscovered Thailand', *Sydney Morning Herald*, 20 November 2009, www.smh.com.au/travel/traveller-tips/undiscovered-thailand-20091117-ijy9.html, accessed 22 November 2009.

## 9:   SONS AND DAUGHTERS

1    Australian Bureau of Statistics, *Characteristics of Recent Migrants*, www.abs.gov.au/AUSSTATS/absé.nsf/Lookup/3416.0Main+Features22011?OpenDocument, accessed 16 January 2014.

2    Paul Jones 2005, *Chinese-Australian Journeys: Records on Travel, Migration and Settlement, 1860–1975* National Archives of Australia, Canberra.; John Fitzgerald 2007, *Big White Lie: Chinese Australians in White Australia*, UNSW Press, Sydney, p. 13

3    Fitzgerald, *Big White Lie*.

4    Fitzgerald, *Big White Lie*, pp. 78; 148.

5    Loy-Wilson, 'The Smiling Professions', p. 356.

6    Zhiming Chen, cited in Fitzgerald, *Big White Lie*, p. 141.

7    'Persona Non Grata I am/ In my own native land', 13 June 1963, cited in Charlotte Jordon Greene 2005, *Fantastic Dreams: William Liu, and the origins and influence of protest against the White Australia Policy in the 20th Century*, PhD thesis, Department of History, University of Sydney, pp. 69–70.

8    William Liu, 'The Way I See Things – China and Things Chinese', 1959, Papers of William Liu, Mitchell Library: ML MSS 6294/3.

9    William Liu to Fred Quinlan, 15 June 1932, cited in Greene, *Fantastic Dreams*.

10    Tavan, *The Long, Slow Death of White Australia*; Anna Haebich 2007, *Spinning the*

*Dream: assimilation in Australia, 1950–1970*, Fremantle Press, North Fremantle.

11    Greene, *Fantastic Dreams*, p. 219.

12    Helene Chung 1989, *Shouting from China*, 2nd ed., Penguin, Ringwood, Vic., p. 62.

13    Angela Chan, cited in Carole Tan 2003, 'Living with 'difference': Growing up 'Chinese' in White Australia', *Journal of Australian Studies*, no. 77.

14    Chung, *Shouting from China*, p. 62.

15    Doulman and Lee, *Every Assistance & Protection, p. 145.*

16    Brady, *Making the Foreign Serve China.*

17    Sobocinska, 'Australian fellow-travellers to China: devotion and deceit in the People's Republic'.

18    William Liu, 'From Manchu to Mao: The life story of "Uncle Bill" Liu', *The Asian*, November 1977, p. 9, cited in Greene, *Fantastic Dreams*.

19    Pamela Tan 2008, *The Chinese Factor: an Australian Chinese woman's life in China from 1950 to 1979*, Rosenberg Publishing, Sydney, pp. 24–5.

20    Tan, *The Chinese Factor*, p. 27.

21    Tan, *The Chinese Factor*, p. 259.

22    Chung, *Shouting from China*, p. xiii

23    Chung, *Shouting from China*, p. 134.

24    Chung, *Shouting from China*, p. xxv.

25    Chung, *Shouting from China*, p. 2.

26    *Chung, Shouting from China*, pp. 27, 185–89.

27    Tim Soutphommasane 2012, *Don't go back to where you came from: Why multiculturalism works*, NewSouth Publishing, Sydney, p. x.

28    'Kylie Kwong – My China', www.lifestylefood.com.au/tv/kylie-kwong-my-china/, accessed 15 December 2013.

29    Kylie Kwong, *George Negus Tonight*, broadcast 11 November 2004, transcript at www.abc.net.au/gnt/profiles/Transcripts/s1242188.htm, accessed 15 December 2013.

30    Kylie Kwong, 'My Life', www.kyliekwong.org/MyLife.aspx, accessed 15 December 2013.

31    Interview with Willa Zheng conducted by Agnieszka Sobocinska, Sydney, 11 November 2013.

## PEOPLE'S DIPLOMATS

1    Julia Gillard, 'Speech to the AsiaLink and Asia Society Lunch, Melbourne', 28 September 2011.

2    Clune, *To the Isles of Spice*, p.275; Clune, *All Aboard for Singapore*, p.138

3    Audio letters of William Wade.

4    Gilmore and Warner, *Near North*, p. 1.

# REFERENCES

## BIBLIOGRAPHY

Aarons, Eric, 'As I Saw the Sixties' *Australian Left Review* no. 27, Oct–Nov. 1970, pp. 60–73.

Akami, Tomoko and Tony Milner, 'Australia in the Asia-Pacific Region' in Alison Bashford and Stuart Macintyre (eds.) 2013, *The Cambridge History of Australia*, Cambridge University Press, Melbourne.

Altman, Dennis 1979, *Coming out in the Seventies*, Wild and Woolley, Sydney.

Angell, Barbara 2003, *A Woman's War: The Exceptional Life of Wilma Oram Young, AM*, New Holland, Sydney.

Appadurai, Arjun 1996, *Modernity at Large: Cultural Dimensions of Globalization*, University of Minnesota Press, Minneapolis.

Arneil, Stan 2003 (1980), *One Man's War*, Pan Macmillan Australia, Sydney.

Arthur Andersen & Co. 1986, *China Business Guide*, Longman, Hong Kong.

Atkinson, Alan 2002, *Three Weeks in Bali: A Personal Account of the Bali Bombing*, ABC Books, Sydney.

Atkinson, Les 2001, *My Side of the Kwai: Reminiscences of an Australian Prisoner of War of the Japanese*, Kangaroo Press, Sydney.

Australian Government 2012, *Australia in the Asian Century White Paper*, Government Publisher, Canberra.

Bagnall, Kate, 'Crossing Oceans and Cultures', in David Walker and Agnieszka Sobocinska (eds) 2012, *Australia's Asia: From Yellow Peril to Asian Century*, UWA Publishing, Crawley, WA pp. 121–44.

Balfe, John 1985, *...And Far from Home: Flying RAAF Transports in the Pacific War and After*, Macmillan, Melbourne.

Balint, Ruth, 'Epilogue: The Yellow Sea', in David Walker and Agnieszka Sobocinska (eds) 2012, *Australia's Asia: From Yellow Peril to Asian Century*, UWA Publishing, Crawley, WA, pp. 345–65.

Ballantyne, Tony and Antoinette Burton (eds) 2005, *Bodies in Contact: Rethinking Colonial Encounters in World History*, Duke University Press, Durham and London.

Baranay, Inez 1992, *The Edge of Bali*, Angus & Robertson, Sydney.

Barrett, John 1987, *We Were There: Australian Soldiers of World War II*, Viking, Ringwood, Vic.

Barthes, Roland 1983, *The Fashion System*, translated by Matthew Ward and Richard Howard, Hill and Wang, New York.

Bates, Peter 1993, *Japan and the British Commonwealth Occupation Force 1946–52*, Brassey's, London.

Bernstein, Richard 2009, *The East, the West, and Sex: A History of Erotic Encounters*, Alfred A Knopf, New York.

Berry, Chris, 'Denis O'Rourke's Original Sin: *The Good Woman of Bangkok*, or "Is This What They Mean by 'Australia in Asia'? "', in Chris Berry, Annette Hamilton and Laleen Jayamanne (eds) 1997, *The Filmmaker and the Prostitute: Denis O'Rourke's the Good Woman of Bangkok*, Power Institute of Fine Arts, Sydney, pp. 35–55.

Braddon, Russell 1974, *The Naked Island*, Pan Books, London.

Brady, Anne-Marie 2003, *Making the Foreign Serve China: Managing Foreigners in the People's Republic*, Rowman & Littlefield Publishers Inc., Lanham, Maryland.

Brawley, Sean 1995, *The White Peril: Foreign Relations and Asian Immigration to Australasia and North America, 1918–1978*, UNSW Press, Sydney.

Brawley, Sean, and Chris Dixon 2012, *Hollywood's South Seas and the Pacific War: Searching for Dorothy Lamour*, Palgrave Macmillan, New York.

Brett, Judith, 'Menzies' Forgotten People', *Meanjin* 43, 1984, pp. 256–65.

Bridge, Carl, Robert Crawford and David Dunstan (eds) 2009, *Australians in Britain: The Twentieth-Century Experience*, Monash University ePress, Clayton, Vic.

Broinowski, Alison 1992, *The Yellow Lady: Australian Impressions of Asia*, Oxford University Press, Melbourne.

Browne, GS, and ND Harper 1953, *Our Pacific Neighbours*, F.W. Cheshire, Melbourne.

Burchett, Wilfred 1951, *News from New China*, World Unity Publications, Banksia Park, Vic.

Burke, Anthony 2008, *Fear of Security: Australia's Invasion Anxiety*, Cambridge University Press, Melbourne.

Buzard, James 1993, *The Beaten Track: European Tourism, Literature and the Ways to 'Culture', 1800–1918*, Oxford University Press, Oxford.

Byles, Marie Beuzeville 1962, *Journey into Burmese Silence*, George Allen & Unwin, London.

Carter, Carolyne, 'Between War and Peace: The Experience of Occupation for Members of the British Commonwealth Occupation Force, 1945–1952', PhD thesis submitted to the Australian Defence Force Academy/ University of New South Wales, 2002.

Caulfield, Michael 2008, *War Behind the Wire: Australian Prisoners of War*, Hachette Australia, Sydney.

Chung, Helene 1989, *Shouting from China* (2nd ed.), Penguin, Ringwood, Vic.

Clarke, Gregory 1967, *In Fear of China*, Lansdowne, Melbourne.

Clarke, Hugh V, 'Of Elephants and Men' in Gavan McCormack and Hank Nelson (eds) 1993, *The Burma-Thailand Railway: Memory and History*, Allen & Unwin, Sydney, pp. 37–44.

Clifton, Allan S 1950, *Time of Fallen Blossoms*, Cassell & Company Ltd, London, Toronto, Melbourne.

Clune, Frank 1939, *Sky High to Shanghai*, Angus & Robertson, Sydney.

Clune, Frank 1941, *All Aboard for Singapore: A Trip by Qantas Flying Boat from Sydney to Malaya*, Angus & Robertson, Sydney.

Clune, Frank 1942, *Prowling through Papua*, Angus & Robertson, Sydney.

Clune, Frank 1944, *To the Isles of Spice: A Vagabond Journey by Air from Botany Bay to Darwin, Bathurst Island, Timor, Java, Borneo, Celebes and French Indo-China*, Angus & Robertson, Sydney.

Clune, Frank 1947, *Song of India*, Thacker & Co. Ltd, Bombay.

Clune, Frank 1948, *High-Ho to London: Incidents and Interviews on a Leisurely Journey by Air from Australia to Britain*, Angus & Robertson, Sydney.

Clune, Frank 1950, *Ashes of Hiroshima*, Angus & Robertson, Sydney.

Clune, Frank 1958, *Flight to Formosa*, Angus & Robertson, Sydney.

# References

Cobbs Hoffman, Elizabeth 1998, *All You Need Is Love: The Peace Corps and the Spirit of the 1960s*, Harvard University Press, Cambridge, MA.

Cohen, Erik, 'Lovelorn Farangs: The Correspondence between Foreign Men and Thai Girls', *Anthropological Quarterly* 59, no. 3, July 1986, pp. 115–27.

Cohen, Erik 1996, *Thai Tourism: Hill Tribes, Islands and Open-Ended Prostitution*, White Lotus Press, Bangkok.

Cook, Ivan 2006, *Australia, Indonesia and the World: Public Opinion and Foreign Policy*, Lowy Institute for International Policy, Sydney.

Coopers & Lybrand 1995, *Doing Business in North Asia*, Coopers & Lybrand, Sydney.

Crofts, Stephen, 'Media Constructions of the Schapelle Corby Trial: Populism Versus Multiculturalism', *Australian Journal of Communications* 33, no. 2/3, 2006, pp. 7–20.

Crombie, Gavin 2005, *The Way of the Dragon: A Guide for Australians Doing Business in China*, Wrightbooks, Milton, Qld.

Cull, Nicholas J 2008, *The Cold War and the United States Information Agency: American Propaganda and Public Diplomacy, 1945–1989*, Cambridge University Press, Cambridge.

Cusack, Dymphna 1958, *Chinese Women Speak*, Angus & Robertson, Sydney.

Dallas, Nick 2007, *How to Do Business in China: 24 Lessons in Engaging the Dragon*, McGraw-Hill Australia, Sydney.

Dalton, Bill 1974, *Travellers' Notes: Indonesia*, Moon Publications/ Tomato Press, Sydney.

Dalton, Bill 1977, *Indonesia Handbook*, Moon Publications, Michigan.

Dass, Ram 1971, *Be Here Now, Remember*, Lama Foundation, San Cristobal, New Mexico.

Dawson, Christopher 1995, *To Sandakan: The Diaries of Charlie Johnstone, Prisoner of War, 1942–1945*, Allen & Unwin, Sydney.

de Matos, Christine 2007, 'A Very Gendered Occupation: Australian Women as "Conquerors" and "Liberators"', in Faculty of Arts - Papers, University of Wollongong, Wollongong.

de Matos, Christine 2008, *Imposing Peace and Prosperity: Australia, Social Justice and Labour Reform in Occupied Japan*, Australian Scholarly Publishing, Melbourne.

De Neefe, Janet 2003, *Fragrant Rice: My Continuing Love Affair with Bali*, Flamingo, Sydney.

Deakin, Alfred 1983, *Temple and Tomb in India*, Melville, Mullen and Slade, Melbourne.

Department of Foreign Affairs and Trade 2003, *Advancing the National Interest: Australia's Foreign and Trade Policy White Paper* Commonwealth of Australia, Canberra.

Department of Foreign Affairs and Trade 2004, *Transnational Terrorism: The Threat to Australia*, National Capital Printing, Canberra.

Department of Foreign Affairs and Trade/Newspoll 2013, *Australian Attitudes Towards Indonesia*, Newspoll, Sydney.

Department of Industry, Tourism and Resources 2003, *Tourism White Paper: A Medium to Long Term Strategy for Tourism*, Canberra.

Dixon, Robert 1995, *Writing the Colonial Adventure: Race, Gender and Nation in Anglo-Australian Popular Fiction, 1875–1914*, Cambridge University Press, Cambridge.

Dizard, Wilson 2004, *Inventing Public Diplomacy: The Story of the U.S. Information Agency*, Lynne Rienner Publishers, Boulder, CO.

Doulman, Jane, and David Lee 2008, *Every Assistance & Protection: A History of the Australian Passport*, The Federation Press/Department of Foreign Affairs and Trade, Sydney.

Dower, John 1999, *Embracing Defeat: Japan in the Wake of World War II*, W. W. Norton & Company, New York.

Dunlop, EE 1990, *The War Diaries of Weary Dunlop: Java and the Burma-Thailand*

*Railway, 1943–1945*, Penguin Books, Ringwood, Vic.

Dutton, David, 'A British Outpost in the Pacific' in David Goldsworthy (ed.) 2001, *Facing North: A Century of Australian Engagement with Asia*, DFAT/Melbourne University Press, Melbourne, pp. 21–60.

Duyker, Edward, 'William Glen Wade (1911–1983): A Biographical Memoir', *Sutherland Shire Historical Society Quarterly Bulletin* 2, 1995, pp. 209–13.

East Asia Christian Conference 1959, *Our Asian Neighbours: Articles on the Churches of East Asia*, Joint Committee of the Australian Council for World Churches and the National Missionary Council of Australia, Sydney.

Easterly, William 2006, *White Man's Burden: Why the West's efforts to aid the rest have done so little good*, Penguin Press, New York.

Education Department of Western Australia 1970, *Northern Neighbours: A Study of an Indonesian Community*, Education Department of Western Australia, Perth.

Endy, Christopher, 'Travel and World Power: Americans in Europe, 1890–1917', *Diplomatic History* 22, no. 4, 1998, pp. 565–94.

Endy, Christopher 2004, *Cold War Holidays: American Tourism in France*, The University of North Carolina Press, Chapel Hill and London.

Ewans, Martin 2002, *Afghanistan: A Short History of Its People and Politics*, HarperCollins Publishers, New York.

Feith, Herb, 'Molly Bondan: Pioneer, Mentor and Role Model' in Anton Lucas (ed.) 1996, *Half a Century of Indonesian-Australian Interaction*, Department of Asian Studies and Languages, Flinders University of South Australia, Adelaide, pp. 8–16.

Fernandes, Clinton 2004, *Reluctant Saviour: Australia, Indonesia and the Independence of East Timor*, Scribe, Melbourne.

Finnane, Antonia, 'Chinese in Australia' in Graeme Davison, John Hirst and Stuart Macintyre (eds) 1998, *The Oxford Companion to Australian History*, Oxford University Press, Melbourne pp. 122–23.

Fitzgerald, John 2007, *Big White Lie: Chinese Australians in White Australia*, UNSW Press, Sydney.

FitzGerald, Stephen, 'Australia's China', *Australian Journal of Chinese Affairs*, no. 24, July 1990, pp. 315–35.

Fitzpatrick, Peter, 'Really Rather Like Slavery: Law and Labor in the Colonial Economy in Papua New Guinea', *Contemporary Crises* 4, 1980, pp. 77–95.

Frank, Thomas 1997, *The Conquest of Cool: Business Culture, Counterculture and the Rise of Hip Consumerism*, University of Chicago Press, Chicago and London.

Fung, Edmund, 'Australia and China', in PJ Boyce and JR Angel (eds) 1992 *Diplomacy in the Marketplace: Australia in World Affairs, 1981–90*, Longman Cheshire, Melbourne, pp. 277–99.

Fussell, Paul (ed.) 1987, *The Norton Book of Travel*, Norton, New York, pp. 15–16.

Ganter, Regina 2006, *Mixed Relations: Asian-Aboriginal Contact in North Australia*, UWA Publishing, Crawley, WA.

George, Margaret 1980, *Australia and the Indonesian Revolution*, Melbourne University Press, Melbourne.

Gerster, Robin, 'Asian Destinies/Destinations: The Vietnam Tour', *Australian Studies* 10, 1996, pp. 61–69.

Gerster, Robin, 'Six Inch Rule: Revisiting the Australian Occupation of Japan, 1946–1952', *History Australia* 4, no. 2, 2007, 42.1–42.16.

Gerster, Robin 2008, *Travels in Atomic Sunshine: Australia and the Occupation of Japan*, Scribe, Melbourne.

Gilmore, Robert J and Denis Warner (eds) 1948, *Near North: Australia and a Thousand Million Neighbours*, Angus & Robertson, Sydney.

# References

Ginsberg, Allen 1970, *Indian Journals, March 1962–May 1963: Notebooks, Diary, Blank Pages, Writings*, Dave Haselwood Books, San Francisco.

Goldsworthy, David, David Dutton, Peter Gifford, and Roderic Pitty, 'Reorientation' in David Goldsworthy (ed.) 2001, *Facing North: A Century of Australian Engagement with Asia, Volume 1: 1901 to the 1970s*, Department of Foreign Affairs and Trade/ Melbourne University Press, Melbourne, pp. 310–71.

Goldsworthy, David, 'Regional Relations' in Peter Edwards and David Goldsworthy (eds) 2003, *Facing North: A Century of Engagement with Asia; Volume 2: 1970s to 2000*, Department of Foreign Affairs and Trade/ Melbourne University Press, Melbourne, pp. 130–77.

Graburn, Nelson, 'Tourism and Prostitution', *Annals of Tourism Research* 10, no. 3, 1983, pp. 437–56.

Grant, Ian 1992, *A Dictionary of Australian Military History*, Random House, Sydney.

Grant, Lachlan 2010, 'The AIF in Asia and the Pacific 1941–1945: A Reorientation in Attitudes Towards Asia, Empire and Nation', Monash University, Melbourne.

Greene, Charlotte Jordon 2005, 'Fantastic Dreams: William Liu, and the Origins and Influence of Protest against the White Australia Policy in the 20th Century', PhD thesis submitted to the Department of History, University of Sydney, Sydney.

Haebich, Anna 2007, *Spinning the Dream: Assimilation in Australia, 1950–1970*, Fremantle Press, North Fremantle, WA.

Hamilton, Annette, 'Fear and Desire: Aborigines, Asians and the National Imaginary' *Australian Cultural History*, no. 9, David Walker, Julia Horne & Adrian Vickers (eds), 1990, pp. 14–35.

Hamilton, Walter 2012, *Children of the Occupation: Japan's untold story*, NewSouth Publishing, Sydney.

Hanson, Fergus 2010, *Indonesia and Australia: Time for a Step Change*, Lowy Institute for International Policy, Sydney.

Hanson, Marianne, 'Issues in Australian Foreign Policy, January to June 2005', *Australian Journal of Politics and History* 51, no. 4, 2005, pp. 564–77.

Hardjono, Joan, and Charles Warner (eds) 1995, *In Love with a Nation: Molly Bondan and Indonesia*, Charles Warner, Picton, NSW.

Haylen, Leslie 1959, *Chinese Journey: The Republic Revisited*, Angus and Robertson, Sydney.

Hazell, Robert C 1966, 'The Tourist Industry in Hong Kong, 1966', The Far Eastern Research Organisation for the Hong Kong Tourist Association, Hong Kong.

Higman, BW 2002, *Domestic Service in Australia*, Melbourne University Press, Melbourne.

Hingston, James 1885, *The Australian Abroad*, William Inglis & Co., Melbourne.

Hirst, Martin, and Robert Schutze 'Duckspeak Crusader: Greg Sheridan's Unique Brand of Seculo-Christian Morality', *Overland*, no. 176, Spring 2004, pp. 18–25.

Hitchcock, Michael, and I Nyoman Darma Putra 2007, *Tourism, Development and Terrorism in Bali*, Ashgate, Hampshire, UK.

Horne, Donald 1964, *The Lucky Country: Australia in the Sixties*, Penguin, Ringwood, Vic.

Horner, David, Peter Londey and Jean Bou (eds) 2009, *Australian Peacekeeping: Sixty Years in the Field*, Cambridge University Press, Cambridge.

Hottola, Petri, 'Amoral and Available? Western Women Travellers in South Asia', *Gender/ Tourism/Fun*, 2002, pp. 164–71.

Huggan, Graham, 'The Australian Tourist Novel' in Maryanne Dever (ed.) 1997, *Australia and Asia: Cultural Transactions*, University of Hawai'i Press, Honolulu, pp. 162–75.

Hugo, Graeme, Dianne Rudd, and Kevin Harris 2003, *Australia's Diaspora: Its Size, Nature and Policy Implications*, Committee for Economic Development of Australia, Canberra.

Hutnyk, John 1996, *The Rumour of Calcutta: Tourism, Charity and the Poverty of Representation*, Zed Books, London.

Inglis, KS, 'Going Home: Australians in England, 1870–1900' in David Fitzpatrick (ed.) 1992, *Home or Away? Immigrants in Colonial Australia: Visible Immigrants*, Division of Historical Studies, Australian National University, Canberra.

Irwin, Harry 1996, *Communicating with Asia: Understanding People and Customs*, Allen & Unwin, Sydney.

Jackson, John 1971, *Ping Pong to China*, Sun Books, Melbourne.

Jarvis, Jeff, 'Yellow Bible Tourism: Backpackers in South East Asia', in Brad West (ed.) 2005, *Down the Road: Exploring backpacker and independent travel*, API Network, Perth.

Jeans, Peter 1998, *Long Road to London*, Rawlhouse Publishing, Perth.

Jeffrey, Betty 1997, *White Coolies*, Angus & Robertson, Sydney.

Jenkins, David 1975, *Asia Traveller's Guide*, Acme Books, Melbourne.

Jenkins, David 1976, *Asia: A Traveller's Guide*, Rigby Limited, Adelaide.

Jobs, Richard Ivan, 'Youth Movements: Travel, Protest, and Europe in 1968', *American Historical Review* 114, no. 2, April 2009, pp. 376–404.

Johnson, Mandy 2005, *Family, Village, Tribe: The Story of Flight Centre Limited*, Random House Australia, Sydney.

Johnston, George 1947, *Journey through Tomorrow*, F.W. Cheshire Pty. Ltd, Melbourne.

Jones, Paul 2005, *Chinese-Australian Journeys: Records on Travel, Migration and Settlement, 1860–1975*, National Archives of Australia, Canberra.

Josephi, Beate, 'Expressing Concern: Australian Press Reporting of the Bali Bomb Blasts', *Australian Journalism Review* 26, no. 1, 2004, pp. 55–68.

Kabbani, Rana 1986, *Europe's Myths of Orient*, Indiana University Press, Bloomington.

Kapur, Tribhuwan 1981, *Hippies: A Study of Their Drug Habits and Sexual Customs*, Vikas Publishing House, New Delhi.

Keddie, Nikki R 2006, *Modern Iran: Roots and Results of Revolution* (3rd ed.), Yale University Press, New Haven, CT.

Kenny, Gillian, '"Our Travellers" out There on the Road: *Lonely Planet* and Its Readers, 1973–1981', *Journal of Australian Studies*, no. 72, 2002, pp. 111–19.

Kerouac, Jack 1959, *The Dharma Bums*, Andre Deutsch Ltd, London.

Klein, Christina 2003, *Cold War Orientalism: Asia in the Middlebrow Imagination, 1945–1961*, University of California Press, Berkeley.

Kumar, Subas C, 'The tourism industry in India: Economic significance and emerging issues' in Kartik C Roy and Clement A Tisdell (eds.) 1998, *Tourism in India and India's economic development*, Nova Science Publishers Inc., Commack, NY.

Kwitko, Ludmilla, and Diane McDonald 2009, *Australian Government Volunteer Program Review: Final Report*, www.ausaid.gov.au/partner/pdf/volunteer_review.pdf: AusAID.

Lake, Marilyn, and Henry Reynolds 2008, *Drawing the Global Colour Line: White Men's Countries and the Question of Racial Equality*, Melbourne University Press, Melbourne.

Leary, Timothy, Ralph Metzner and Richard Alpert 1964, *The Psychedelic Experience: A Manual Based on the Tibetan Book of the Dead*, Citadel Press, New Jersey.

Lee, Gerard 1990, *Troppo Man*, University of Queensland Press, St. Lucia, Qld.

Leheny, David, 'A Political Economy of Asian Sex Tourism', *Annals of Tourism Research* 22, no. 3, 1995, pp. 367–84.

Letters, Frances 1968, *The Surprising Asians: A Hitch-Hike through Malaya, Thailand, Laos, Cambodia and South Vietnam*, Angus & Robertson, Sydney.

Letters, Frances 1971, *People of Shiva: Encounters in India*, Angus & Robertson, Sydney.

Lewis, Jeff, 'Paradise Defiled: The Bali Bombings and the Terror of National Identity', *European Journal of Cultural Studies* 9, no. 2, 2006, pp. 223–42.

# References

Lewis, Jeff, and Sonya de Masi, 'Unholy Wars: Media Representations of the First Bali Bombings and Their Aftermath', *Media International Australia*, no. 122, February 2007, pp. 59–72.

Leys, Simon 1977, *Chinese Shadows*, The Viking Press, New York.

Littlewood, Ian 2001, *Sultry Climates: Travel and Sex*, Da Capo Press, Cambridge, MA.

Lockwood, Rupert 1982, *Black Armada: Australia and the Struggle for Indonesian Independence, 1942–49*, Hale & Iremonger, Sydney.

Londey, Peter 2004, *Other People's Wars: A History of Australian Peacekeeping*, Allen & Unwin, Sydney.

Long, Gavin 1966, *The Final Campaign*, Australia in the War of 1939–1945, Vol. 7, Australian War Memorial, Canberra.

Loy-Wilson, Sophie 2012, 'The Smiling Professions: Salesmanship and Promotional Culture in Australia and China, 1920–1939', PhD thesis submitted to the Department of History, University of Sydney.

Loy-Wilson, Sophie, 'White Cargo: Australian Residents, Trade and Colonialism in Shanghai between the Wars', *History Australia* 9, no. 3, December 2012, pp. 154–77.

Loy-Wilson, Sophie, 'Commercial encounters: Business guidebooks and cross-cultural relations between Australia and China' in Chengxin Pan (ed.) 2014, *Australia and China in the 21st century: Challenges and ideas in cross-cultural engagement*, China Social Science Press, Beijing.

Luxingshe (China International Travel Service) 1980, *The Official Guidebook of China*, Books New China, New York.

Lyons, Martyn, and Lucy Taksa 1992, *Australian Readers Remember: An Oral History of Reading 1890–1930*, Oxford University Press, Melbourne.

McCreery, Cindy, and Kirsten McKenzie, 'Colonial Lives in a Connected Maritime World', in Alison Bashford and Stuart Macintyre (eds) 2013, *The New Cambridge History of Australia*, Cambridge University Press, Cambridge.

McDougall, Derek, and Kingsley Edney, 'Howard's Way? Public Opinion as an Influence on Australia's Engagement with Asia, 1996–2007', *Australian Journal of International Affairs* 64, no. 2, 2010, pp. 205–24.

Macintyre, Stuart 1998, *The Reds: The Communist Party of Australia from Origins to Illegality*, Allen & Unwin, Sydney.

Mack, Louise 1902, *An Australian Girl in London*, T. Fisher Unwin, London.

McKay, Gary 1998, *In Good Company: One Man's War in Vietnam*, Allen & Unwin, Sydney.

McKenna, Mark 2009, 'Turning Away from Britain: Manning Clark, History, Public Intellectuals and the End of Empire in Australia', Paper Presented to 'Sydney Sawyer Seminar: Varieties of Empire in the Antipodes', 30 October 2009, University of Sydney.

McKenna, Mark 2011, *An Eye for Eternity: The Life of Manning Clark*, The Miegunyah Press, Melbourne.

Mackenzie, John M (ed.) 2011, *European Empires and the People: Popular Responses to Imperialism in France, Britain, the Netherlands, Belgium, Germany and Italy*, Manchester University Press, Manchester and New York.

Mackerras, Colin, and Neale Hunter 1967, *China Observed, 1964/1967*, Thomas Nelson (Australia), Sydney.

McKie, Ronald, and Beryl Bernay 1969, *Bali*. Angus & Robertson, Sydney.

McKie, Ronald 1972, *Singapore*, Angus & Robertson, Sydney.

Macknight, Campbell 1976, *The Voyage to Marege': Macassan Trepangers in Northern Australia*, Melbourne University Press, Melbourne.

McLaren, Don 1998, *Mates in Hell: The Secret Diary of Don Mclaren, Prisoner of War of the Japanese: Changi, Burma Railway, Japan, 1942–1945*, Seaview Press, Henley Beach, SA.

Macmahon Ball, William 1949, *Our Thousand Million Neighbours*, Pioneers' Memorial Trust, Wangaratta, Victoria.

MacRae, Graeme, 'Fear and Loathing in Our Own Holiday Paradise: The Strange Tale of Schapelle Corby (et al.)', *Australian Journal of Anthropology* 17, no. 1, April 2006, pp. 79–85.

Maddock, Keith, (ed.) 1991, *Memories of Vietnam*, Random House, Sydney.

Mann, Graeme 2006, *The Vietnam War on a Tourist Visa*, Mini Publishing, Sydney.

Meaney, Neville 1985, *Australia and the World: A Documentary History from the 1870s to the 1970s*, Longman Cheshire Pty Ltd, Melbourne.

Meaney, Neville 2009, *The Search for Security in the Pacific: A History of Australian Defence and Foreign Policy, Vol.1: 1901–1914* (2nd ed.), University of Sydney Press, Sydney.

Morrison, GE 1895, *An Australian in China: Being the Narrative of a Quiet Journey across China to British Burma*, Horace Cox, London.

Moyo, Dambisa 2009, *Dead Aid: Why aid is not working and how there is another way for Africa*, Farrar, Straus and Giroux, New York .

National Centre for Language Training 2008, *Doing Business in China: A Guide for Australians*, UNSW Press, Sydney.

National Union of Australian University Students 1969, *Student Travel Handbook*, NUAUS, Melbourne.

Nelson, Hank 1982, *Taim Bilong Masta: The Australian Involvement with Papua New Guinea*, Australian Broadcasting Corporation, Sydney.

Nelson, Hank, '"The Nips Are Going for the Parker": The Prisoners Face Freedom', *War & Society* 3, no. 2, September 1985, pp. 127–43.

Neville, Richard 1970, *Play Power*, Jonathan Cape, London.

Neville, Richard 1995, *Hippie Hippie Shake: The Dreams, the Trips, the Trials, the Love-Ins, the Screw-Ups…the Sixties*, William Heinemann Australia, Melbourne.

O'Brien, Daniel A 1958, *I Circle the Earth*, W.R. Smith & Paterson, Brisbane.

Oakman, Daniel 2004, *Facing Asia: A History of the Colombo Plan*, Pandanus Books, Canberra.

Oppermann, Martin, 'Sex Tourism', *Annals of Tourism Research* 26, no. 2, 1999, pp. 251–66.

Palmos, Frank, and Pat Price 1976, *Indonesia Do-It-Yourself*, Palmii, Melbourne.

Parkinson, Jack 2001, *Farewell Hippy Heaven: Rites of Way on the Overland Route*, Lothian Books, Melbourne.

Pearson, Charles 1894, *National Life and Character: A Forecast* (2nd ed., reprinted 1913), Macmillan and Co., London.

Pesman, Ros, 'Australian Women Encounter the East: The Boat Stops at Colombo', *Journal of the Royal Australian Historical Society* 84, no. 1, 1998.

Philpott, Simon, 'Fear of the Dark: Indonesia and the Australian National Imagination', *Australian Journal of International Affairs* 55, no. 3, 2001, pp. 371–88.

Pitty, Roderic, 'The Postwar Expansion of Trade with East Asia' in David Goldsworthy (ed.) 2001, *Facing North: A Century of Australian Engagement with Asia*, Department of Foreign Affairs and Trade and Melbourne University Press, Melbourne, pp. 220–61.

Pratt, Mary Louise 1992, *Imperial Eyes: Travel Writing and Transculturation*, Routledge, London.

Purdey, Jemma 2011, *From Vienna to Yogyakarta: The Life of Herb Feith*, UNSW Press, Sydney.

Qantas Airways Ltd 1972, *Qantas Travel Handbook*, Qantas, Sydney.

Ravi, Srilata, 'Modernity, Imperialism and the Pleasures of Travel: The Continental Hotel in Saigon', *Asian Studies Review* 32, no. 4, December 2008, pp. 475–90.

Rawson, Richard (ed.) 1976, *On Your Own: Air Siam's Student Guide to Asia*, Volunteers in Asia, Inc., Stanford, CA.

# References

Raymond, EM, and CM Hall, 'The Development of Cross-Cultural (Mis)Understanding through Volunteer Tourism', *Journal of Sustainable Tourism* 6, no. 5 2008, pp. 530–43.

Reck, David, 'Beatles Orientalis: Influences from Asia in a Popular Song Tradition', *Asian Music* 16, no. 1, 1985, pp. 83–149.

Reeves, Keir, and Benjamin Mountford, 'Sojourning and Settling: Locating Chinese Australian History', *Australian Historical Studies* 42, no. 1, 2011, pp. 111–25.

Reilly, James, and Jingdong Yuan, 'Australia's Relations with China in a New Era' in James Reilly and Jingdong Yuan (eds) 2012, *Australia and China at 40*, UNSW Press, Sydney, pp. 2–20.

Rivett, Rohan D 1946, *Behind Bamboo: An inside Story of the Japanese Prison Camps*, Angus & Robertson, Sydney.

Robinson, Mike, 'Tourism Encounters: Inter and Intra-Cultural Conflicts and the World's Largest Industry' in Nezar AlSayyad (ed.) 2001, *Consuming Tradition, Manufacturing Heritage: Global Norms and Urban Forms in the Age of Tourism*, Routledge, London, pp. 34–67.

Rodd, LC 1938, *Australian Imperialism*, Survey of Australia Series, No. 2, Modern Publishers and Importers, Sydney.

Roe, Jill 1986, *Beyond Belief: Theosophy in Australia, 1879–1939*, UNSW Press, Sydney.

Roper, Myra 1966, *China: The Surprising Country*, Heinemann, London.

Roscoe, GT 1959, *Our Neighbours in Netherlands New Guinea*, Jacaranda Press, Brisbane.

Roszak, Theodore 1969, *The Making of a Counter Culture*, Faber and Faber, London.

Rutledge, Helen (ed.) 1976, *A Season in India: Letters of Ruby Madden*, Fontana/Collins, Netley, SA.

Said, Edward 1978, *Orientalism* (1st ed.), Routledge & Kegan Paul, London and Henley.

Said, Edward W 1994, *Culture and Imperialism*, Vintage Books, New York.

Schutze, Robert, 'Terror in "our backyard": negotiating "home" in Australia after the Bali bombings', *Crossings*, vol. 8, no. 1, 2003.

Schwartz, John, 'Pot and Prejudice: Australian Media Coverage of the Corby Saga', *Metro*, no. 145, 2006, pp. 138–43.

Scutt, Craig, 'Love Thy Neighbour: Australia's Shameful Fetish', *Griffith Review*, no. 22, Summer 2008, pp. 105–15.

Selle, Earl Albert 1948, *Donald of China*, Invincible Press, Sydney.

Sengupta, Ipsita, 'Entangled: Deakin in India', in David Walker and Agnieszka Sobocinska (eds) 2012, *Australia's Asia: From Yellow Peril to Asian Century*, UWA Publishing, Crawley, WA, pp. 50–72.

Shann, Keith 1968, *Our Indonesian Neighbours*, Syme Oration, Adelaide.

Simpson, Colin 1956, *The Country Upstairs*, Angus & Robertson, Sydney.

Simpson, Colin 1962, *Asia's Bright Balconies*, Angus & Robertson, Sydney.

Simpson, Colin 1962, *The Country Upstairs* (revised and enlarged ed.), Angus & Robertson, Sydney.

Simpson, Colin 1972, *Bali and Beyond*, Angus & Robertson, Sydney.

Simpson, Colin 1973, *Off to Asia*, Angus & Robertson, Sydney.

Simpson, Colin 1975, *This Is Japan*, Angus & Robertson, Sydney.

Sinclair, Kevin, and Iris Wong Po-yee 1990, *Culture Shock! China*, Time Books International, Singapore.

Smith, Lynne Maree 1995, *Bali at Cost*, Little Hills Press, Sydney.

Smith, Shannon L, 'Towards Diplomatic Representation', in David Goldsworthy (ed.) 2001, *Facing North: A Century of Australian Engagement with Asia, Vol. 1: 1901 to the 1970s*, Department of Foreign Affairs and Trade with Melbourne University Press, Melbourne, pp. 61–96.

Smythe Sherwood, Barbara 2003, *Too Long in the Tropicals: A Tale of Papua New Guinea in the Fifteen Years after World War II*, Parker Pattinson Publishing, Douglas Park, NSW.

Sobocinska, Agnieszka, 'Australian Fellow-Travellers to China: Devotion and Deceit in the People's Republic', *Journal of Australian Studies* 32, no. 3, September 2008, pp. 323–34.

Sobocinska, Agnieszka, '"Two Days' Rest in the City of Sin": Australian Soldiers on R & R in Vietnam' in Daniela Carl and Domenico Colasurdo (eds) 2009, *Conference Proceedings: Resorting to the Coast: Tourism, Heritage and Cultures of the Seaside*, Centre for Tourism and Cultural Change, Leeds.

Sobocinska, Agnieszka, 'The Language of Scars: Australian Prisoners of War and the Colonial Order', *History Australia* 7, no. 3, December 2010, 59.1–59.20.

Sobocinska, Agnieszka, 'Innocence Lost and Paradise Regained: Tourism to Bali and Australian perceptions of Asia', *History Australia*, vol. 8, no. 2, 2011, pp. 199–222.

Sobocinska, Agnieszka, 'Hearts of Darkness, Hearts of Gold' in David Walker and Agnieszka Sobocinska (eds) 2012, *Australia's Asia: From Yellow Peril to Asian century*, UWA Publishing, Crawley, WA.

Sobocinska, Agnieszka, 'Visiting the Neighbours: The political meanings of Australian travel to Cold War Asia', *Australian Historical Studies*, vol. 44, no. 3, 2013, pp. 382–404.

Sobocinska, Agnieszka, 'Following the "hippie sahibs": Colonial cultures of travel and the Hippie Trail', *Journal of Colonialism and Colonial History*, vol. 15, no. 2, Summer 2014.

Sobocinska, Agnieszka, and Richard White 'Travel and Connections' in Alison Bashford and Stuart Macintyre (eds) 2013, *Cambridge History of Australia, Volume 2: The Commonwealth of Australia*, Cambridge University Press, Melbourne, pp. 472–93.

Southall, Ivan 1964, *Indonesia Face to Face*, Lansdowne Press, Melbourne.

Soutphommasane, Tim 2012, *Don't Go Back to Where You Came From: Why Multiculturalism Works*, NewSouth Publishing, Sydney.

Steadman, John M 1970, *The Myth of Asia*, Macmillan, London.

Stella, Regis Tove 2007, *Imagining the Other: The representation of the Papua New Guinean Subject*, University of Hawai'i Press, Honolulu, pp. 8, 90–110.

Stephens, Julie 1998, *Anti-Disciplinary Protest: Sixties Radicalism and Postmodernism*, Cambridge University Press, Cambridge.

Stevens, Rachel, '"Captured by Kindness": Australian Press Representations of the Vietnam War, 1965–1970', *History Australia* 3, no. 2, 2006, 45.1–45.17s.

Stoler, Ann Laura, 'Rethinking Colonial Categories: European Communities and the Boundaries of Rule', *Comparative Studies in Society and History* 31, no. 1, January 1989, pp. 134–61.

Stoler, Ann Laura 2002, *Carnal Knowledge and Imperial Power: Race and the Intimate in Colonial Rule*, University of California Press, Berkeley.

Strahan, Lachlan 1996, *Australia's China: Changing Perceptions from the 1930s to the 1990s*, Cambridge University Press, Cambridge.

Sutherland, Stan 2007, *In This Man's Army: A Vietnam War Memoir*, Self-published, Yackandandah, Vic.

Tamura, Keiko, 'Home Away from Home: The Entry of Japanese War Brides into Australia', in Paul Jones and Vera Mackie (eds) 2001, *Relationships: Japan and Australia*, Department of History, University of Melbourne, Melbourne, pp. 241–64.

Tan, Carole, 'Living with "Difference": Growing up "Chinese" in White Australia', *Journal of Australian Studies*, no. 77, 2003, pp. 101–13.

Tan, Pamela 2008, *The Chinese Factor: An Australian Chinese Woman's Life in China from 1950 to 1979*, Rosenberg Publishing, Sydney.

# References

Tavan, Gwenda 2005, *The Long, Slow Death of White Australia*, Scribe, Melbourne.

Taylor, Rosemary 1988, *Orphans of War: Work with the Abandoned Children of Vietnam, 1967–1975*, William Collins Sons & Co., London.

Tebbutt, John, 'Frank Clune: Modernity and Popular National History', *Australian Journal of Communication* 24, no. 3, 1997, pp. 53–64.

Tebbutt, John, 'The Travel Writer as Foreign Correspondent: Frank Clune and the ABC', *Journal of Australian Studies* 34, no. 1, 2010, pp. 95–107.

Teo, Hsu-Ming 2012, *Desert Passions: Orientalism and Romance Novels*, University of Texas Press, Austin.

Thompson, John 1946, *Hubbub in Java*, Currawong Publishing Company, Sydney.

Tipping, EW, 'Australians in the Near North' in Robert J Gilmore and Denis Warner (eds) 1948, *Near North: Australia and a thousand million neighbours*, Angus & Robertson, Sydney.

Tom, Emma 2006, *Bali: Paradise Lost?*, Pluto Press, Melbourne.

Tomory, David 1998, *A Season in Heaven: True Tales from the Road to Kathmandu*, Lonely Planet, Melbourne.

Torney-Parlicki, Prue 2000, *Somewhere in Asia: War, Journalism and Australia's Neighbours, 1941–75*, UNSW Press Sydney.

Torney-Parlicki, Prue, '"Fighting on the Front Is Coldly Animal": Australian Press Representations of Japan During the Pacific War' in Vera Mackie and Paul Jones (eds) 2001, *Relationships: Japan and Australia, 1870s–1950s*, Department of History, University of Melbourne, Melbourne, pp. 163–88.

Truong, Thanh-Dam 1990, *Sex, Money and Morality: Prostitution and Tourism in Southeast Asia*, Zed Books, London.

Turnbull, Clive, 'White Australia: Policy and passion', in Robert J Gilmore and Denis Warner (eds) 1948, *Near North: Australia and a thousand million neighbours*, Angus & Robertson, Sydney.

Twomey, Christina, 'Emaciation or Emasculation: Photographic Images, White Masculinity and Captivity by the Japanese in World War Two', *Journal of Men's Studies* 15, no. 3, 2007, pp. 295–311.

Vickers, Adrian, 'Australian Novels and South-East Asia, 1895–1945' *Australian Cultural History*, no. 9, 1990, pp. 65–79.

Vickers, Adrian 1989, *Bali: A Paradise Created*, Penguin Books, Ringwood, Vic.

Vickers, Adrian, 'Jemaah Korbyah: Another Low in Australian-Indonesian Relations', *Asian Currents*, June 2005: www.coombs.anu.edu.au/SpecialProj/ASAA/asian-currents-archive/asian-currents-05-06.html, accessed 3 February 2008. (2005).

Vickers, Adrian, 'A Paradise Bombed', *Griffith Review*, no. 1, 2003, pp. 105–13.

Ville, Simon, 'The Economy' in Alison Bashford and Stuart Macintyre (eds) 2013, *The Cambridge History of Australia*, Cambridge University Press, Melbourne.

Volunteer Graduate Association for Indonesia 1962, *Living and Working in Indonesia*, Volunteer Graduate Association for Indonesia, Melbourne.

Walker, David 1999, *Anxious Nation: Australia and the Rise of Asia, 1850–1939*, University of Queensland Press, St. Lucia, Qld.

Walker, David, 'Shooting Mabel: Warrior Masculinity and Asian Invasion', *History Australia* 2, no. 3, 2005, 89.1–89.11.

Walker, David, 'Rising Suns', in David Walker and Agnieszka Sobocinska (eds) 2012, *Australia's Asia: From Yellow Peril to Asian Century*, UWA Publishing, Crawley, WA, pp. 73–95.

Walpole, Brian, and David Levell 2004, *My War: An Australian Commando in New Guinea and Borneo*, ABC Books, Sydney.

Ward, Stuart, 'Sentiment and Self-Interest: The Imperial Ideal in Anglo-Australian

Commercial Culture', *Australian Historical Studies* 32, no. 116, April 2001, pp. 91–108.

Warner, Peggy 1961, *Asia Is People*, F.W. Cheshire, Melbourne.

Waters, Christopher, 'War, Decolonisation and Postwar Security' in David Goldsworthy (ed.) 2001, *Facing North: A Century of Australian Engagement with Asia*, Department of Foreign Affairs and Trade and Melbourne University Press, Melbourne.

Welk, Peter, 'The Lonely Planet Myth: "Backpacker Bible" and "Travel Survival Kit"' in Kevin Hannam and Irena Atelejevic (eds) 2008, *Backpacker Tourism: Concepts and Profiles*, Channel View Publications, Clevedon pp. 82–94.

Wesley, Michael 2011, *There Goes the Neighbourhood: Australia and the Rise of Asia*, NewSouth Publishing, Sydney.

West, Brad, 'Collective Memory and Crisis: The 2002 Bali Bombing, National Heroic Archetypes and the Counter-Narrative of Cosmopolitan Nationalism', *Journal of Sociology* 44, no. 4, 2008, pp. 337–53.

Wheeler, Tony 1973, *Across Asia on the Cheap: A Complete Guide to Making the Overland Trip with Minimum Cost and Hassles*, Lonely Planet, Sydney.

Wheeler, Tony 1975, *Across Asia on the Cheap: A Complete Guide to Making the Overland Trip with Minimum Cost and Hassles* (2nd ed.) Lonely Planet, Melbourne.

Wheeler, Tony 1977, *South-East Asia on a Shoestring*, Lonely Planet, Melbourne.

Wheeler, Tony and James Lyon 1992, *Bali & Lombok – a Travel Survival Kit* (4th ed.), Lonely Planet, Melbourne.

Wheeler, Tony and Maureen Wheeler 2005, *Once While Travelling: The Lonely Planet Story*, Viking Press, Melbourne.

White, Richard 1981, *Inventing Australia: Images and Identity, 1688–1980*, George Allen & Unwin, Sydney.

White, Richard, 'Bluebells and Fogtown: Australians' First Impressions of England, 1860–1940', *Australian Cultural History*, no. 5, 1986, pp. 44–59.

White, Richard, 'Sun, Sand and Syphilis: Australian Soldiers and the Orient: Egypt 1914', *Australian Cultural History*, no. 9, Special Issue: 'Australian Perceptions of Asia', David Walker, Julia Horne & Adrian Vickers (eds) (1990): pp. 49–54.

White, Richard, 'The Retreat from Adventure: Popular Travel Writing in the 1950s', *Australian Historical Studies* 28, no. 109, 1997, pp. 90–105.

Whitecross, Roy 2000 (1951), *Slaves of the Son of Heaven*, Kangaroo Press, Sydney.

Williams, Maslyn 1967, *The East Is Red – the Chinese: A New Viewpoint*, Sun Books, Melbourne.

Wilson, Tony 2008, *Schapelle: The Facts, the Evidence, the Truth*, New Holland, Sydney.

Wood, James 1998, *The Forgotten Force: The Australian Military Contribution to the Occupation of Japan, 1945–1952*, Allen & Unwin, Sydney.

Wood, James, 'The Australian Military Contribution to the Occupation of Japan, 1945–1952', *Australian War Memorial*, Australians at War series, www.awm.gov.au/atwar/BCOF_history.pdf, accessed 20 February 2010.

Woollacott, Angela, '"All This Is Empire, I Told Myself": Australian Women's Voyages "Home" and the Articulation of Colonial Whiteness', *The American Historical Review* 102, no. 4, October 1997, pp. 1003–29.

Woollacott, Angela 2001, *To Try Her Fortune in London: Australian Women, Colonialism, and Modernity*, Oxford University Press, New York.

Wright, Meriel, and R Douglas Wright 1973, *China: The New Neighbour*, Tempo Books, Sydney.

Wyett, John 1996, *Staff Wallah at the Fall of Singapore*, Allen & Unwin, Sydney.

References

## UNPUBLISHED AND ARCHIVAL SOURCES

### Australian War Memorial

<u>Private Records:</u>
Papers of R Andrews and T Pleace, AWM MSS 1288
Papers of Mike Fernando, AWM PR 91/180
Papers of John S. Gibson, AWM MSS 1045
Papers of Peter W Groves, AWM PR 86/248
Lavery Family Papers, AWM PR 01487/1
Papers of Jason Neville, AWM PR 91/069
Papers of Roy Maxwell Poy, AWM PR02023

### Mitchell Library (State Library of NSW)

Diary of Phillip M Chancellor, Chancellor-Stuart Field Museum Expedition to Oceania and Malaysia, 1929–1930, ML MSS 2824/0/8/522C.
Ephemera Collection, 'Tourism'.
Papers of Mabel Dowding, ML MSS 4249/8/710/c.
Papers of Una Falkiner, ML MSS 423/14.
Papers of William Liu, Mitchell Library: ML MSS 6294/3.
Papers of Paddy Pallin, Mitchell Library, ML MSS 6016/2-4X.
Papers of PR Stephensen, Mitchell Library, ML MSS 1284.

### National Archives of Australia

Australian Wives of Indonesians, NAA: A433, 1949/2/4823.
Bondan, Mary Allethea, NAA: A6119/19, 356.
Cusack, Ellen Dymphna NAA, A6119: 1555.
Feith, Herbert: Volume 1, NAA , A261, 1938/1424.
Non-military aid to Vietnam – Decision 40, NAA: A5842/52.
South Vietnam – Civil Aid programme, NAA: A4940, C4641.
Visits of Mr Frank Clune abroad, NAA: A1608, CC65/1/1.

### National Library of Australia

<u>Manuscript Collection:</u>
Ephemera Collection, 'Travel'.
Papers of Gordon Clive Bleeck, NLA MS 9149.
Papers of Frank Clune, NLA MS 4951.
Records of Lonely Planet Publications, 1980-1991, NLA MS 8952.
Papers of Myra Roper, NLA MS 7711.
Papers of Joan Mavis Rosanove, NLA MS 2414.
Papers of Colin Simpson, National Library of Australia, NLA MS 5253.
Papers of Colin York Syme, NLA MS 6498.

<u>Oral History Collection</u>
Interview with Tom Molomby, Peter Hamilton and Others, 1 January 1971, NLA ORAL TRC 0245.
Interview with Kenneth Myer conducted by Heather Rusden, NLA ORAL TRC 2655.
Interview with Hugh Veness conducted by Alex and Annette Hood, 15 November 2003, Canberra, NLA ORAL TRC 4864/35.
Interview with Kenneth Whisson, conducted by Barbara Blackman, 20 April 1984, Canberra, NLA ORAL TRC 1660.

## PRIVATE COLLECTIONS AND PERSONAL CORRESPONDENCE

Audio letters of William Wade, 1962–1963, from the personal archives of Edward Duyker, copies in author's possession.

Interview with Abigayle Carmody, conducted by Agnieszka Sobocinska, Melbourne, 11 May 2011.

Interview with Yeshe Khadro conducted by Sean O'Brien, March 2009, copy in author's possession.

Interview with Max Pam conducted by Sean O'Brien, March 2009, copy in author's possession.

Interview with Willa Zheng conducted by Agnieszka Sobocinska, Sydney, 11 November 2013.

Adrian Vickers, Collection of Balinese tourism marketing materials, 1980s–1990s.

## STATISTICAL COLLECTIONS

Australian Bureau of Statistics, *Average Weekly Earnings*, 1975–2013.

Australian Bureau of Statistics, *Characteristics of Recent Migrants*, www.abs.gov.au/AUSSTATS/absé.nsf/Lookup/3416.0Main+Features22011?OpenDocument, accessed 16 January 2014

Australian Bureau of Statistics /Commonwealth Bureau of Census and Statistics, *Commonwealth Year Books* and *Australian Yearbooks*, 1939–2010.

Australian Bureau of Statistics, Dataset: 'Short term movement, resident departures selected destinations: original,' January 2014 release, www.abs.gov.au/AUSSTATS/absé.nsf/DetailsPage/3401.0Jan%202014?OpenDocument last accessed April 2014.

Australian Bureau of Statistics, *Overseas Arrivals and Departures*, 1975–2013.

Commonwealth Bureau of Census and Statistics, *Demography Bulletin*, no. 63 (1945)–no. 87 (1971).

United Nations World Tourism Organization, *Yearbook of Tourism Statistics*, World Tourism Organization, Madrid, 1985–2009.

United Nations World Tourism Organization, *Tourism Highlights*, 2011 edition, www.mkt.unwto.org/sites/all/files/docpdf/unwtohighlights11enhr.pdf, accessed 12 November 2012.

# ACKNOWLEDGMENTS

The process of researching and writing this book has spanned almost a decade, and I have accrued more debts than I can fit onto this page. It began life as a PhD thesis at the University of Sydney, and my first thanks must go to Richard White who supervised my progress with genuine wisdom, unflagging patience and remarkable good humour. Kirsten McKenzie's advice and support as my associate supervisor were immensely helpful. David Walker has been a major influence firstly as a scholar, then as thesis examiner, mentor and friend. Tim Martin, John Hutnyk and Hsu-Ming Teo provided invaluable feedback at an early stage.

I have since been extremely fortunate in finding a supportive working environment at Monash University and I thank my colleagues at the National Centre for Australian Studies, particularly Bruce Scates, Tony Moore, Jenny Hocking and Keir Reeves, as well as the Dean of the Faculty of Arts, Rae Frances, for their unflagging encouragement and support over the past three years. Friends and colleagues from Sydney, Melbourne and elsewhere have generously read and commented on my work and this book bears a particular debt to Amanda Kaladelfos, Adrian Vickers, Marilyn Lake, Bill Garner, Jane Carey, Clare Corbould, Christina Twomey, Fay Anderson, Bain Atwood, Alison Bashford, Sophie Loy-Wilson, Julia Martinez, Sally Percival Wood, Mat Trinca, Frances Clarke,

Vicki Peel, Mia Lindgren, Johan Lidberg, Susie Protschky, Adam Clulow, Damien Williams, Ruth Morgan, Taylor Spence, Rachel Standfield, Sarah Tayton and Jill Barnes.

Many people went out of their way to bring new and varied sources to my attention. Although they are too numerous to mention, I would like to particularly thank Edward Duyker, Bruce Thomas, Jeffrey Mellefont, Abigayle Carmody, Michael Park and Willa Zheng for sharing their own and others' travel tales. Research was facilitated by a Norman McCann Summer Scholarship at the National Library of Australia and a Milt Luger Fellowship at the State Library of NSW. I would like to extend my appreciation to the staff of both institutions, as well as the benefactors of these fellowships. I also gratefully acknowledge the financial support of the Faculty of Arts at Monash University in helping bring this book to publication.

My commissioning editor at NewSouth Publishing, Phillipa McGuinness, has been an unflagging believer in this project. Without her advice and backing this book would have never been published and I would like to extend my gratitude for her confidence that this was a story worth telling. Uthpala Gunethilake and Averil Moffat were both remarkably skilled and patient throughout the editing process, for which I am exceedingly grateful.

My parents, Barbara and Jacek have borne the extended progress of this project with remarkable tolerance and my brother Pawel has provided legendary hospitality all over Europe. Friends in Sydney and Melbourne (you know who you are) are largely responsible for keeping me sane during these years. Jonathan Stoddart was exceptionally supportive during the writing process.

To everyone on this page and many others, I give my whole-hearted thanks.

# INDEX

# Index

# Index

www.ingramcontent.com/pod-product-compliance
Lightning Source LLC
Chambersburg PA
CBHW030354270326
41926CB00009B/1094